AF598910

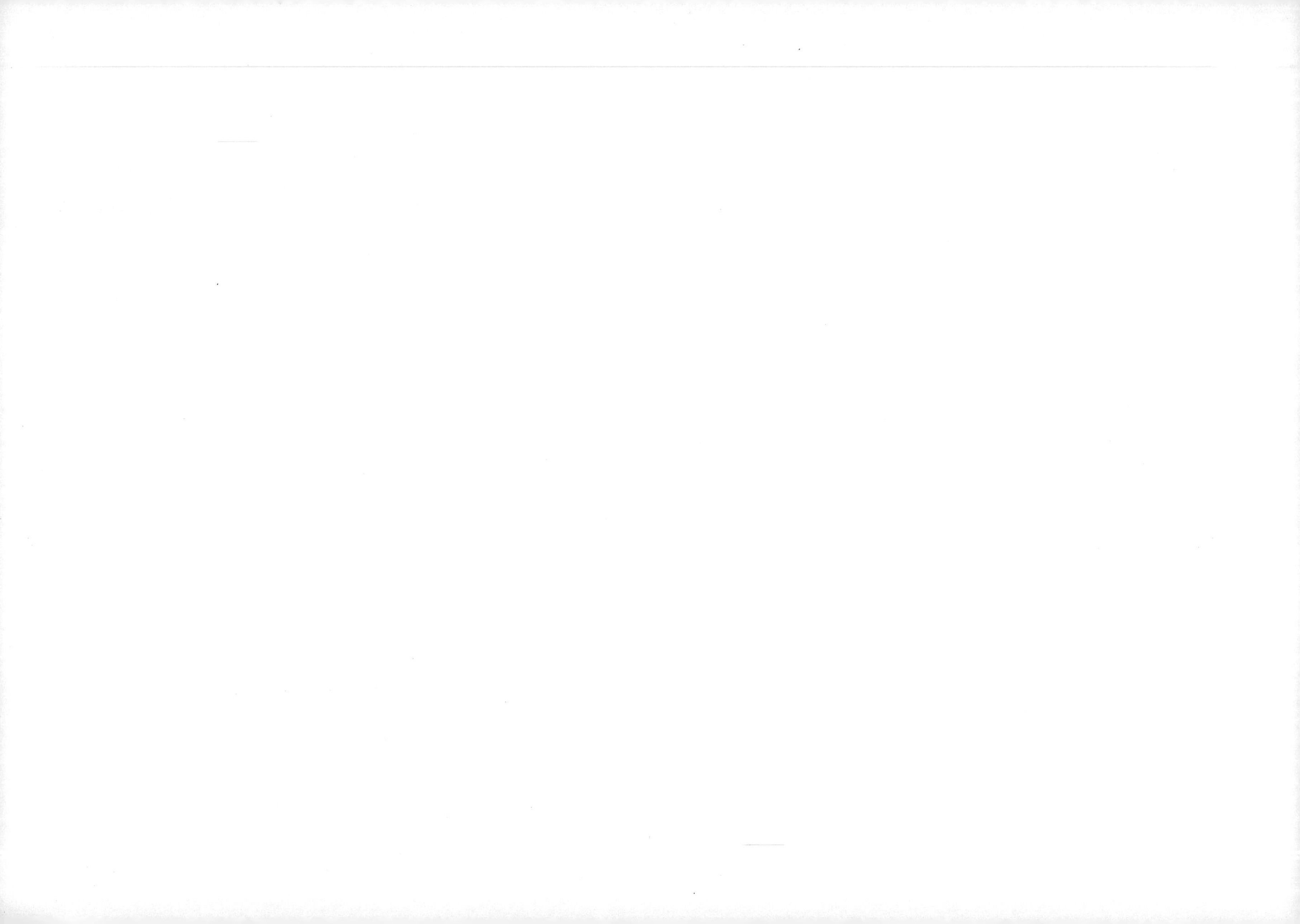

THE ARCHITECTURE OF *Whimsy*

THE ARCHITECTURE OF *Whimsy*

Mid-20th-Century Modern Architecture in South Florida

ARTHUR JAY MARCUS

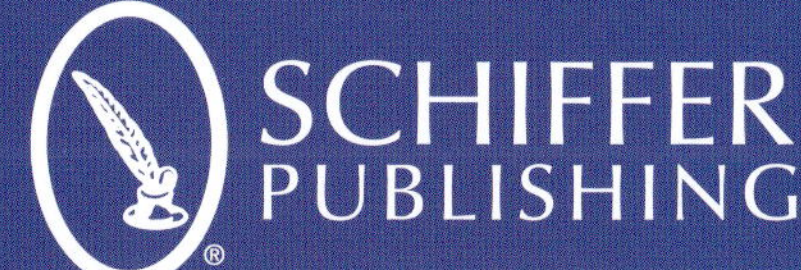

4880 Lower Valley Road • Atglen, PA 19310

Other Schiffer Books on Related Subjects:
Architecture Tours L.A. Guidebook: Downtown, by Laura Massino Smith, 978-0-7643-2084-2

Art Deco Architecture: Miami Beach Postcards, by Paul Clemence, 978-0-7643-2340-9

Library of Congress Control Number: 2020930686

Designed by Molly Shields
Cover design by Justin Watkinson
All photographs in this book are by Arthur Jay Marcus.

Photo opposite: Premiere Inn, 3110 Belmar Street, Fort Lauderdale
Architect: Arthur H. Rude, 1964

Type set in Mr Canfields/ZapfEllipt BT

ISBN: 978-0-7643-6027-5
Printed in China

Published by Schiffer Publishing, Ltd.
4880 Lower Valley Road
Atglen, PA 19310
Phone: (610) 593-1777; Fax: (610) 593-2002
E-mail: Info@schifferbooks.com
Web: www.schifferbooks.com

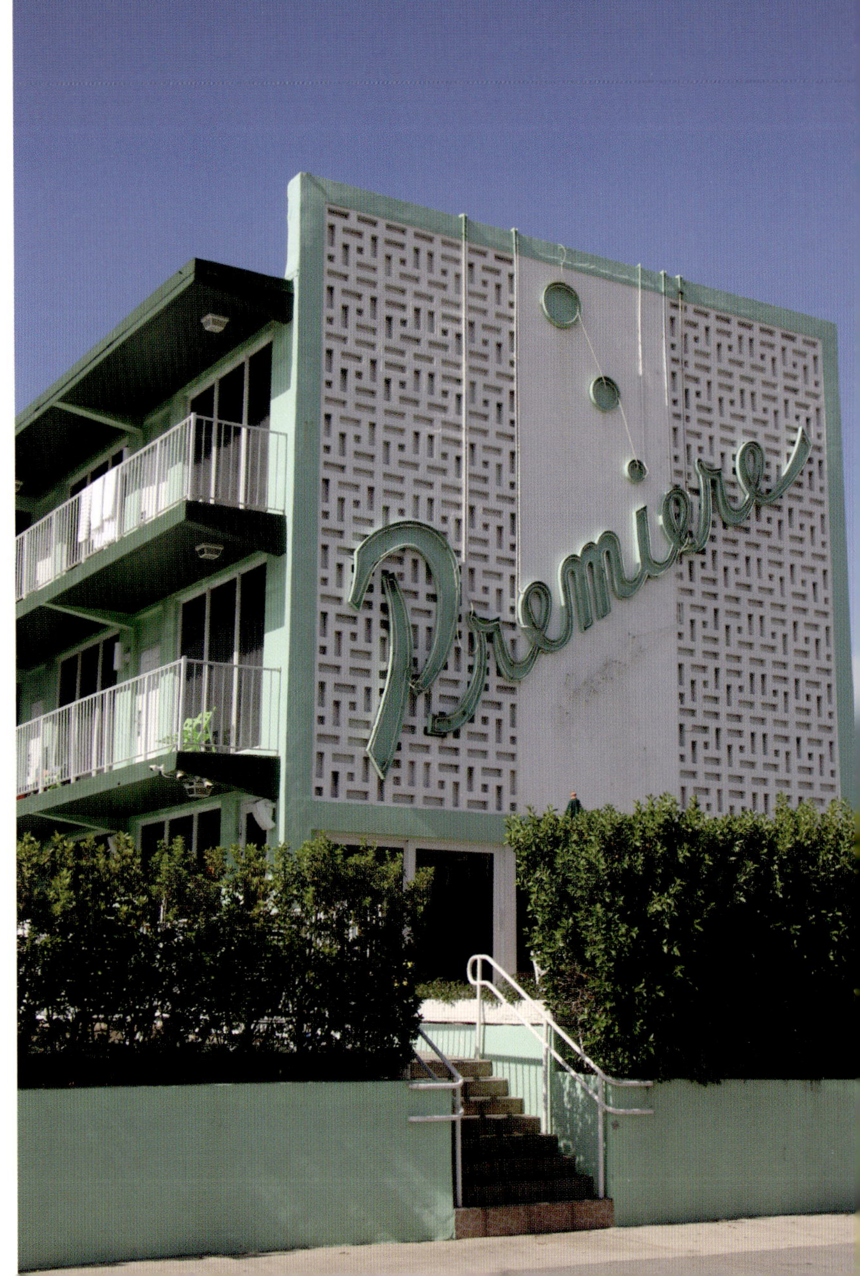

This book is dedicated to

William Churchill Stewart.

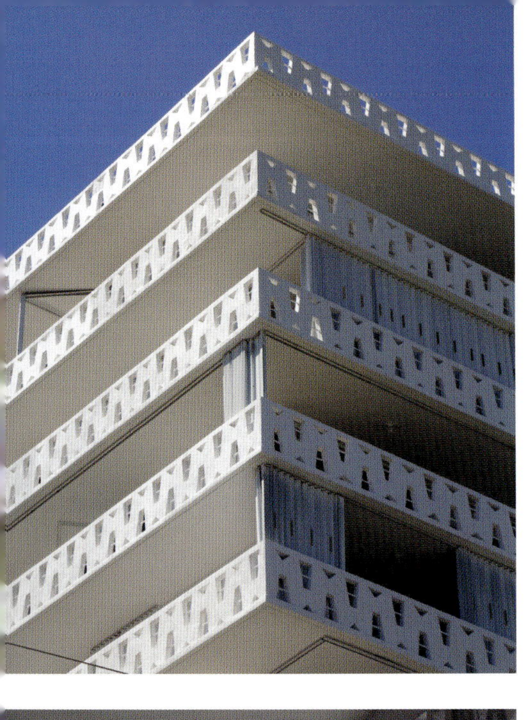
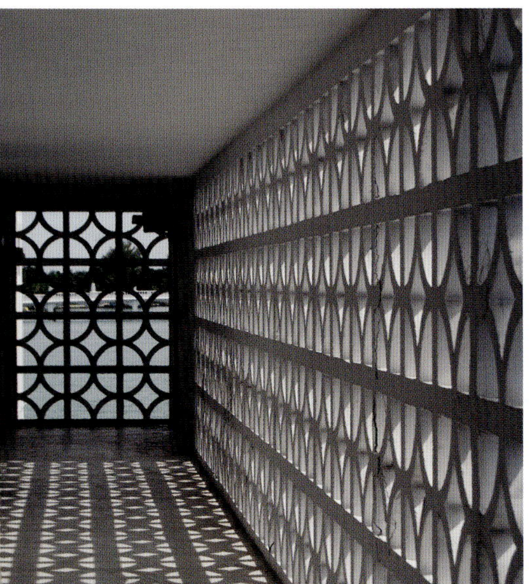
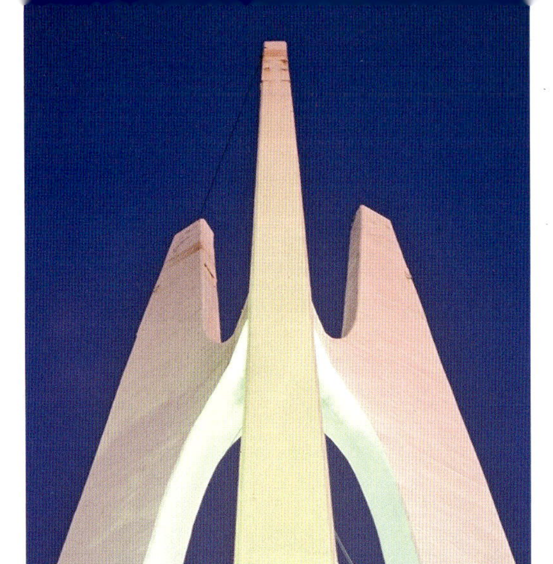
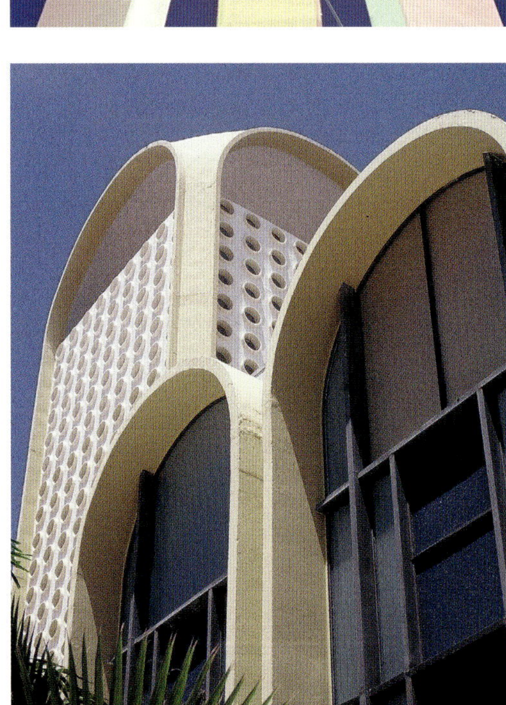
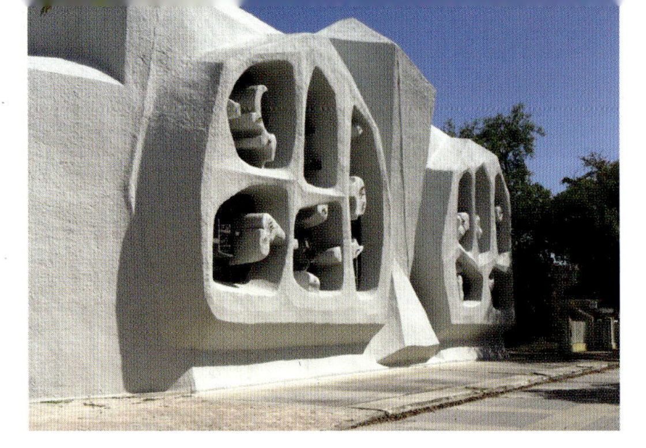
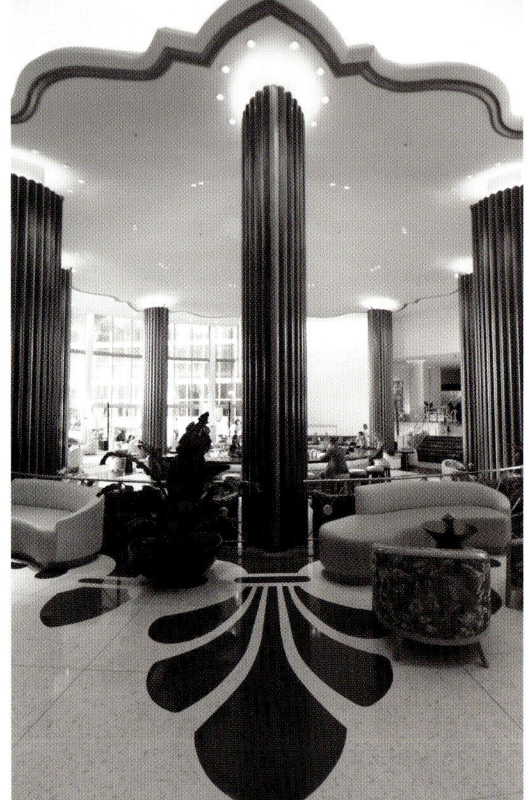
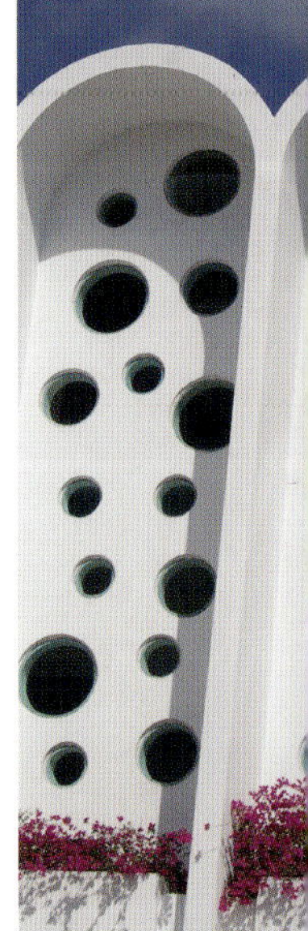
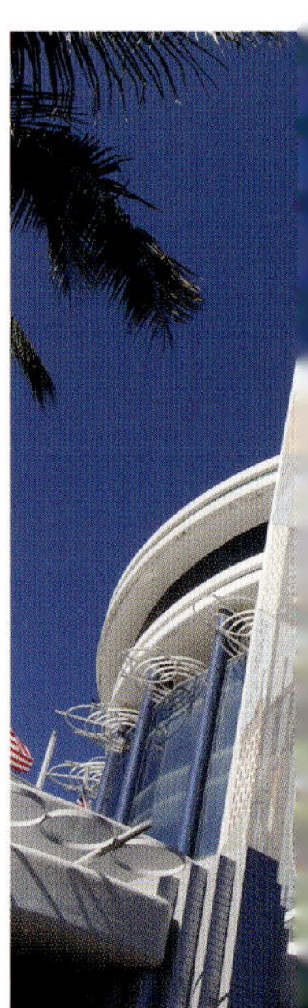

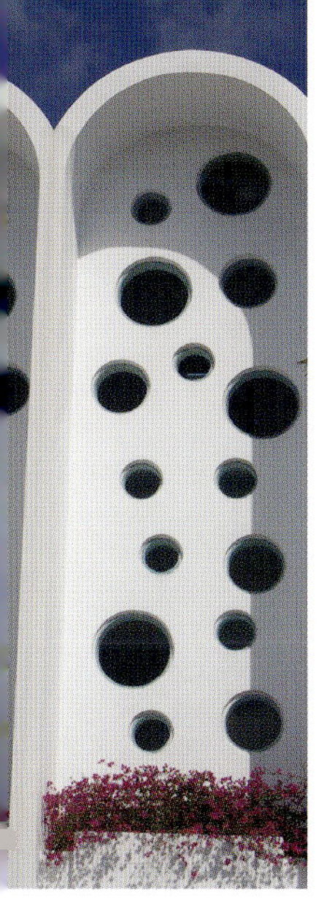

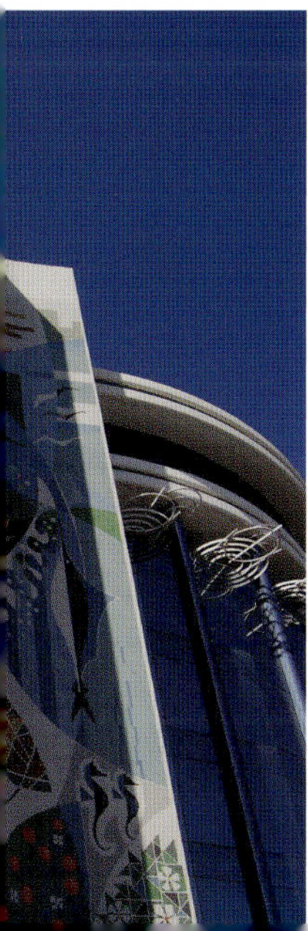

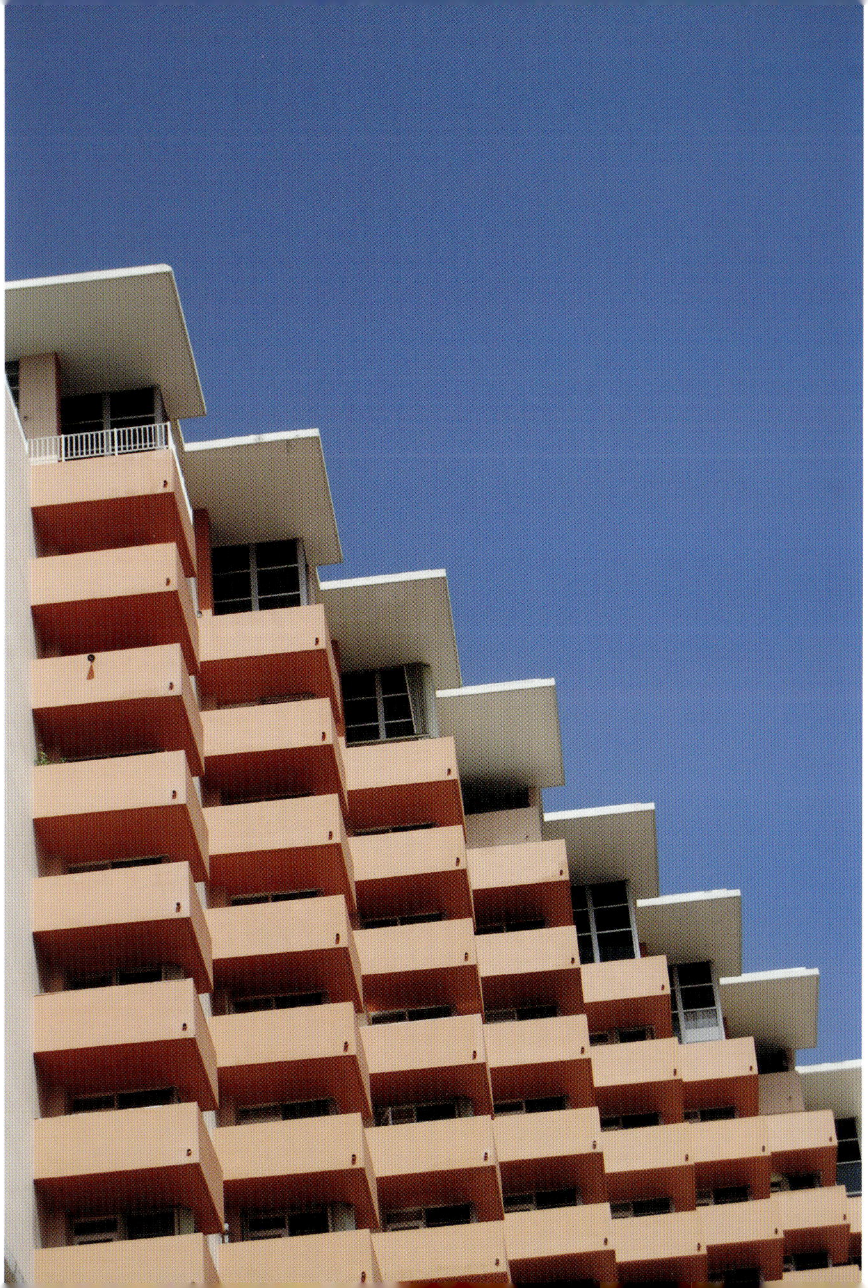

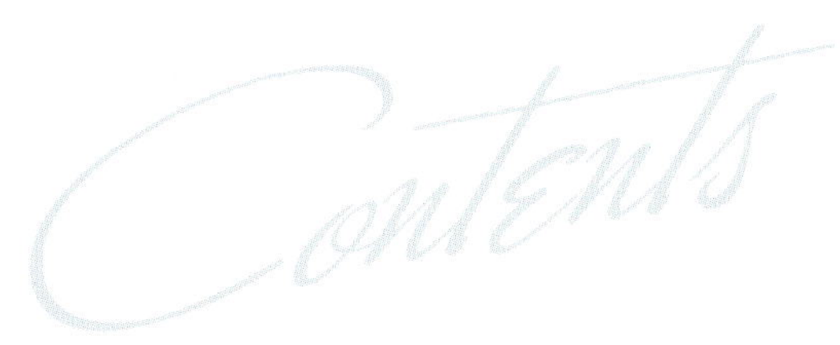
Contents

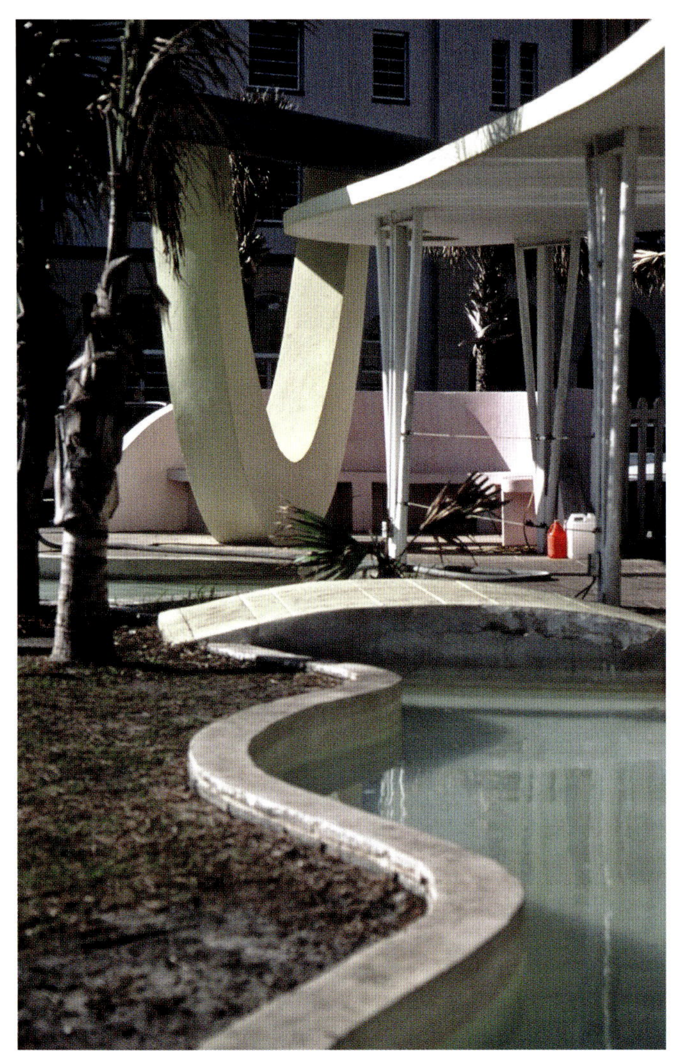

Introduction

THE ARCHITECTURE OF WHIMSY: A HISTORY

Clevelander Hotel Pool
1020 Ocean Drive
Miami Beach
Architect: Albert Anis, 1938
Pool deck renovations:
Robert Swartburg, 1951, 1953
Photograph: 1991

The word "whimsy" evokes something playful, capricious, or fantastic, and these characteristics define a subset of mid-twentieth-century modern architecture in South Florida. Whimsy might mean the quirky juxtaposition of curvaceous sculptural elements with the geometrical lines of a building. It may refer to the decorative details that provide visual relief from the structural matrix, or even to an off-center design. A touch of whimsy often gives a building gravitas.

After World War II ended in 1945, land development and construction boomed in South Florida, coinciding with the widespread use of air conditioning. Over the next twenty-five years, architects and engineers produced a remarkable collection of buildings, using material technologies that grew from wartime research. Engineers took liberties to exploit the uses for new concrete admixtures, which were more structurally robust and made longer spans and cantilevers possible. Architects sculpted concrete into forms that expressed the optimism of the times. Wiggles and tripods, cheese holes, and arches were part of this fantastic sculptural experimentation, with allusions to speed and machinery. Whimsical forms and patterns also grew out of the region's oceanside resort culture. Hotels were designed to provide a fun and stress-free time for visitors, and the architecture expressed this joy.

This book focuses on the Greater Miami Beach and Fort Lauderdale areas as a whole and aims to showcase these whimsical characteristics of mid-twentieth-century modern architecture. For example, the Bay Harbor Continental in Bay Harbor Islands, with its colored-glass-block and brise-soleil built in 1958, recalls in its detailing the Birch House in Fort Lauderdale, built in 1959 by the same architect. The buildings with similar characteristics tended to be designed by the same architects: Charles McKirahan was the major midcentury architect in Fort Lauderdale while completing the Alexander Hotel in Miami Beach. Igor Polevitzsky designed numerous buildings in Miami Beach as well as the Sea Tower in Fort Lauderdale. And Miami-based Tony Sherman designed the nautical Yankee Clipper Hotel in Fort Lauderdale.

Locals have various names for mid-twentieth-century style. In Miami, Miami Beach, Bay Harbor Islands, and Lauderdale-by-the-Sea, it is called MiMo, pronounced "My-Mo" and short for the Miami Modern style of architecture popular in South Florida from the mid-1940s through the mid-1960s. In Fort Lauderdale, the style is referred to as BroCoMo (Broward County Modern). The mention of any of these names refers simply to midcentury modern.

The name MiMo grew out of efforts of the Urban Arts Committee of Miami

Beach in the late 1990s, when I was a member, to promote the rich collection of unique midcentury modern architecture in Miami and Miami Beach.

South Florida's midcentury buildings had not previously been formally recognized as a unique architectural style. Part of the committee's educational efforts involved surveying and photographing buildings identified as MiMo. I was one of the first three photographers retained to document these examples, and several of the photographs are included in this book.

These early efforts were recognized in photography exhibitions in Miami Beach, Tallahassee, and Fort Lauderdale, culminating in the 2002 exhibit at the Municipal Arts Society in New York City titled *Beyond the Box: Mid-century Modern Architecture in Miami and New York*.

It is worth noting that in Miami Dade County, midcentury modern is but one of many architectural styles evolving over time in concert with the city's history. However, in Broward County and Fort Lauderdale, it was the predominant historical architectural style as the city came of age.

South Florida midcentury architecture is typically different from the more geometric midcentury design aesthetic of Palm Springs and Los Angeles. However, there are exceptions where Palm Springs modern looks very much like South Florida modern. This book is certainly not meant to be a complete gallery of MiMo buildings. I have included buildings that I have admired over the years, most of which still exist.

My hope is to raise awareness of the need to preserve this remarkable collection of buildings. Except for the MiMo Biscayne Historic District in Miami and many historic districts in Miami Beach, most of these whimsical midcentury buildings are not within protected historic districts. In spite of the many lost structures, these surviving examples begin to describe the rich and varied legacy of this architectural period.

I have lived in South Florida for more than twenty-five years and am still inspired by the diversity of the region's midcentury architecture. I thank Morris Lapidus, Charles McKirahan, Igor Polevitzsky, Norman Giller, Enrique Gutierrez, and many others who created the works shown here. And I apologize in advance for not being able to include examples from Palm Beach County. I also realize that some reader favorites may not be represented here—but I am still exploring. Perhaps in a sequel!

Enjoy!
Arthur Marcus, Architect

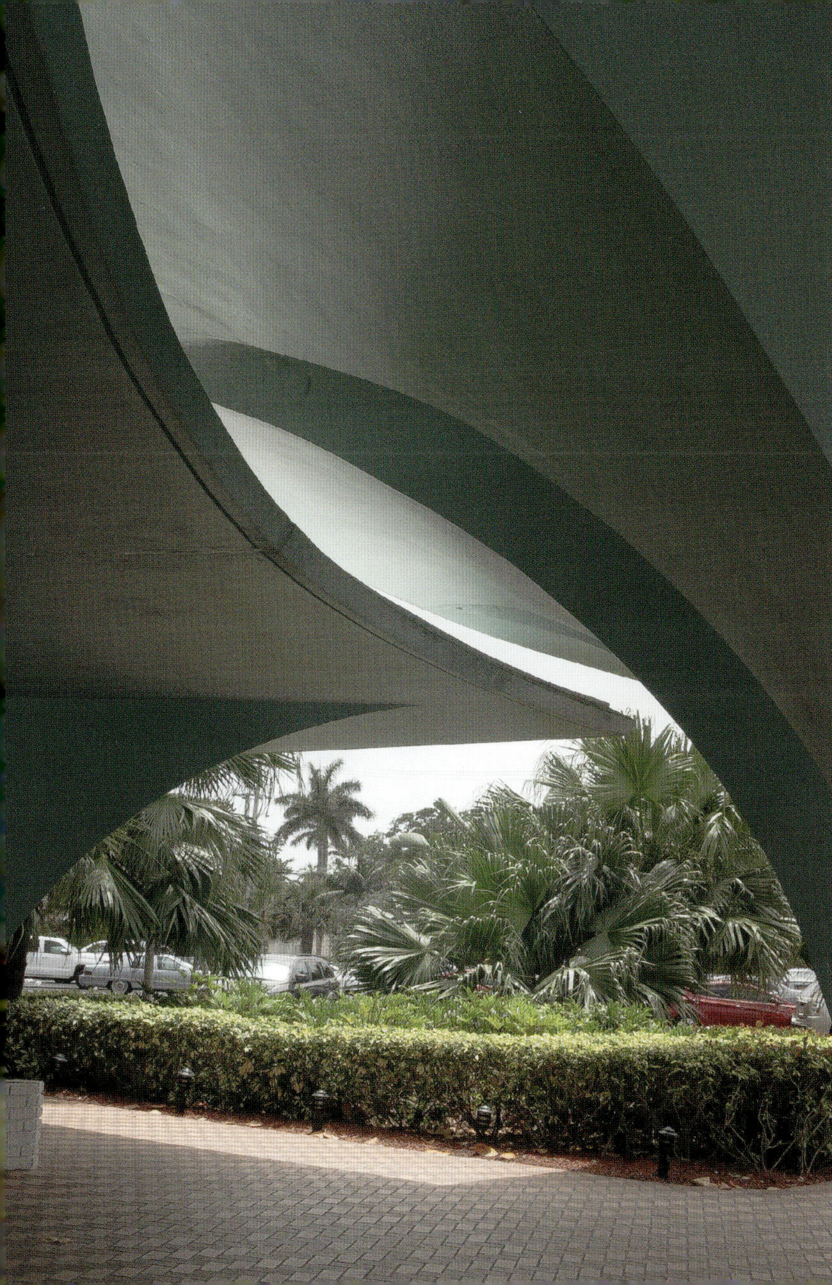

Breakwater Towers
1900 South Ocean Drive
Fort Lauderdale
Architect: Charles McKirahan, 1957
Photograph: 2016

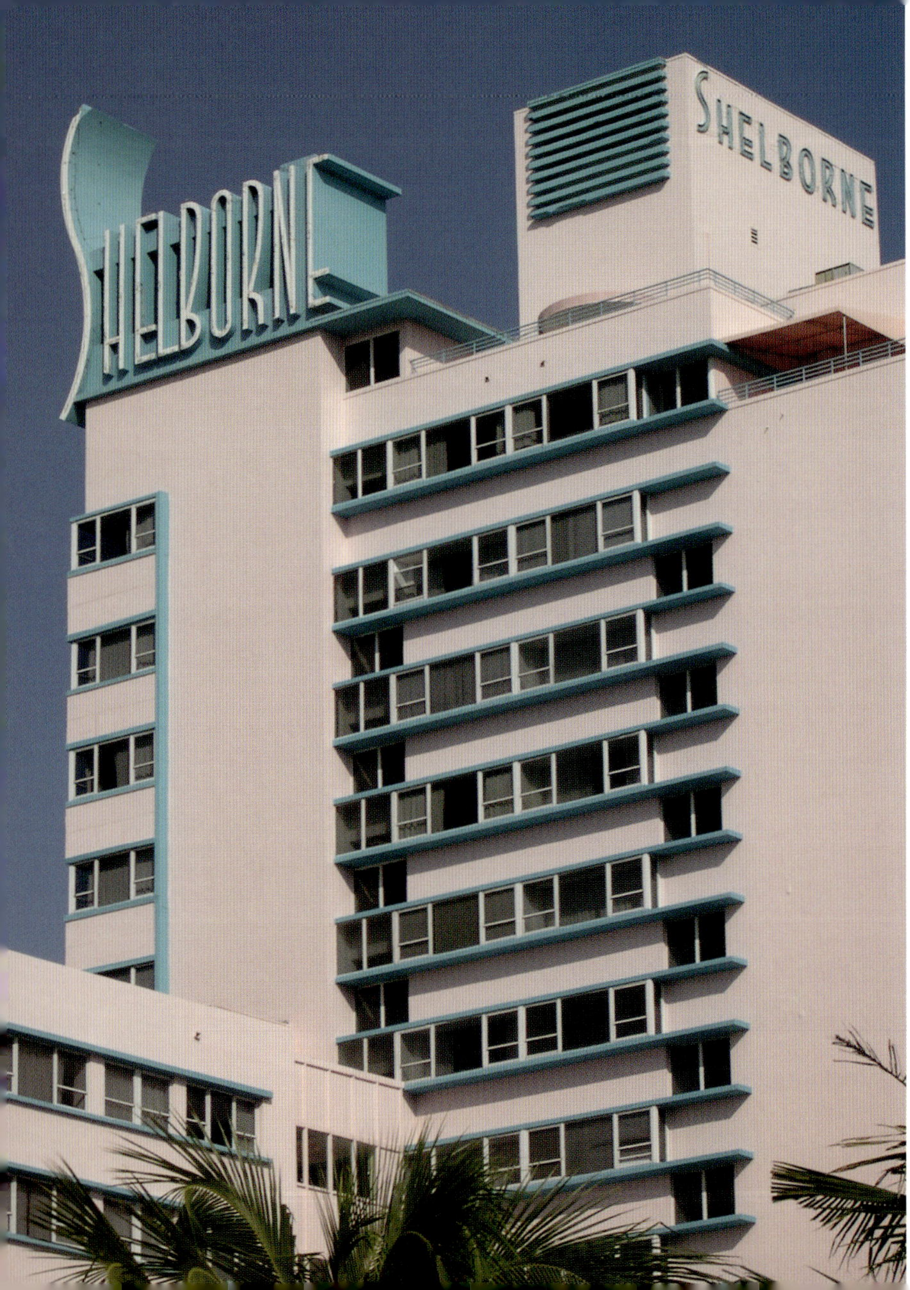

SHELBORNE
SHELBORNE

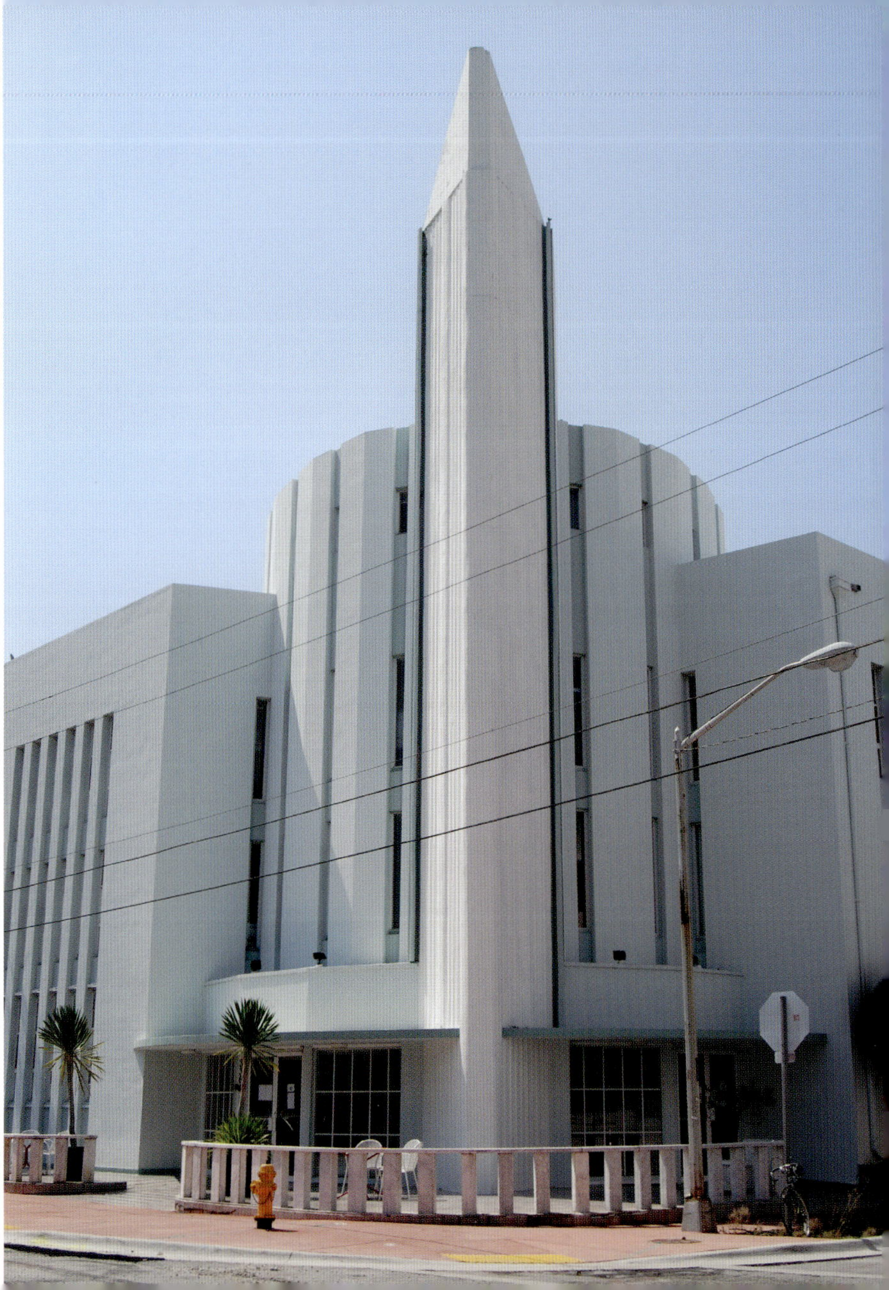

Chapter One
PRECURSORS TO MIDCENTURY MODERN

Shelborne Hotel
1801 Collins Avenue
Miami Beach
Architects: Igor Polevitzsky & T. Trip Russell, 1940
Photograph: ca. 1995

Plymouth Hotel
326 21st Street
Miami Beach
Architect: Anton Skislewicz, 1940
Photograph: 2013

In the years just before World War II, several outstanding examples of contemporary architecture appeared on the Miami Beach skyline and remained at the forefront of progressive civic consciousness during the war. The hundreds of thousands of servicemen who passed through South Florida saw it as the shining modernist city of the future.

The buildings in this chapter were completed during this period, between 1939 and 1941. Art deco was morphing into streamline moderne. Curving forms, strong horizontal lines, brise-soleils, filigree screening, and signage used as architectural elements contributed to the expression of speed and technology that figured prominently in the designs of that era. These gestures later became

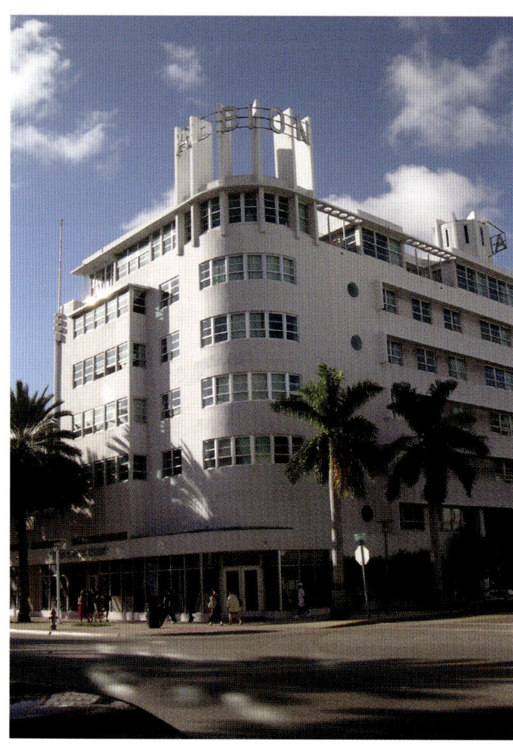

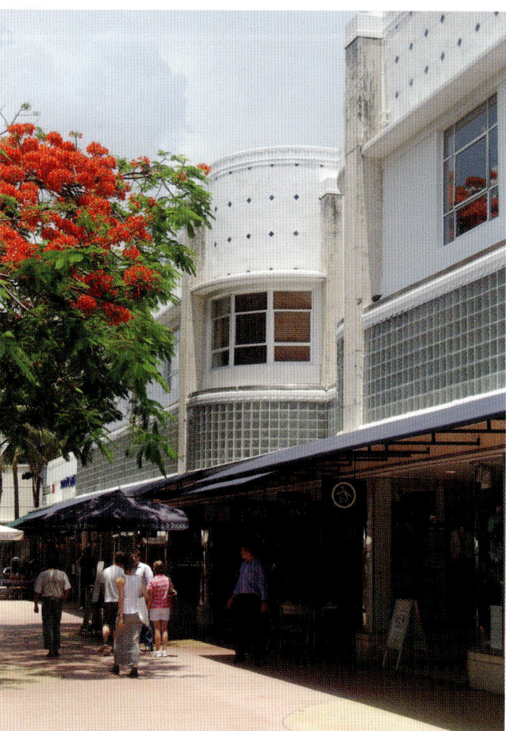

Albion Hotel
1650 James Avenue
Miami Beach
Architects: Igor Polevitzsky & T. Trip Russell (beachside tower and cabanas), 1939
Morris Lapidus (Collins Avenue tower and porte-cochere), 1957
Photograph: 2007

Sterling Building
927 Lincoln Road
Miami Beach
Architect: Alexander Lewis, 1928
Renovation: Victor H. Nellenbogen, 1941
Photograph: 2010

Shelborne Hotel
1801 Collins Avenue
Miami Beach
Architect: Morris Lapidus, 1940
Photograph: ca. 1995

part of the South Florida midcentury modern vocabulary.

The architectural wonders at the 1939 World's Fair in New York City contributed to this development and left a lasting impact on the public imagination. Architect Anton Skislewicz created an inspiring homage to the fair with his 1940 design of the Plymouth Hotel in Miami Beach, with its pylon and perisphere.

Igor Polevitzsky and T. Trip Russell designed the landmark Albion Hotel in Miami Beach in 1939. The prototype for other buildings in the mixed-use urban beach resort, its sleek and varied facade included porthole windows looking into the swimming pool.

In 1941, Victor Nellenbogen redesigned the Sterling Building on Lincoln Road. A new streamline-style facade, with glass block illuminated at night, was constructed over the original 1920s Spanish Mediterranean facade.

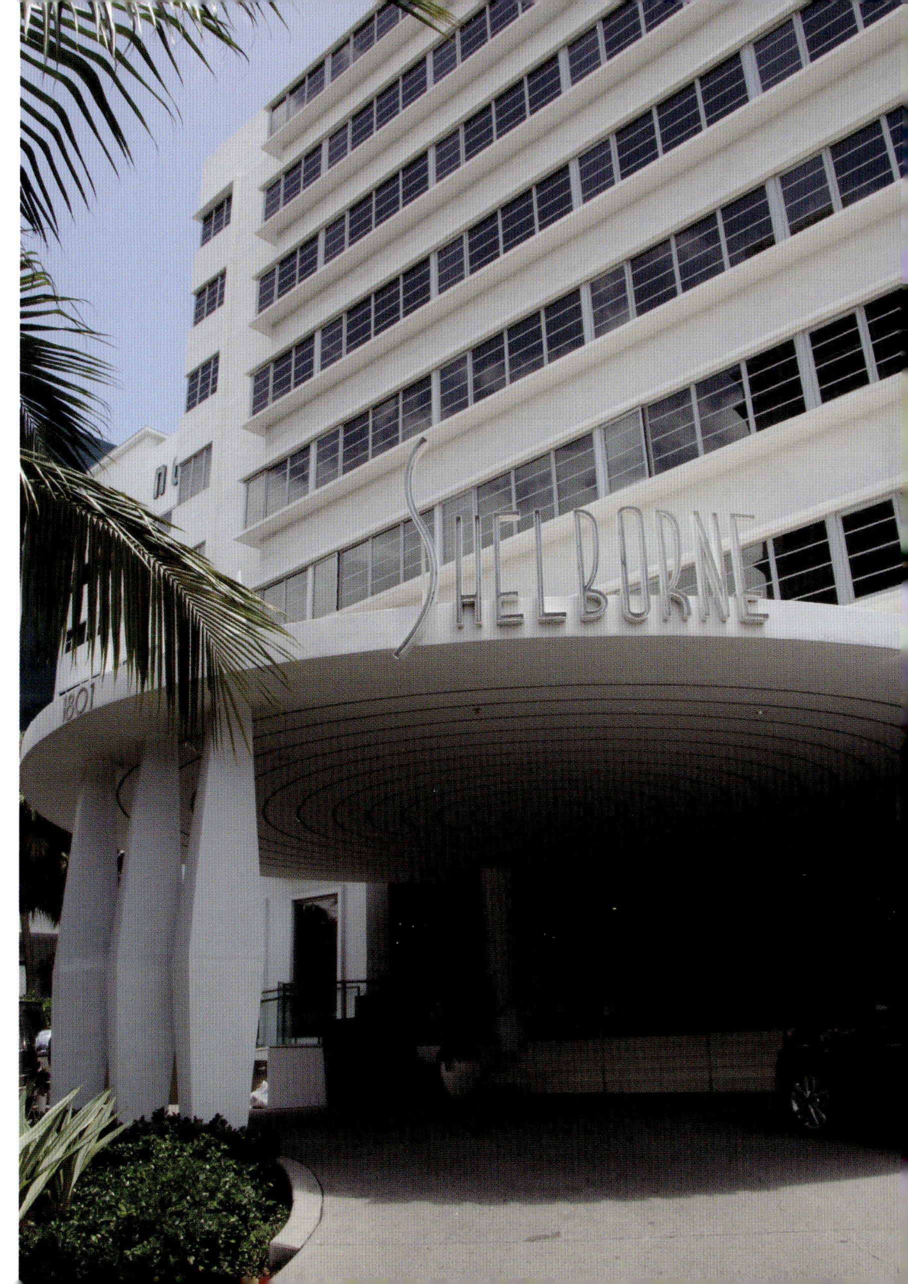

The Shelborne Hotel Building #1, completed in 1940, married the international style with refined architectural detailing. Polevitzsky and Russell gave it an elegantly detailed Bauhaus style with flourishes that foreshadowed MiMo with the use of giant signage as decoration. Building #2, designed by Morri Lapidus, paid homage to the original designs and added the front canopy pilotis and striking, circular automobile entrance canopy.

L. Murray Dixon designed the Raleigh Hotel and pool, completed in 1940. Although modeled on a mythical coat of arms, the pool is a wonderful precursor to the free-flowing shapes of South Florida's midcentury modern architecture.

Each of these buildings prepared the way for the elegant, exuberant flourishes that occasionally made their way into what would become America's optimistic and well-loved mid-twentieth-century style.

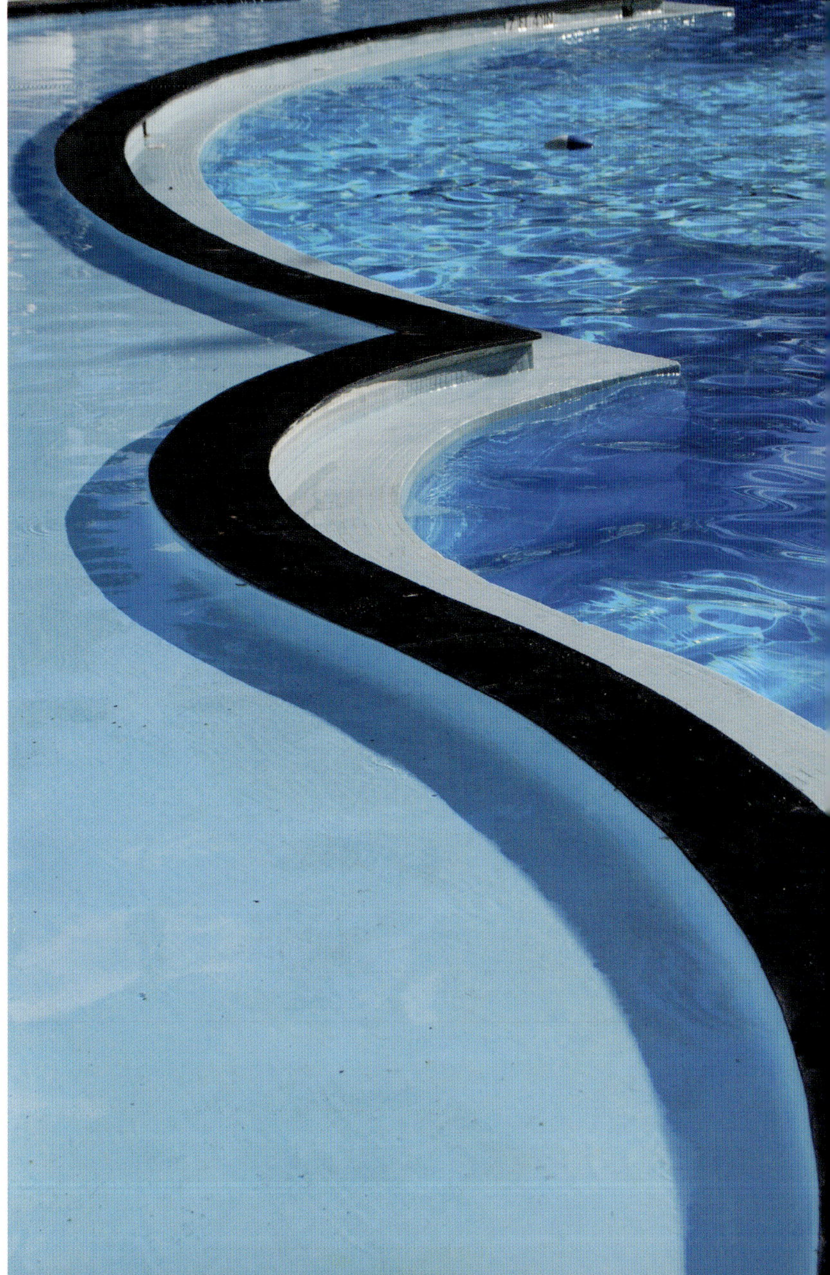

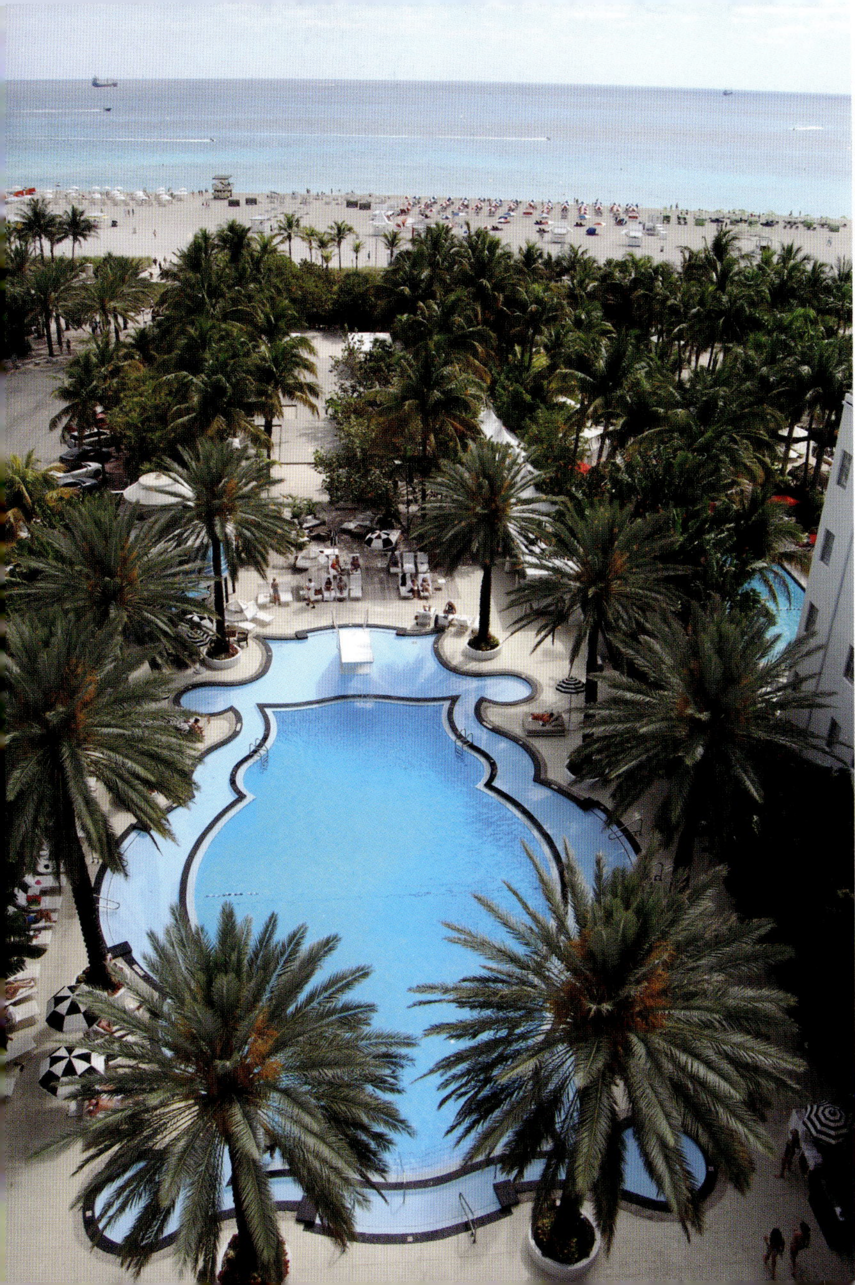

Raleigh Hotel Pool
1775 Collins Avenue
Miami Beach
Architect: Lawrence Murray Dixon, 1940
Photograph: 2013

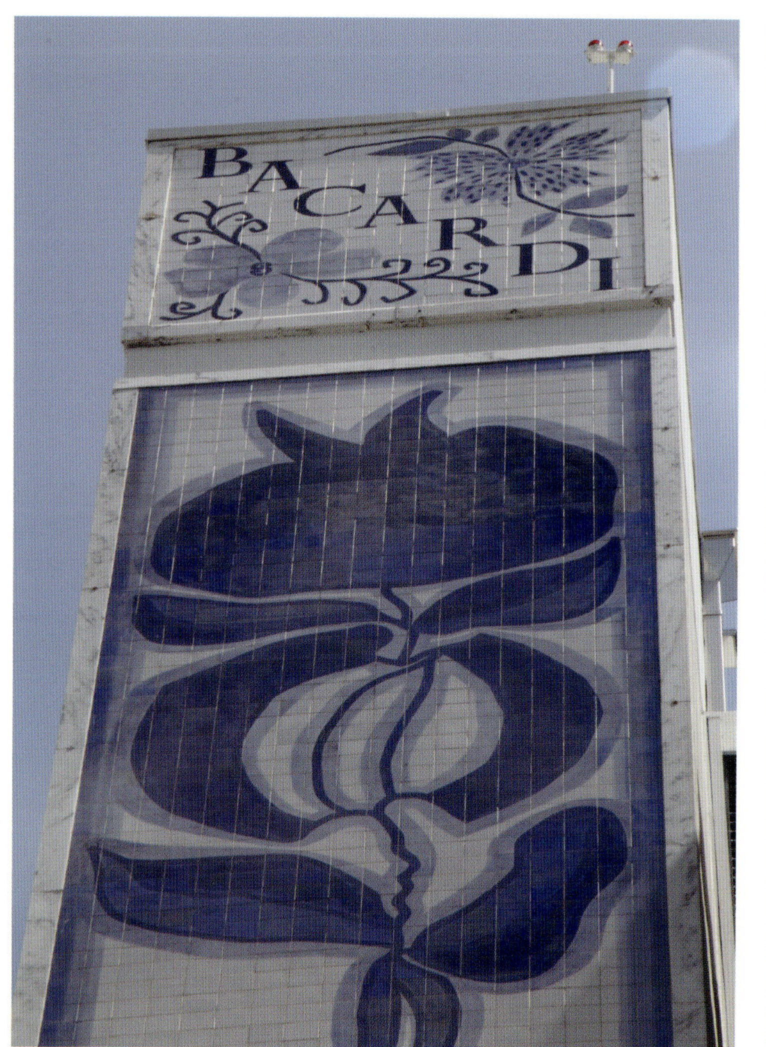
BACARDI

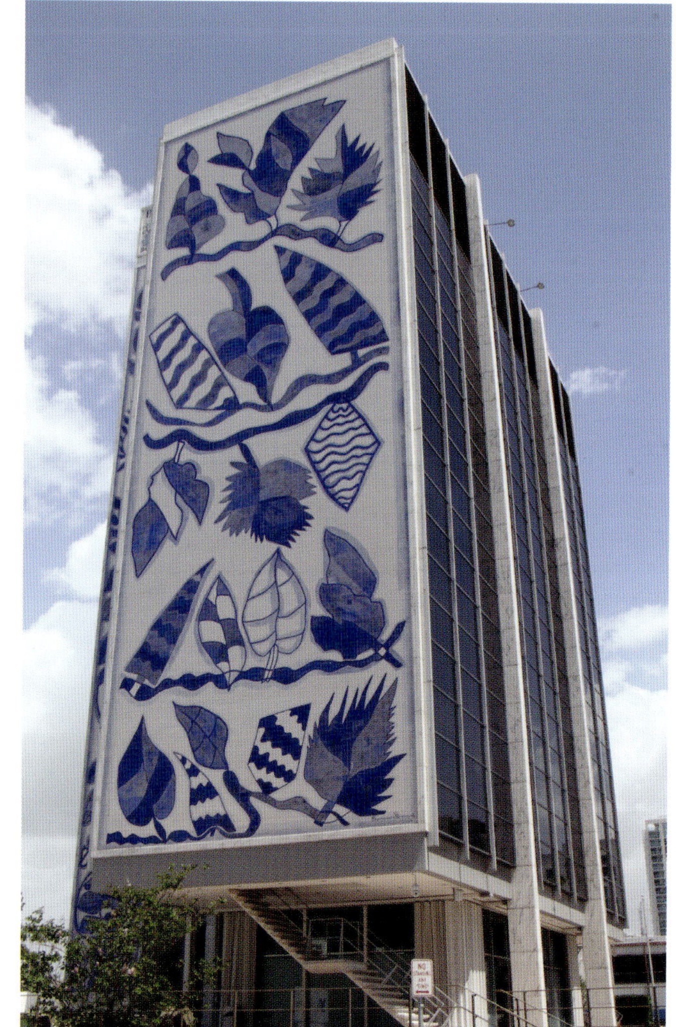

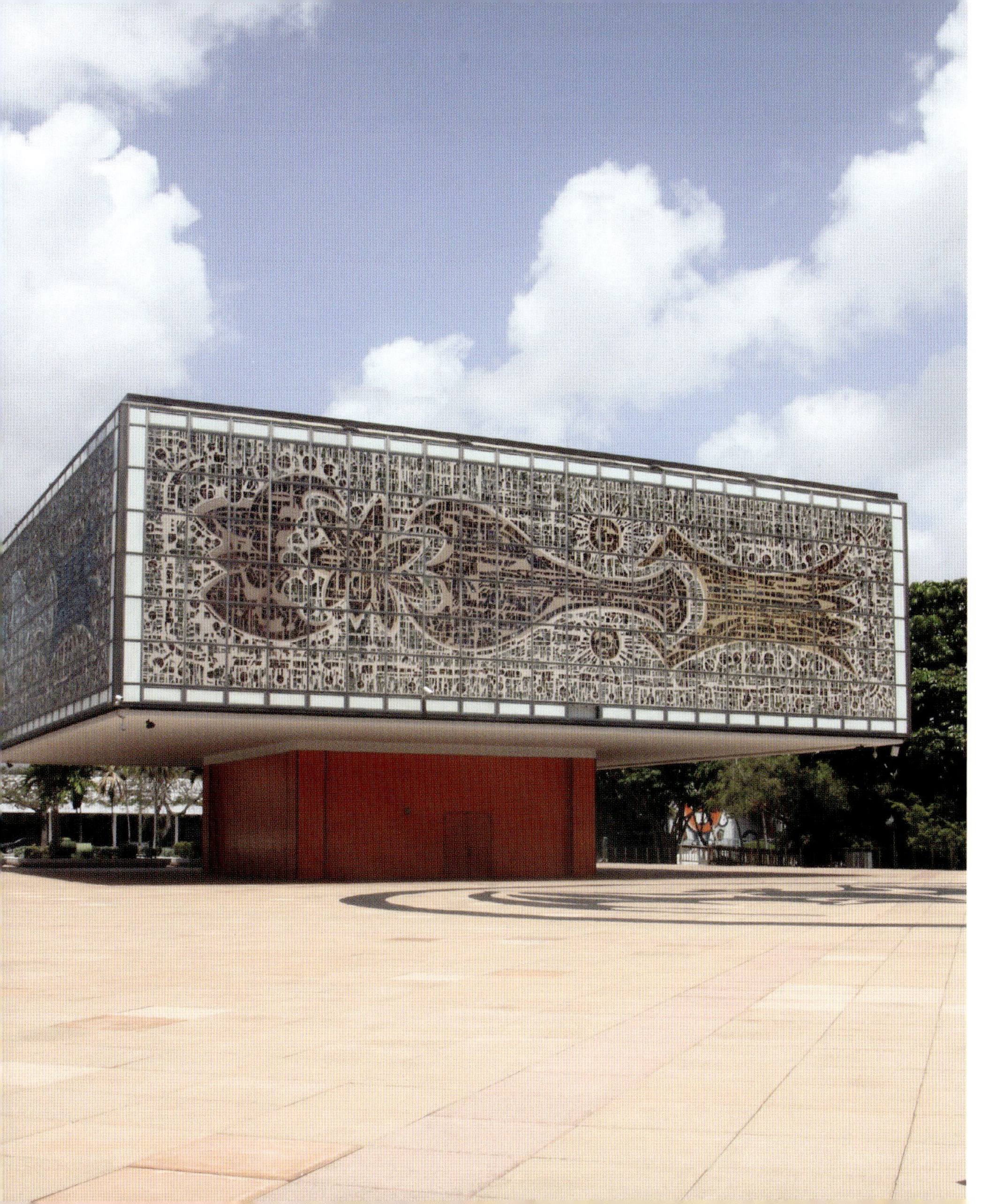

Chapter Two

MIAMI & MIAMI BEACH

Bacardi Building, far left
2100 Biscayne Boulevard
Miami
Architect: Enrique Gutierrez, 1963
Photograph: 2017

Bacardi Building Annex, left
2100 Biscayne Boulevard
Miami
Architect: Ignacio Cabrera-Justiz, 1974
Photograph: 2017

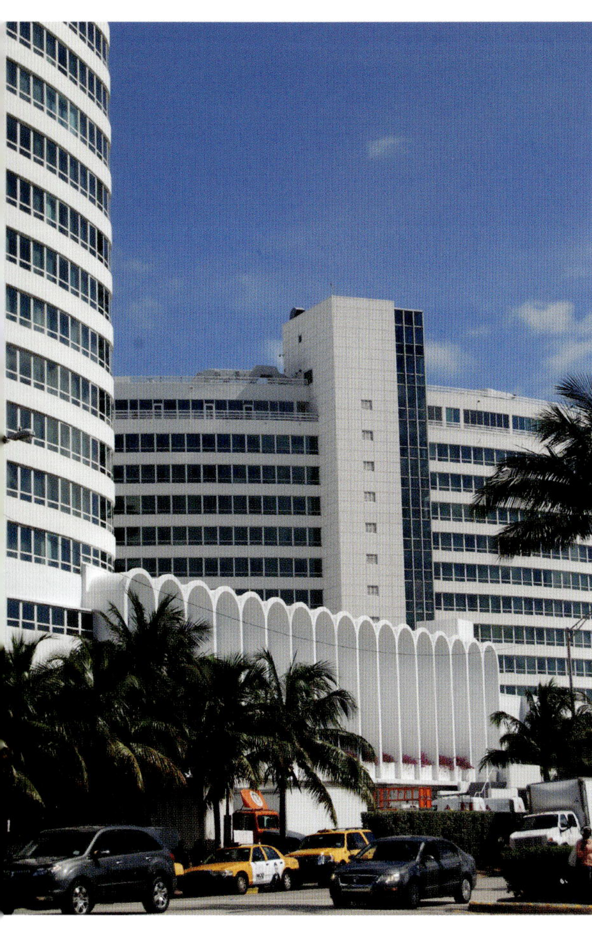

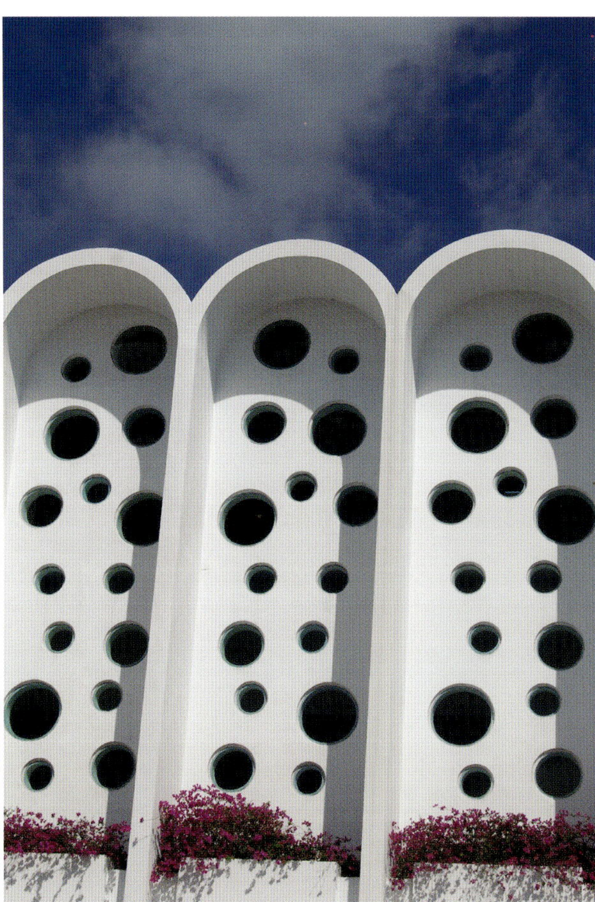

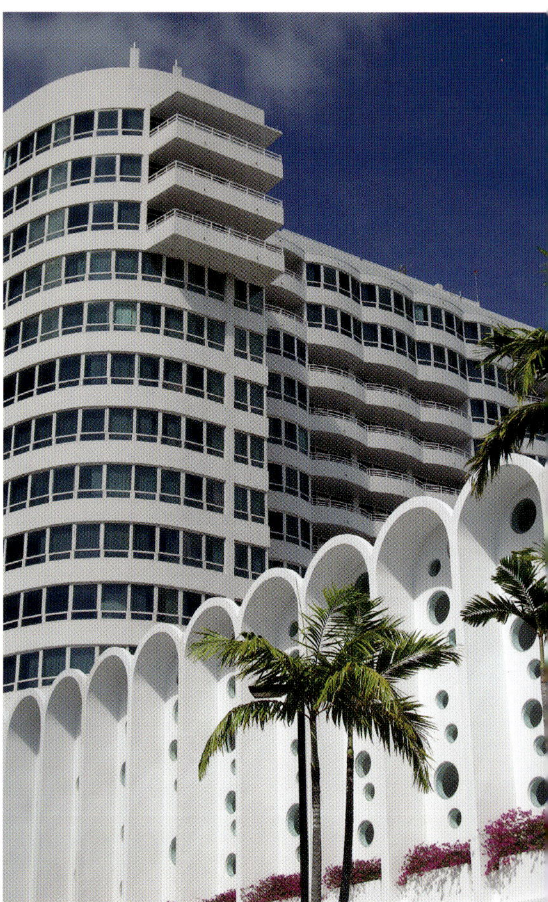

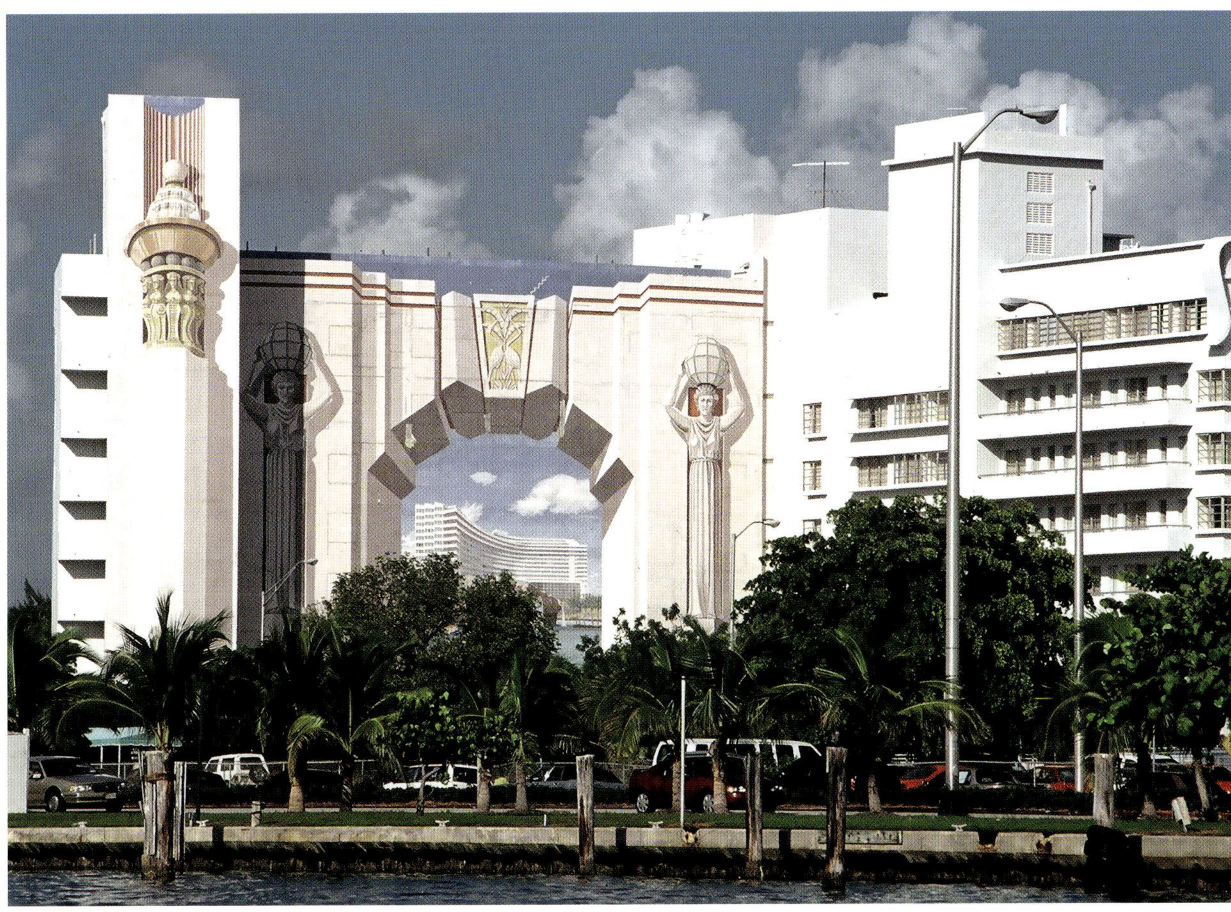

Fontainebleau Hotel
4141 Collins Avenue
Miami Beach
Architect: Morris Lapidus, 1953
North wing by A. Herbert Mathes, 1959
Photograph: 2013

Fontainebleau Hotel Mural
(demolished 2002)

This tromp l'loeil mural replicated the original view of the curved Lapidus tower (depicted under the painted arch), which was lost when the Fontainebleau II Condo / Hotel Tower was built.

Original muralist: Richard Haas, 1986
Photograph: 2000

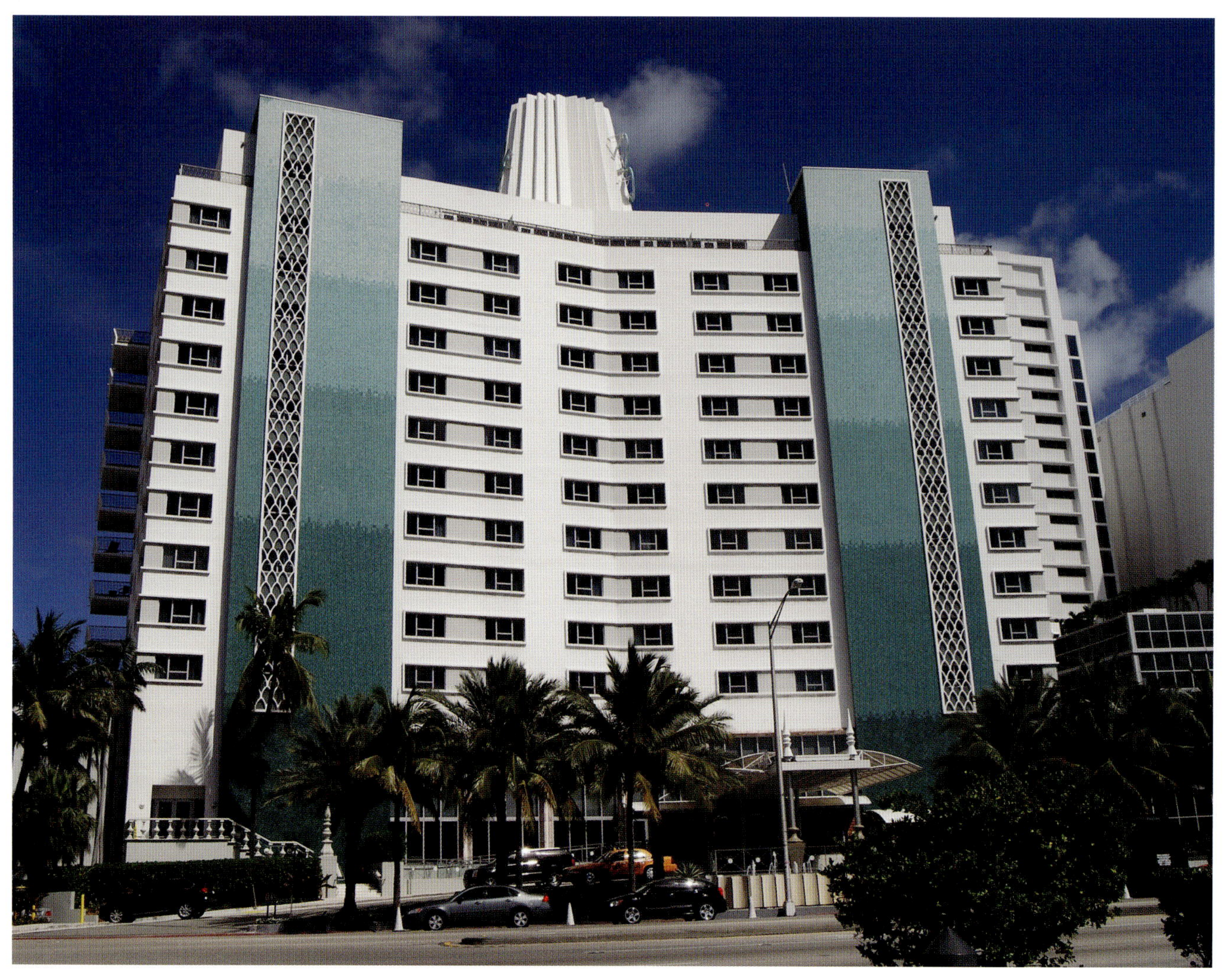

Eden Roc Hotel & Lobby
4525 Collins Avenue
Miami Beach
Architect: Morris
Lapidus, 1955
Photograph: 2015

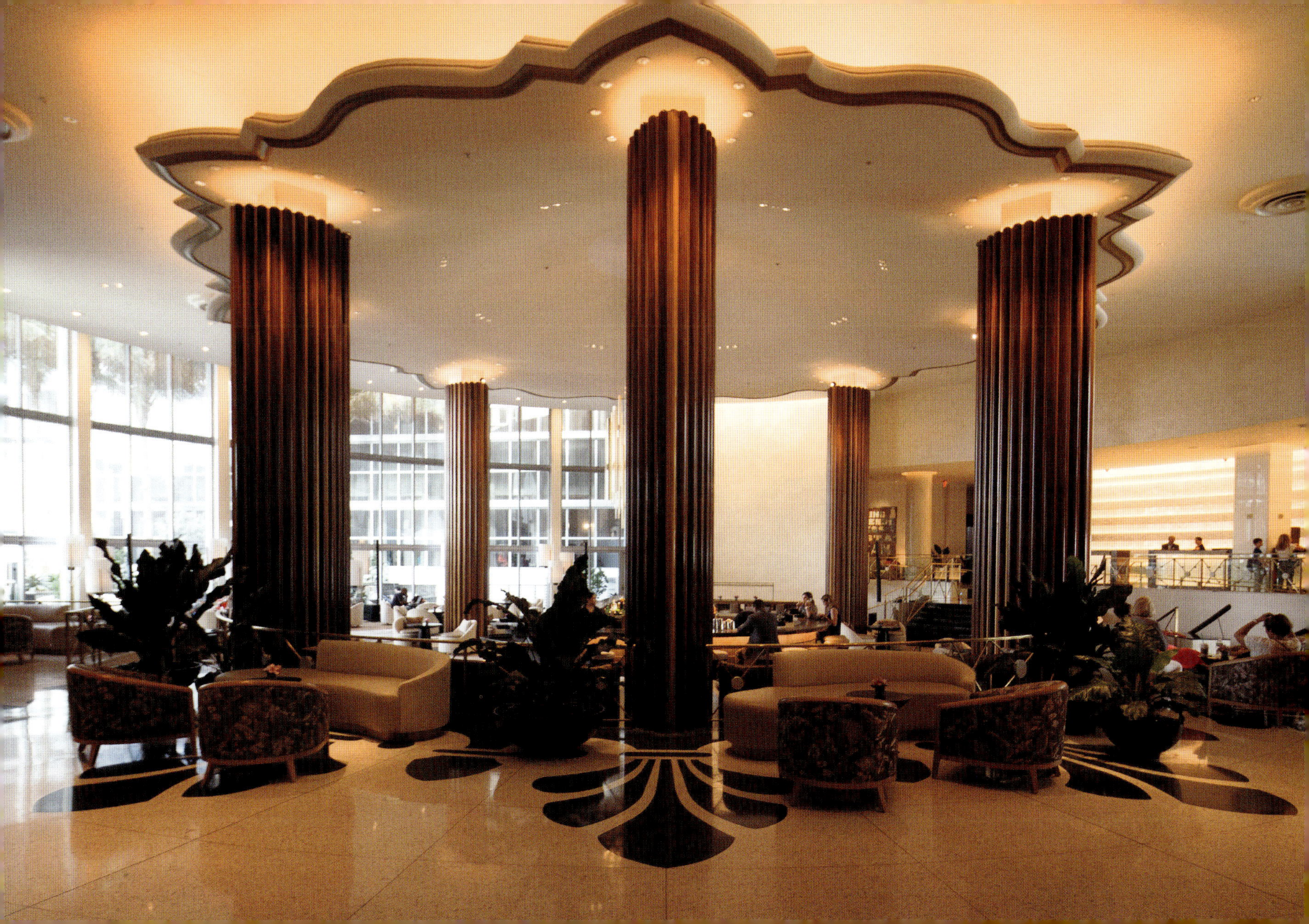

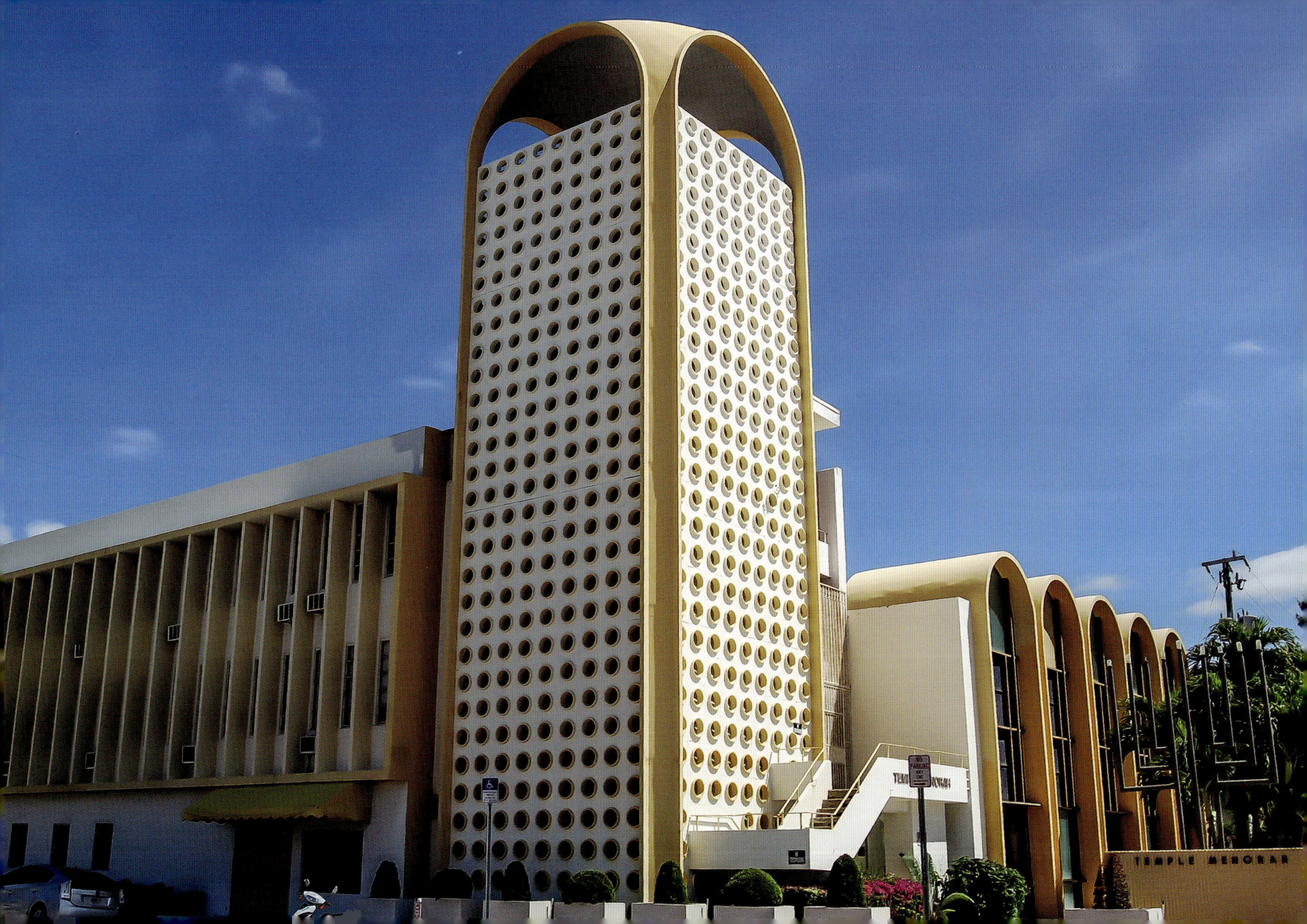
TEMPLE MENORAH

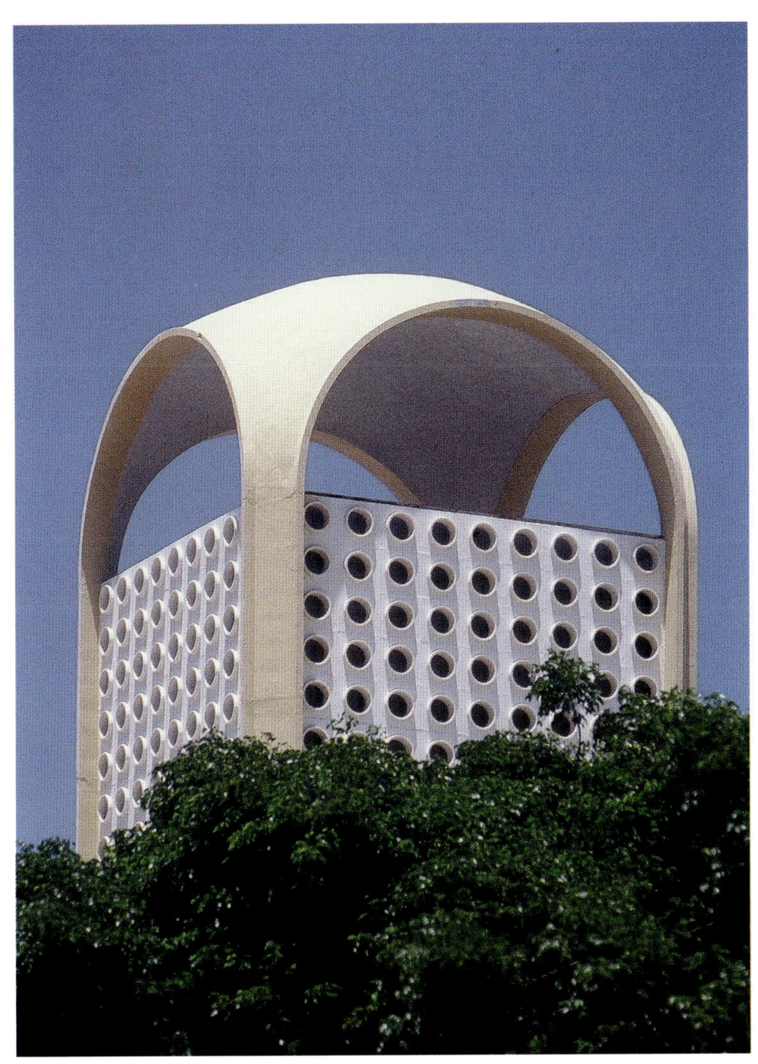

Temple Menorah
620 75th Street
Miami Beach
Architect: Gilbert Fein for Office & School Building, 1951, shown to left of tower
Addition: Morris Lapidus, 1963, central Belvedere Tower and arched sanctuary
Photograph: 2015

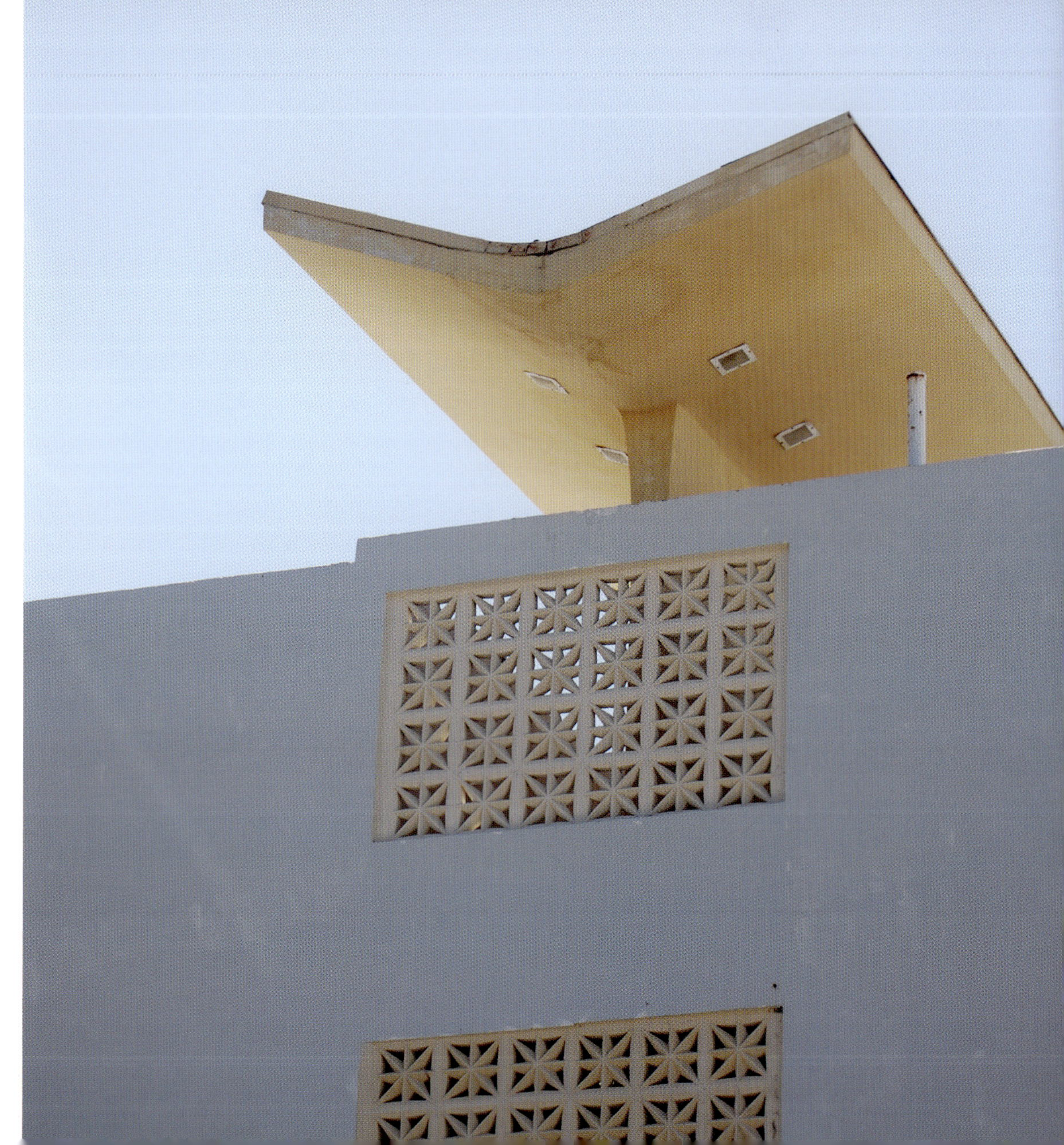

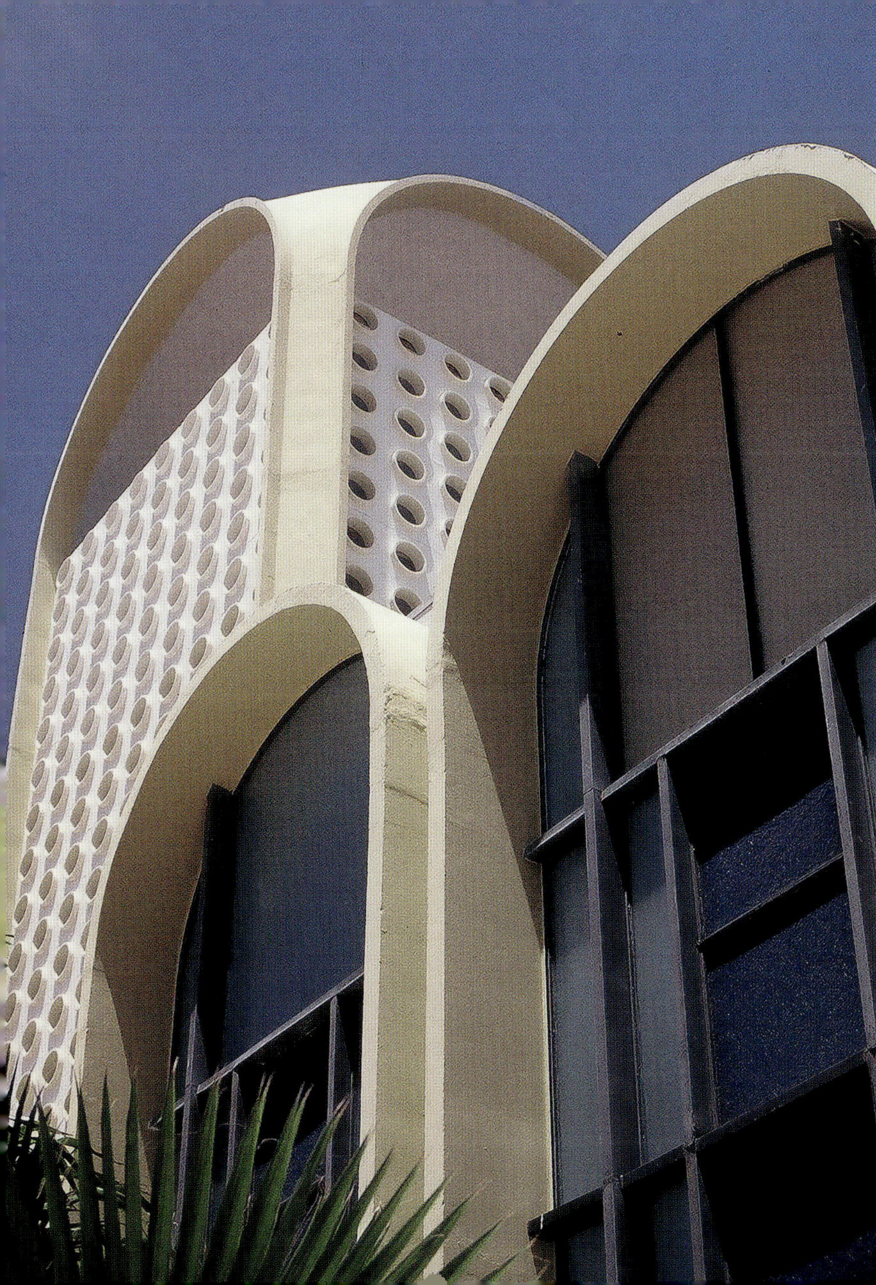

Temple Menorah - Office & School
Building detail
620 75th Street
Miami Beach
Architect: Gilbert Fein, 1951
Photograph: 2015

Temple Menorah - Belevedere Tower and
Sanctuary Addition
620 75th Street
Miami Beach
Architect: Morris Lapidus, 1963
Photograph: 2015

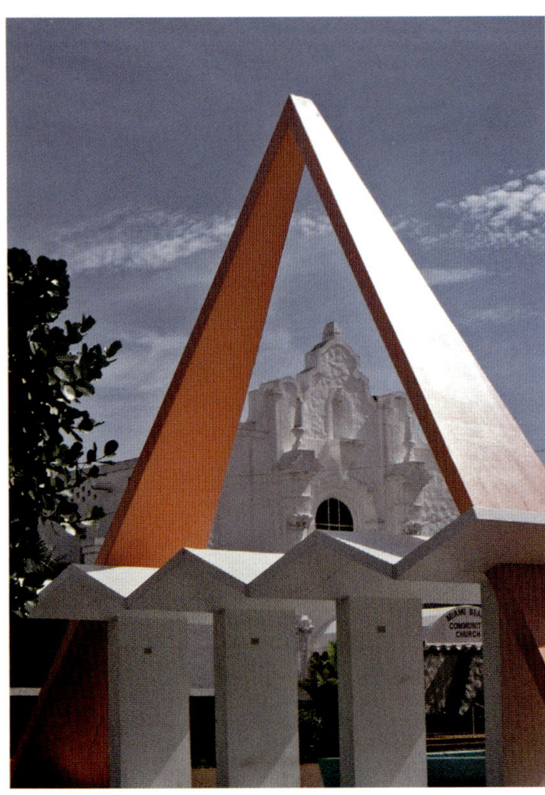

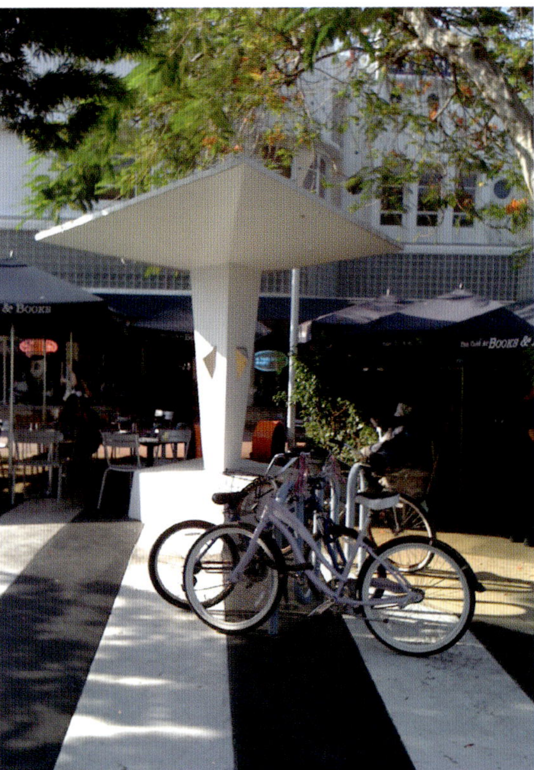

Lincoln Road Folly 1
Lincoln Road near Drexel Avenue
in front of Miami Beach Community Church
Miami Beach
Architect: Morris Lapidus, 1960
Photograph: 2009

Lincoln Road Folly 2
Lincoln Road near Michigan Avenue
Miami Beach
Architect: Morris Lapidus, 1960
Photograph: 2015

Lincoln Road Folly 3 + Fountain
Morris Lapidus Memorial
Lincoln Road near Jefferson Avenue
Miami Beach
Architect: Morris Lapidus, 1960
Photograph: 2015

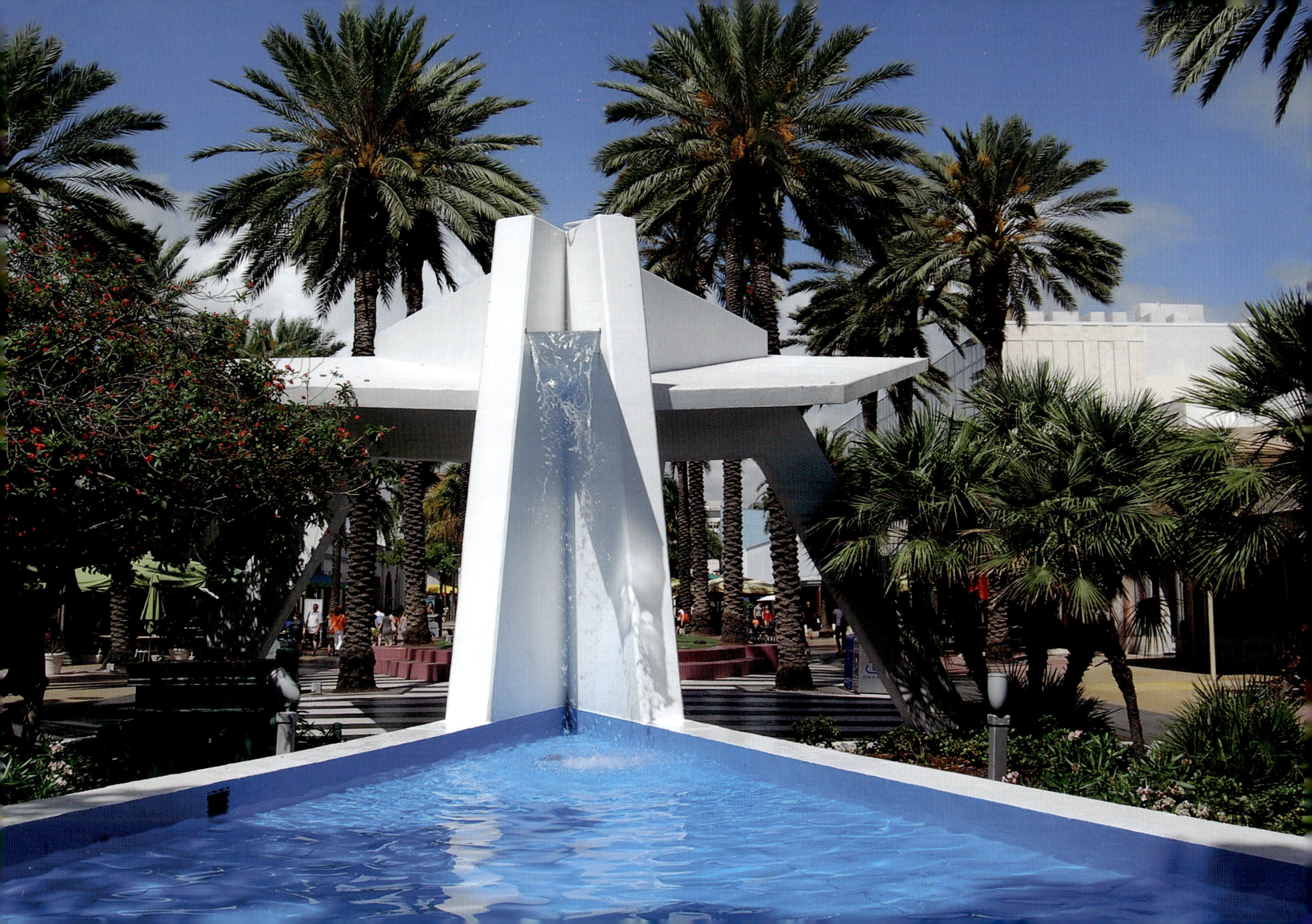

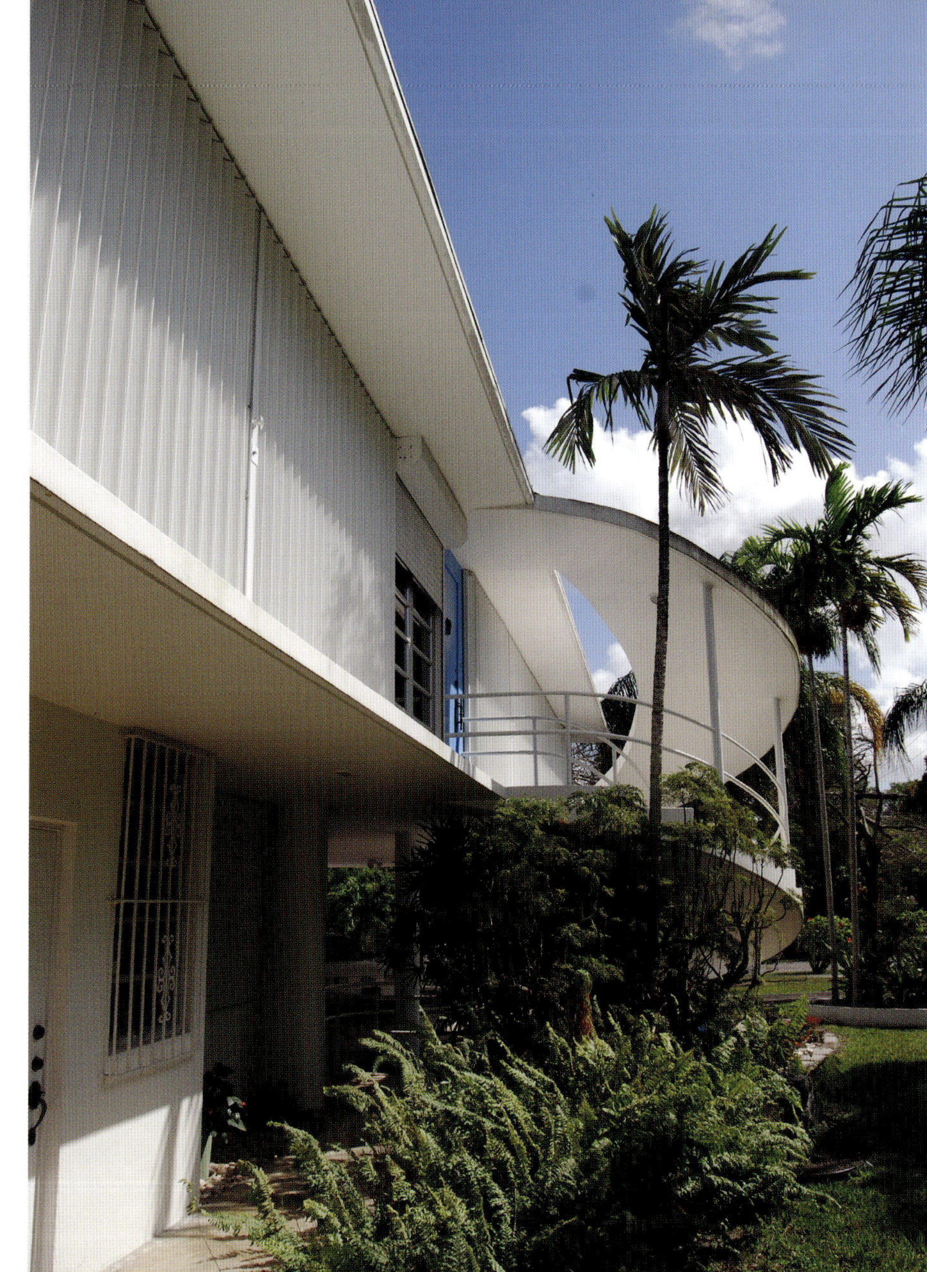

Private Residence with storm shutters closed
5261 NE 5th Avenue
Miami
Architect: Rufus Nims, 1949
Photograph: 2015

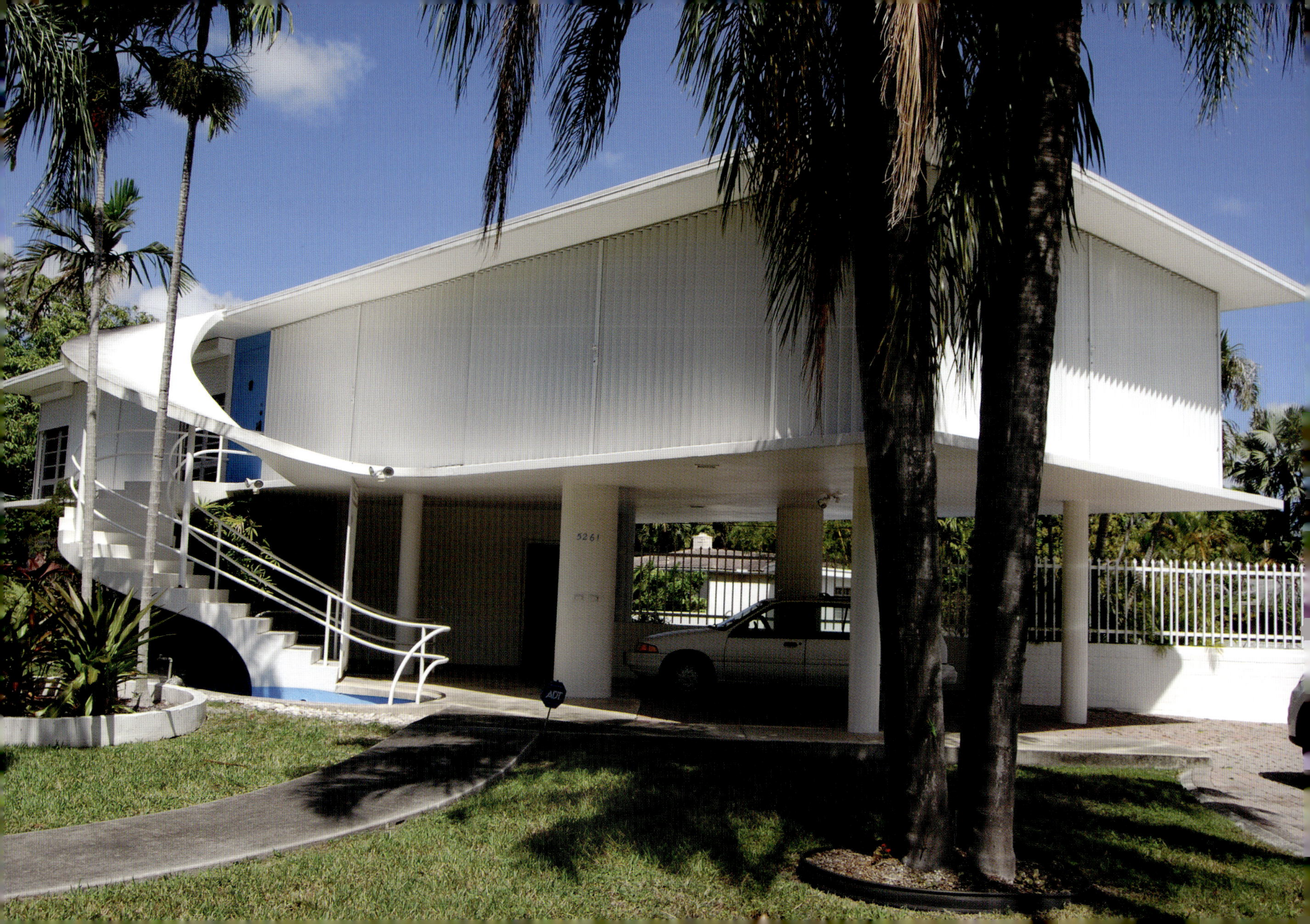
5261
ADT

Alexander Hotel
5225 Collins Avenue
Miami Beach
Architect: Charles McKirahan, 1962
Photograph: 2013

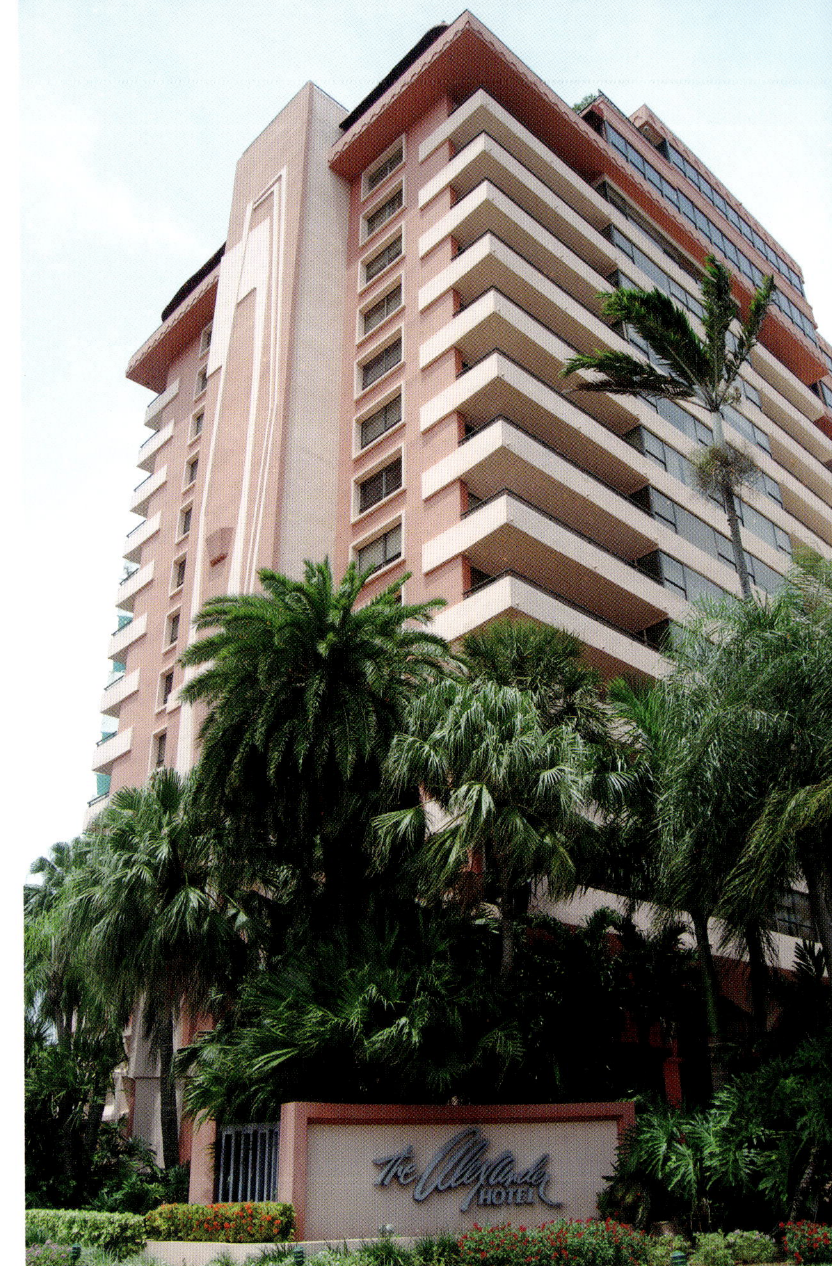

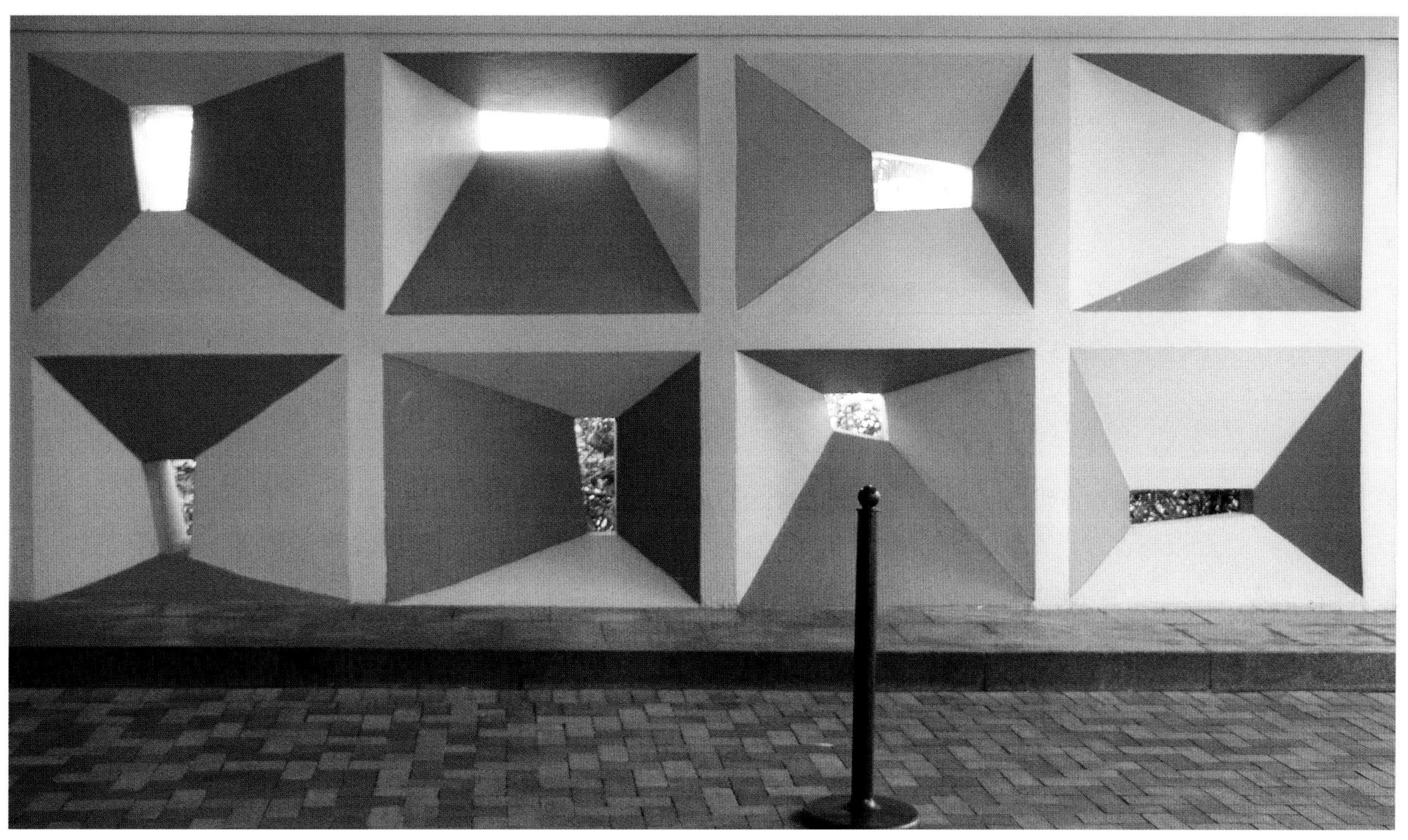

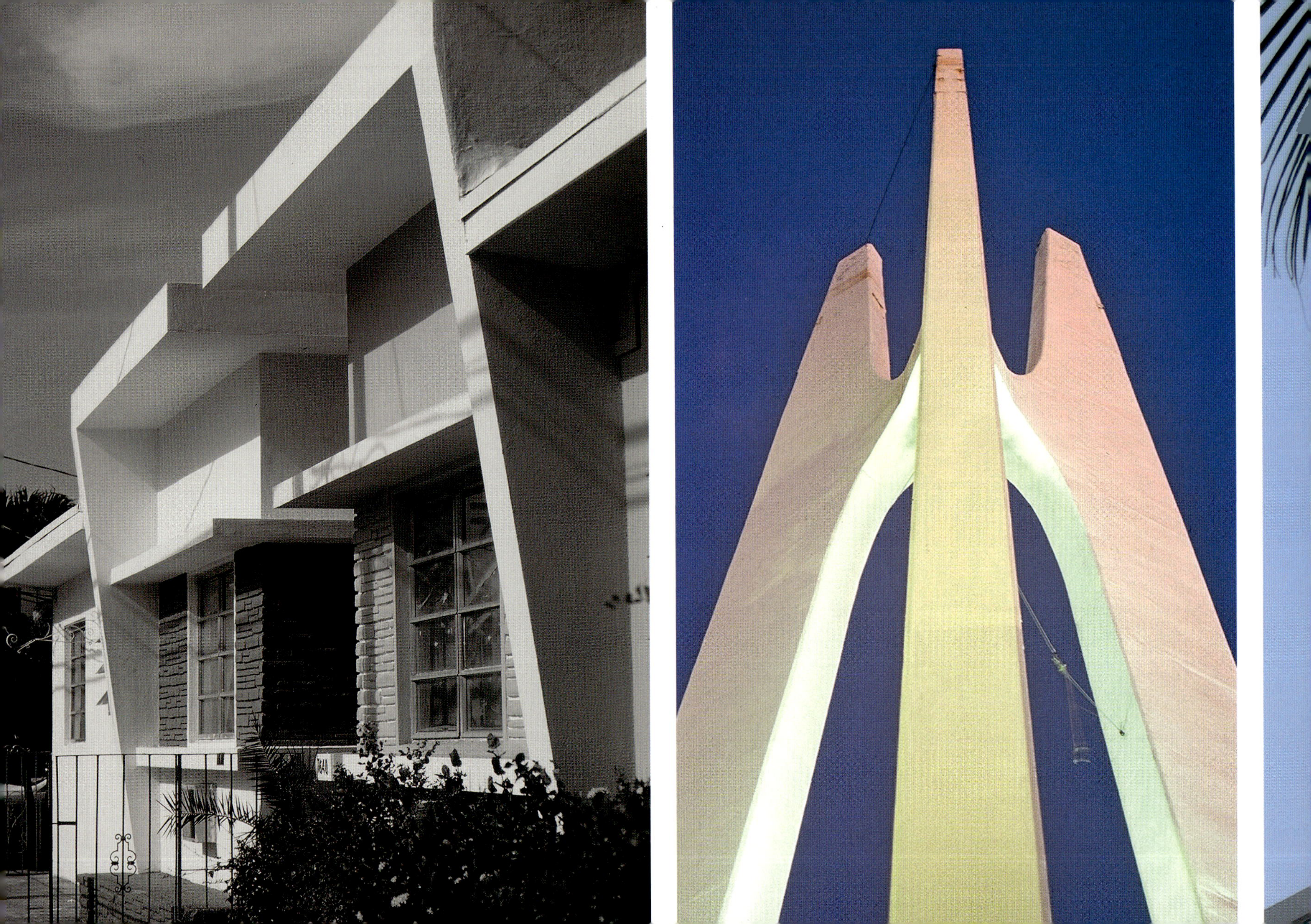

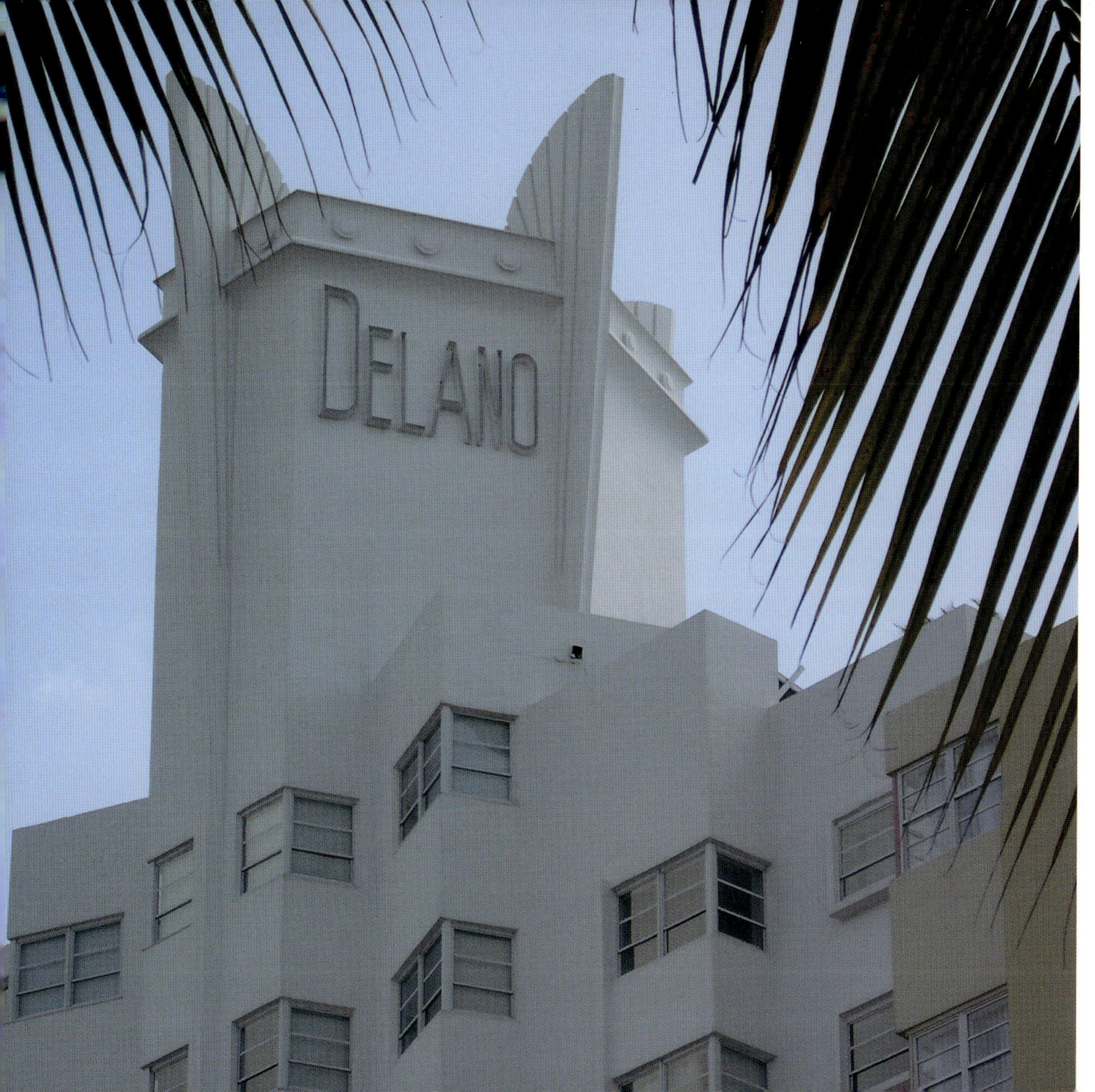

7630–7640 Dickens Avenue
Miami Beach
Architect: Leonard Glasser, 1951
Photograph: 2005

Tripod Signage Pylon for the former
Miami Beach Federal Savings & Loan
743 Washington Avenue
Miami Beach
Architect: Edwin T. Reeder Architect, 1957
Photograph: 2010

Delano Hotel
1685 Collins Avenue
Miami Beach
Architect: Robert Swartburg, 1947
Renovation: Philippe Starck
Photograph: 2004

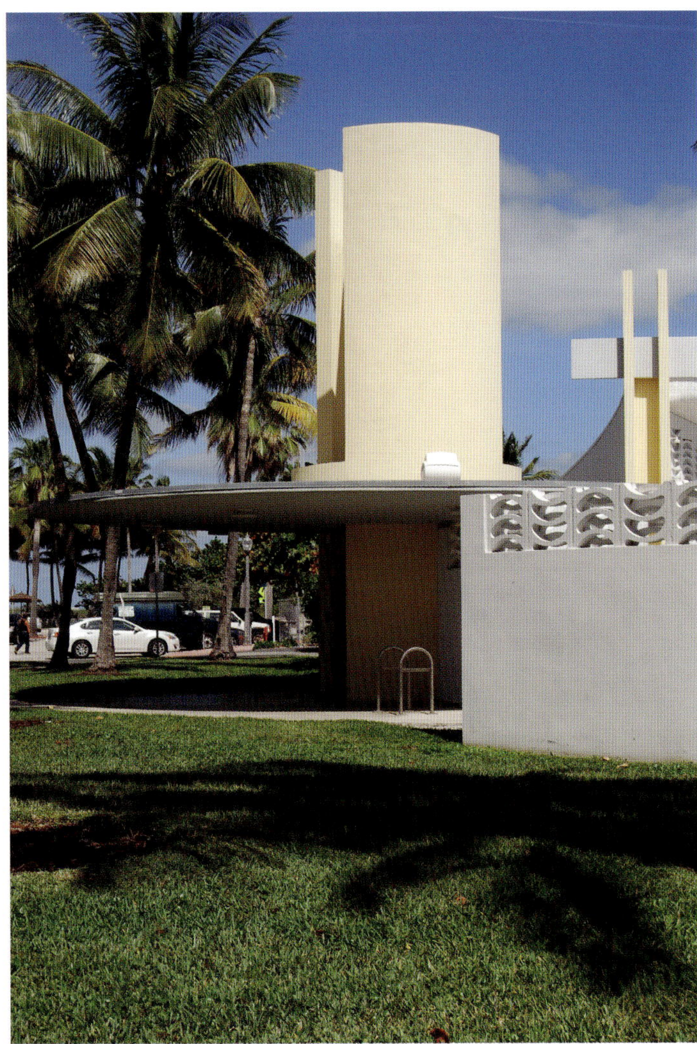

North Shore Band Shell
7251–7275 Collins Avenue
Miami Beach
Architect: Norman Giller, 1957
Photograph: 2014

Duane Motel
315–321 83rd Street
Miami Beach
Architect: Robert Nordlin, 1955
Photograph: 2000

Triton Towers
2899 Collins Avenue
Miami Beach
Architects: Watson, Deutschland & Kruse, 1966
Photograph: 2008

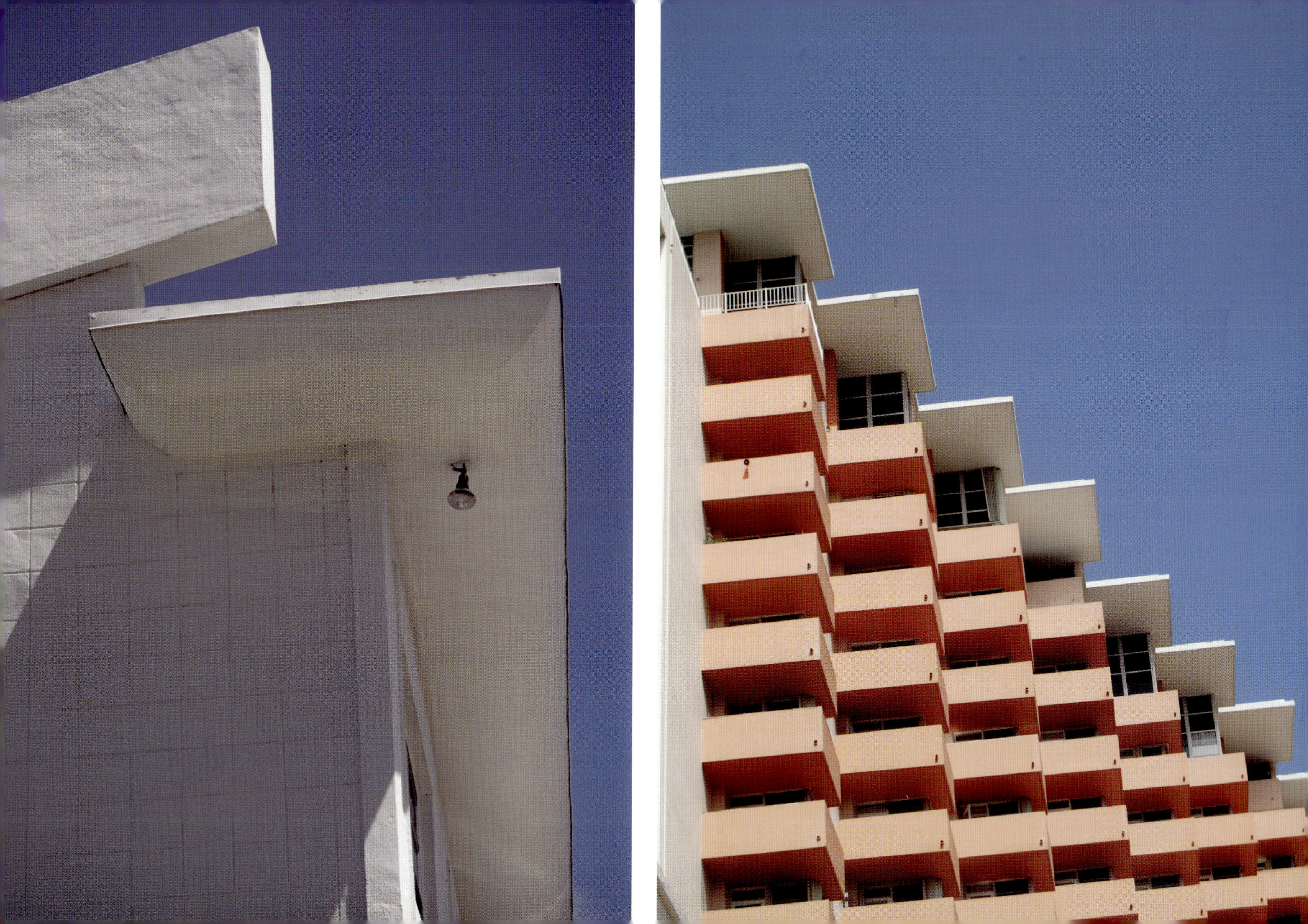

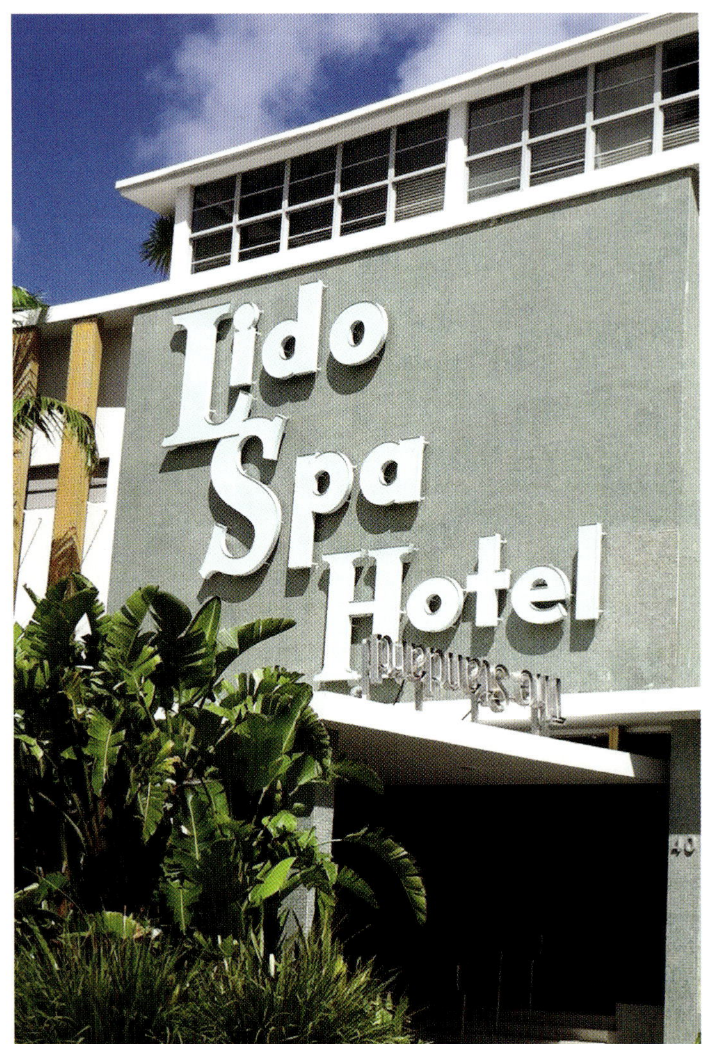

Lido Spa Hotel, a.k.a. Standard Hotel
40 Island Avenue
Miami Beach
Architect: Norman Giller, 1953
Architect for front addition: A Herbert Mathes, 1960
Photograph: 2014

Gumenick Chapel at Temple Israel of Greater Miami
137 NE 19th Street
Miami
Architect: Kenneth Triester, 1969
Photograph: 2011

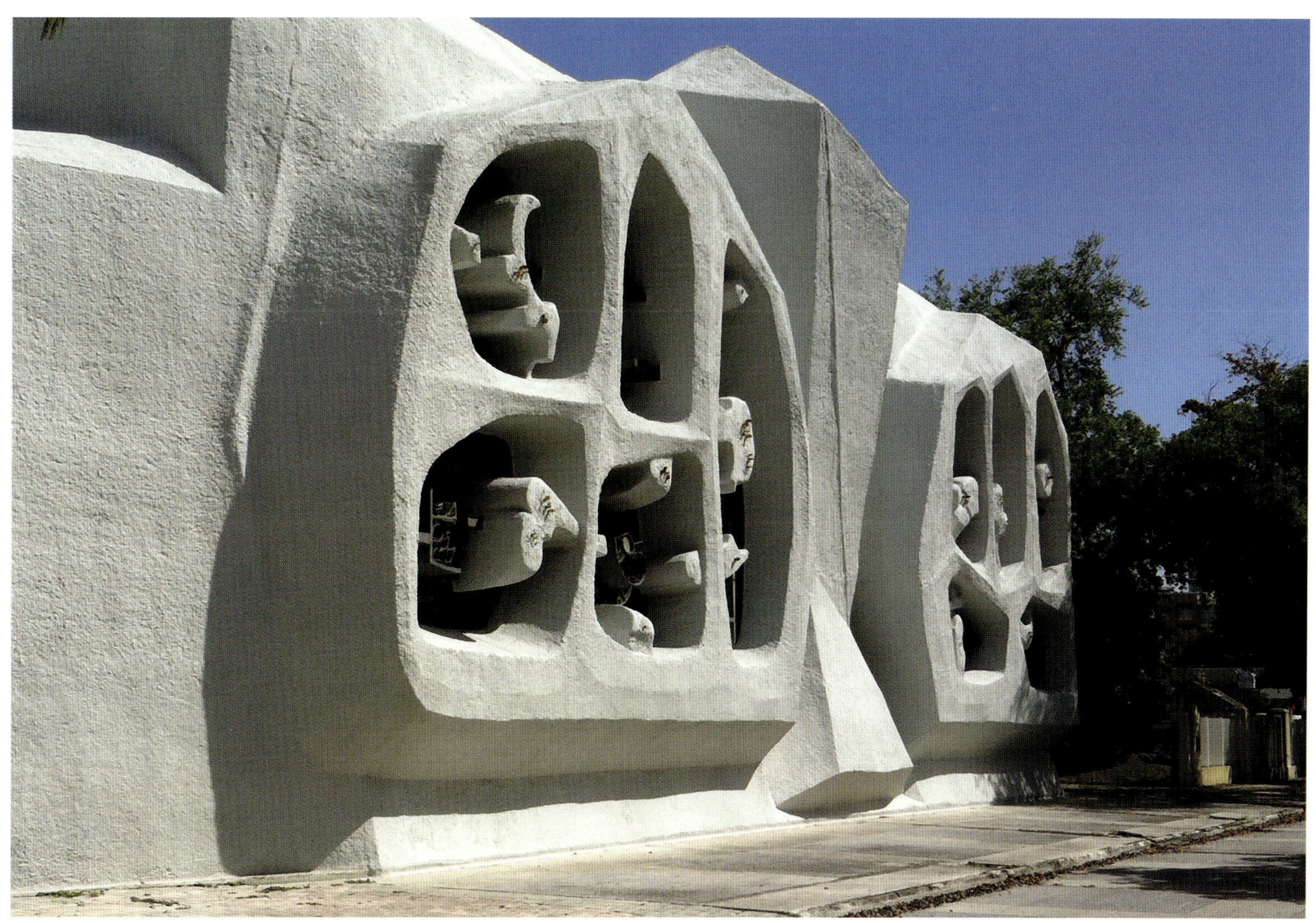

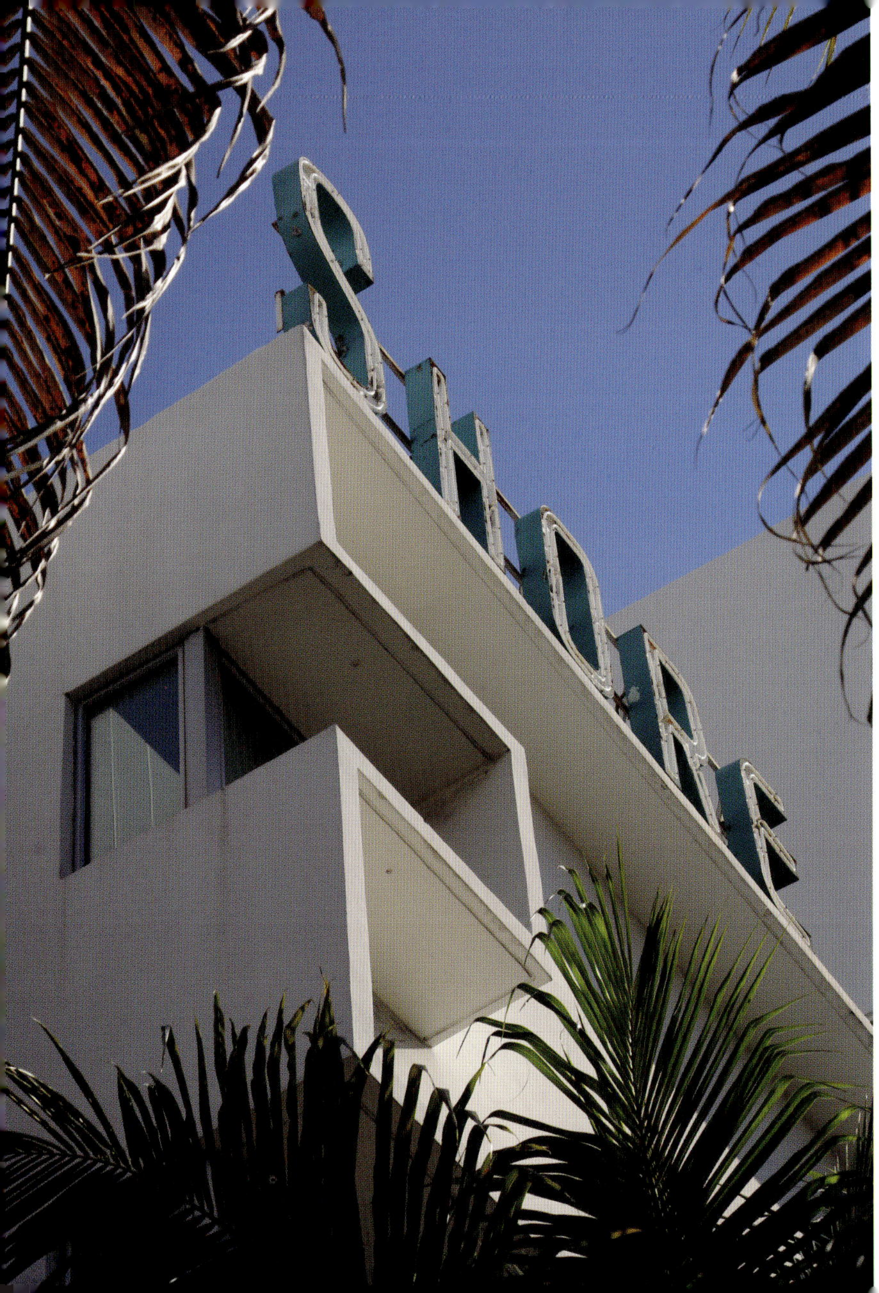

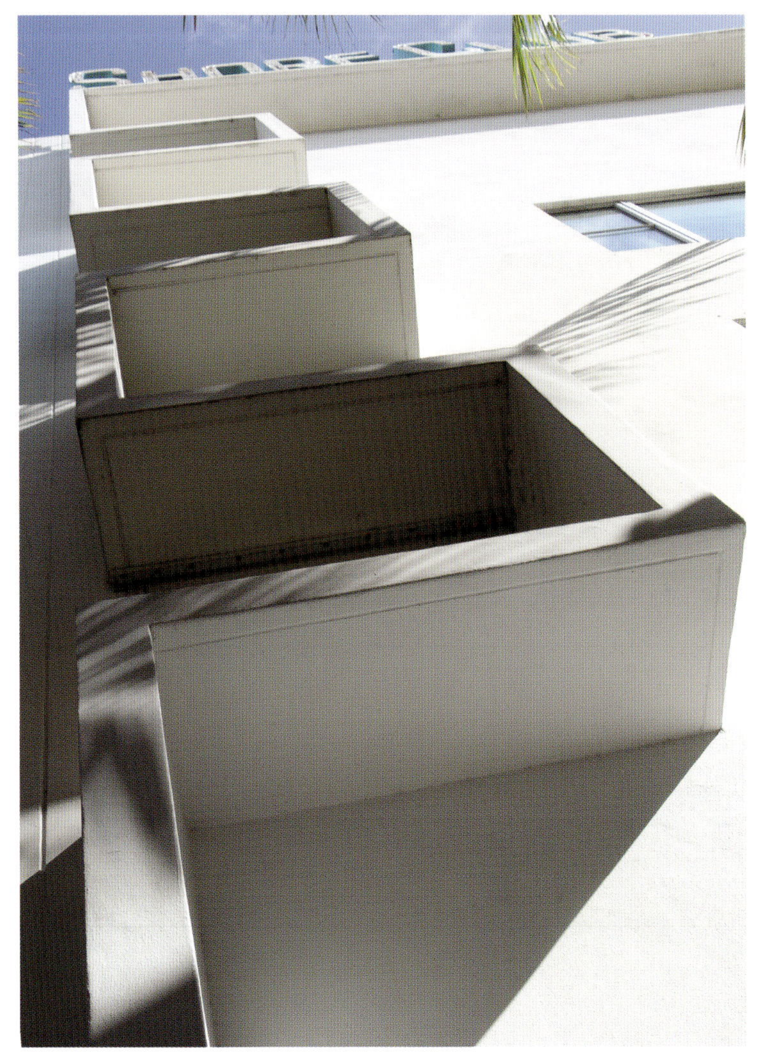

Shore Club Hotel, left
1901 Collins Avenue
Miami Beach
Architect: Albert Anis, 1949
Photograph: 2017

Capri, right
1491 Lincoln Terrace
Miami Beach
Architect: Igor Polevitzsky
Photograph: 2012

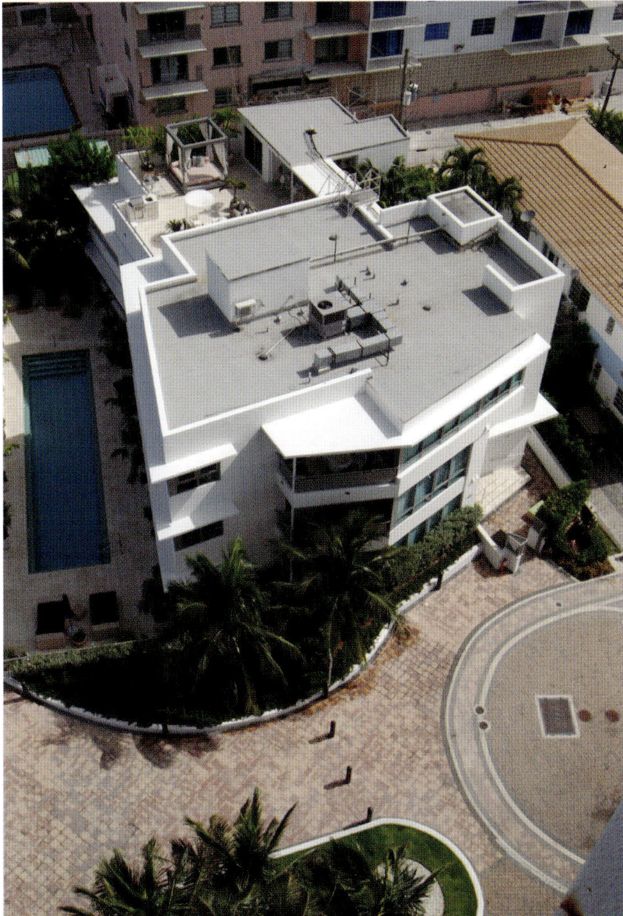

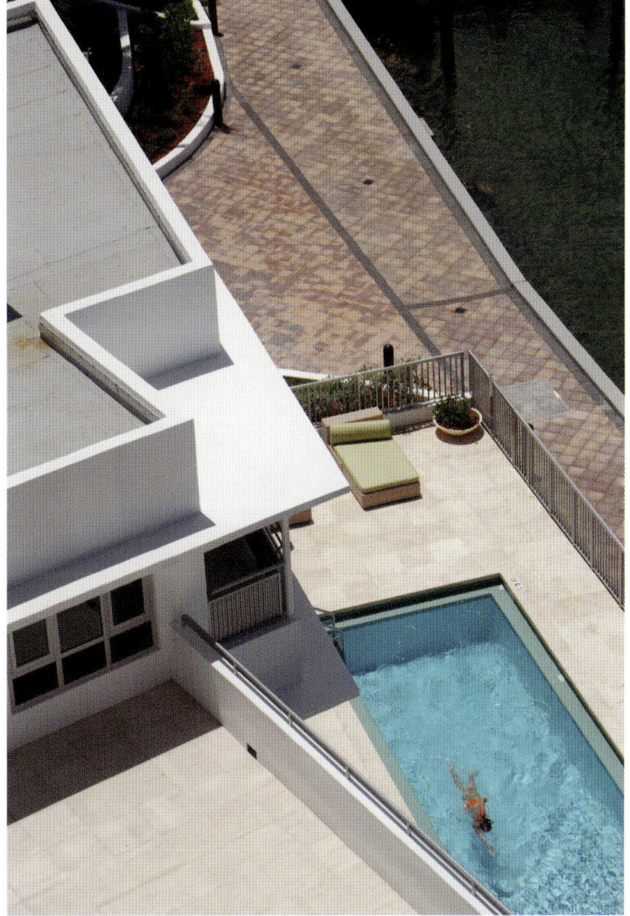

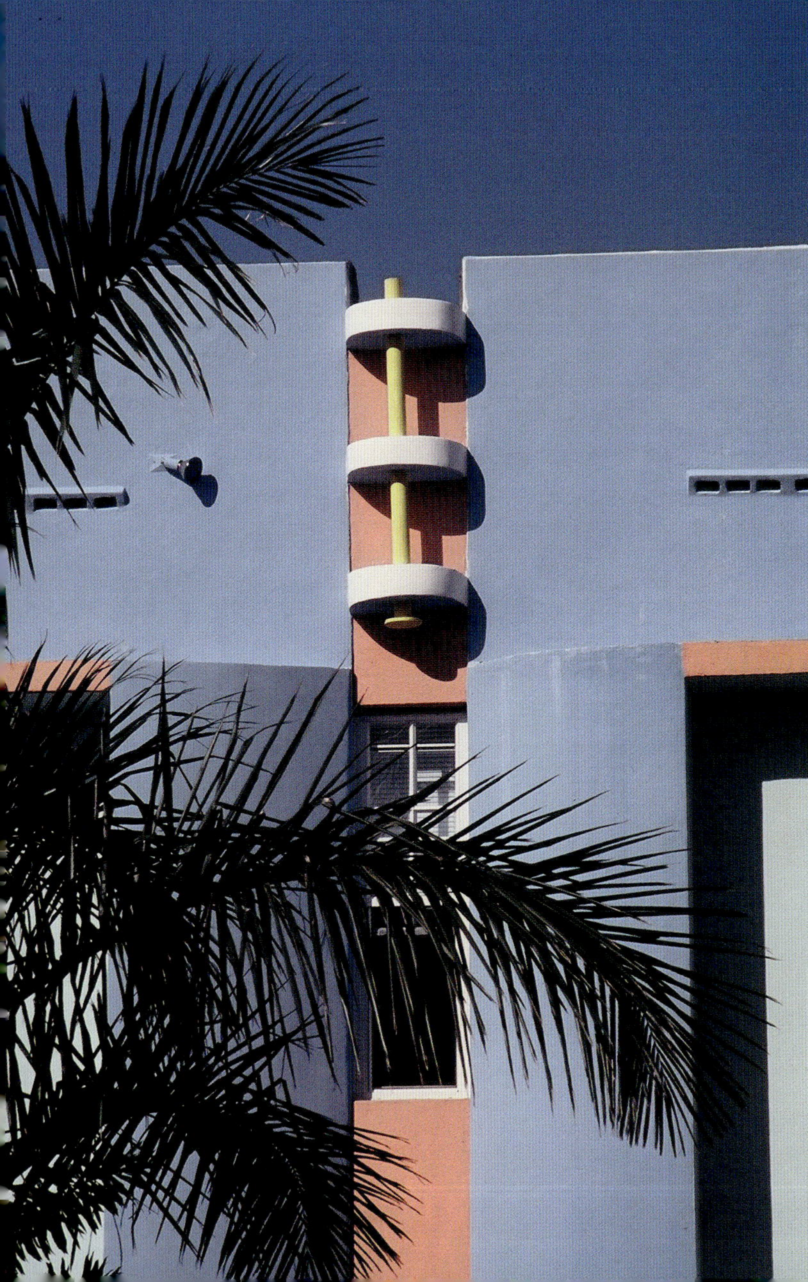

Flag Pole holder
748 Euclid Avenue
Miami Beach
Architect: Gene Bayliss, 1939
Photograph: 2005

Dezerland Hotel
8700 Collins Avenue (demolished)
Miami Beach
Architects: Morris Lapidus and Albert Anis, 1951
Photograph: 2003

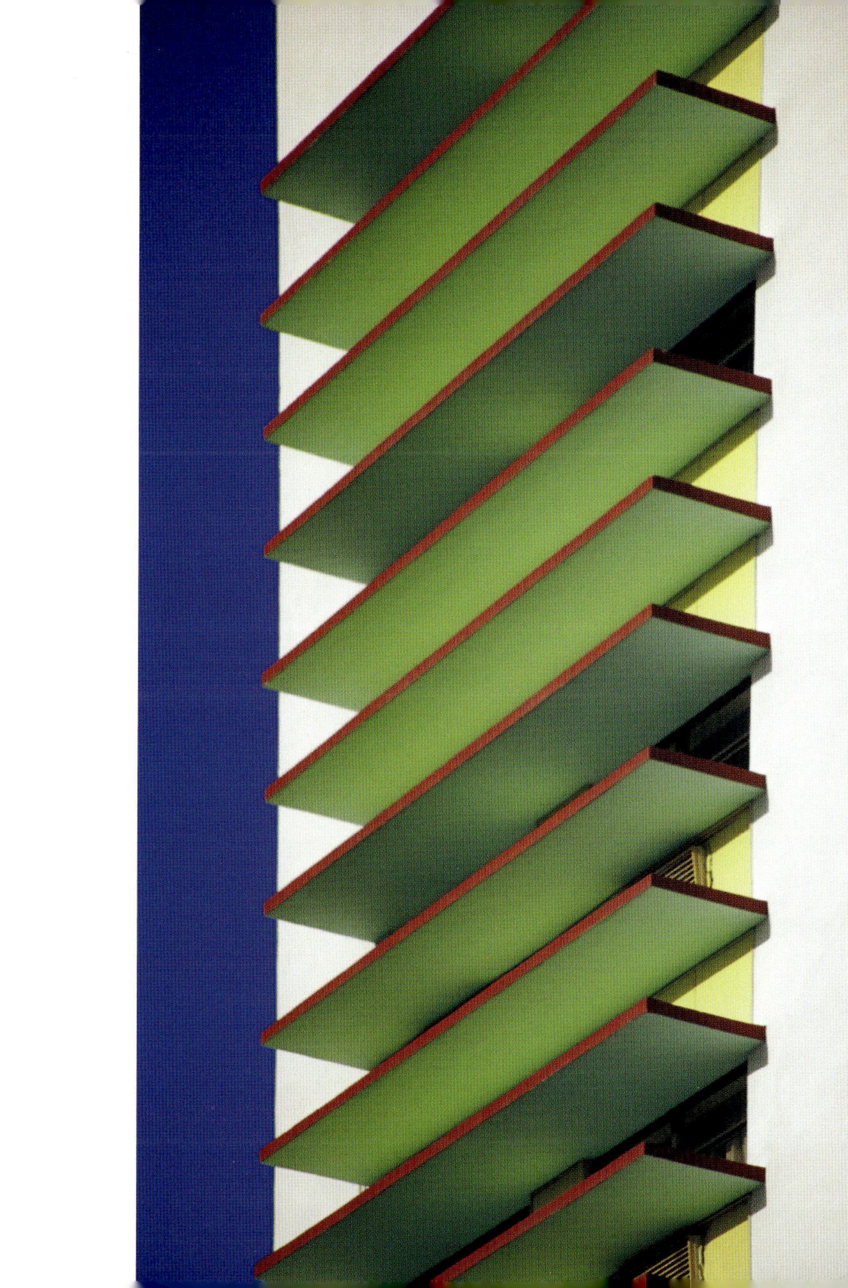

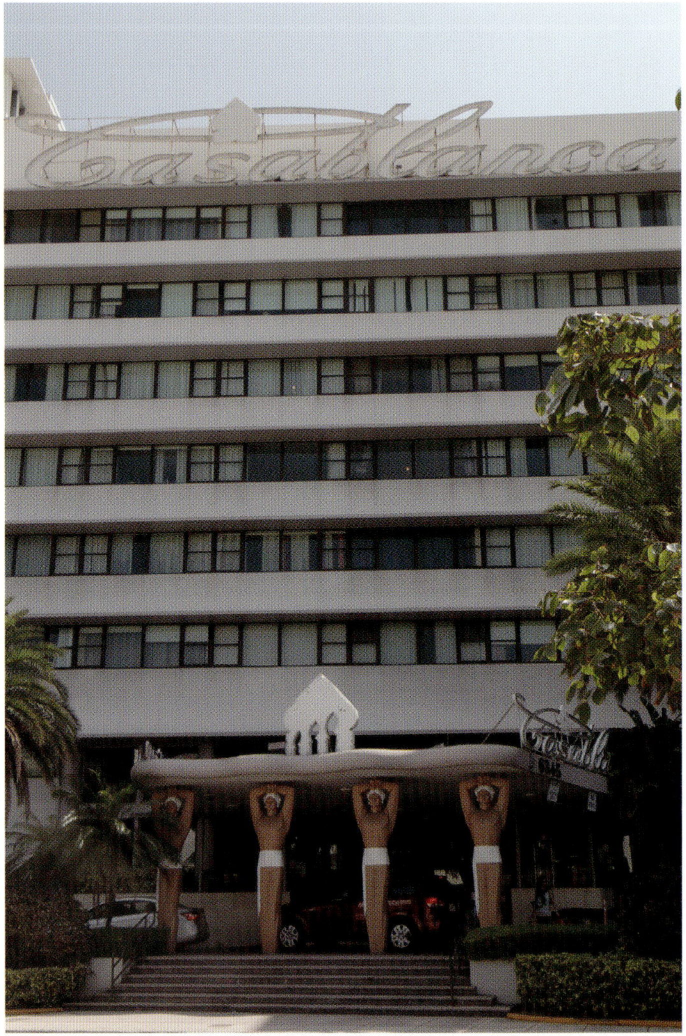

Casablanca Hotel
6345 Collins Avenue
Miami Beach
Architect: Roy France, 1949
Photograph: 2019

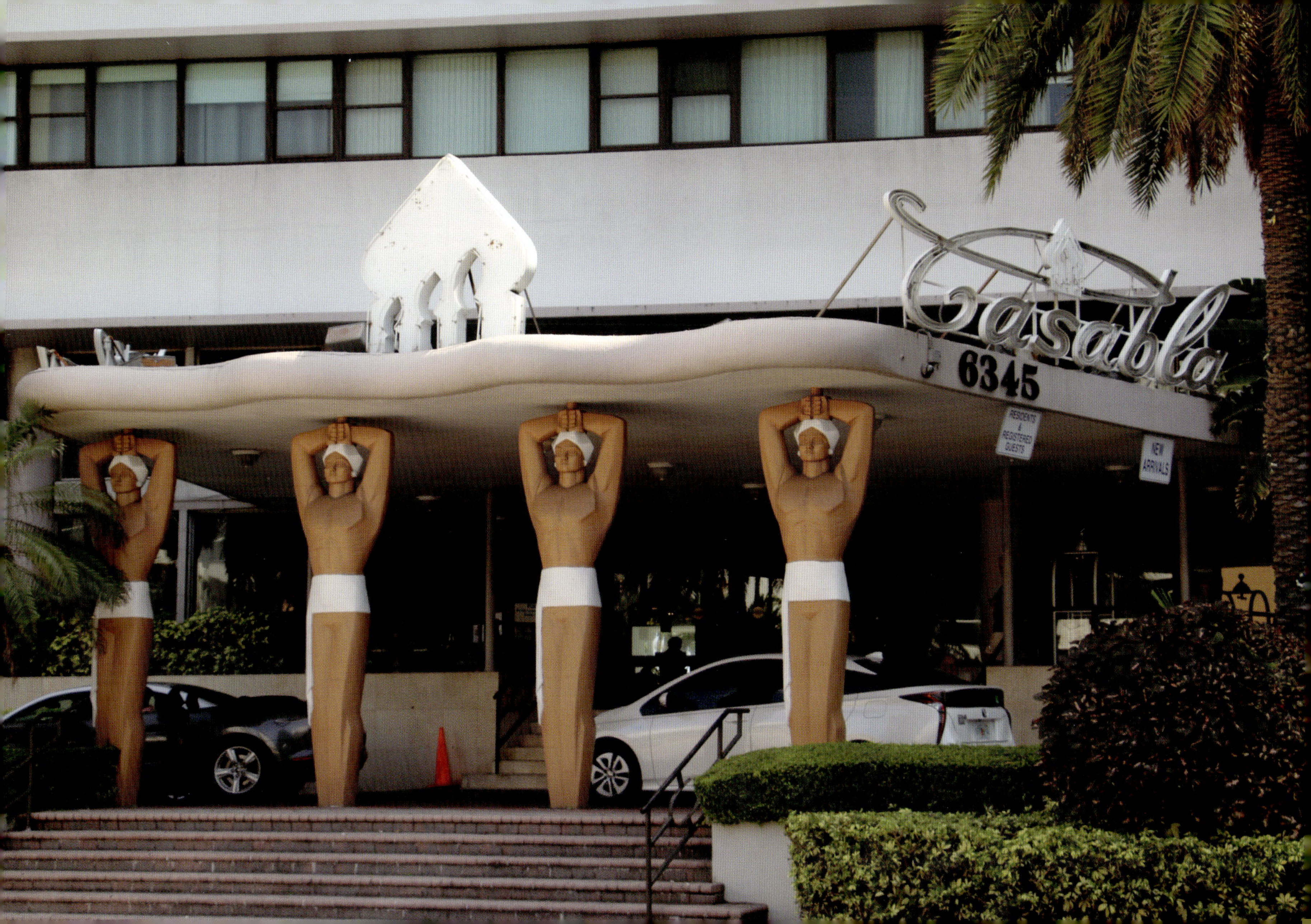
Casabla
6345
RESIDENTS & REGISTERED GUESTS
NEW ARRIVALS

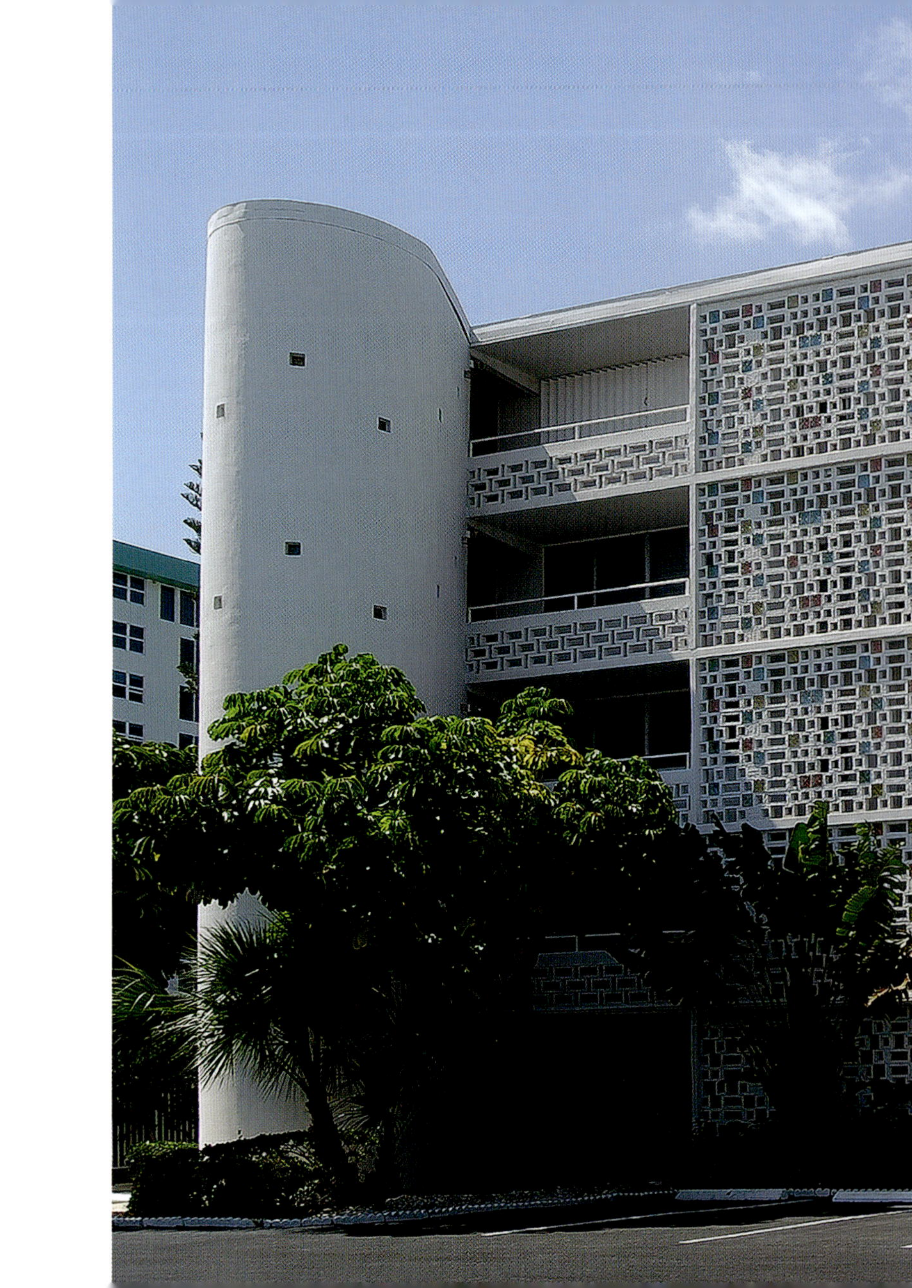

Chapter Three

BAY HARBOR ISLANDS & SURFSIDE

Bay Harbor Continental (demolished)
1135 103rd Street
Bay Harbor Islands
Architect: Charles McKirahan, 1958
Photograph: 2014

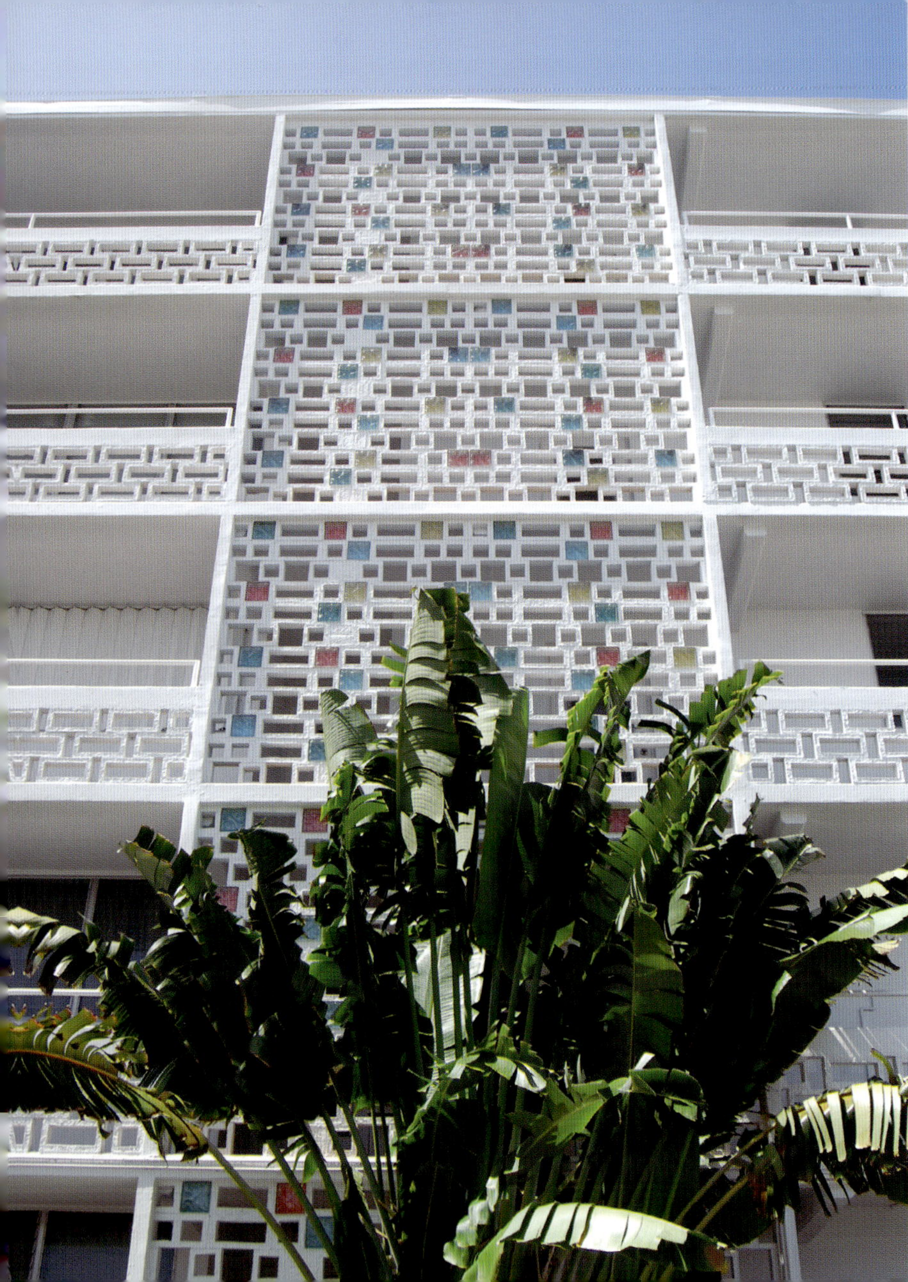

Bay Harbor Continental (demolished)
1135 103rd Street
Bay Harbor Islands
Architect: Charles McKirahan, 1958
Photograph: 2018

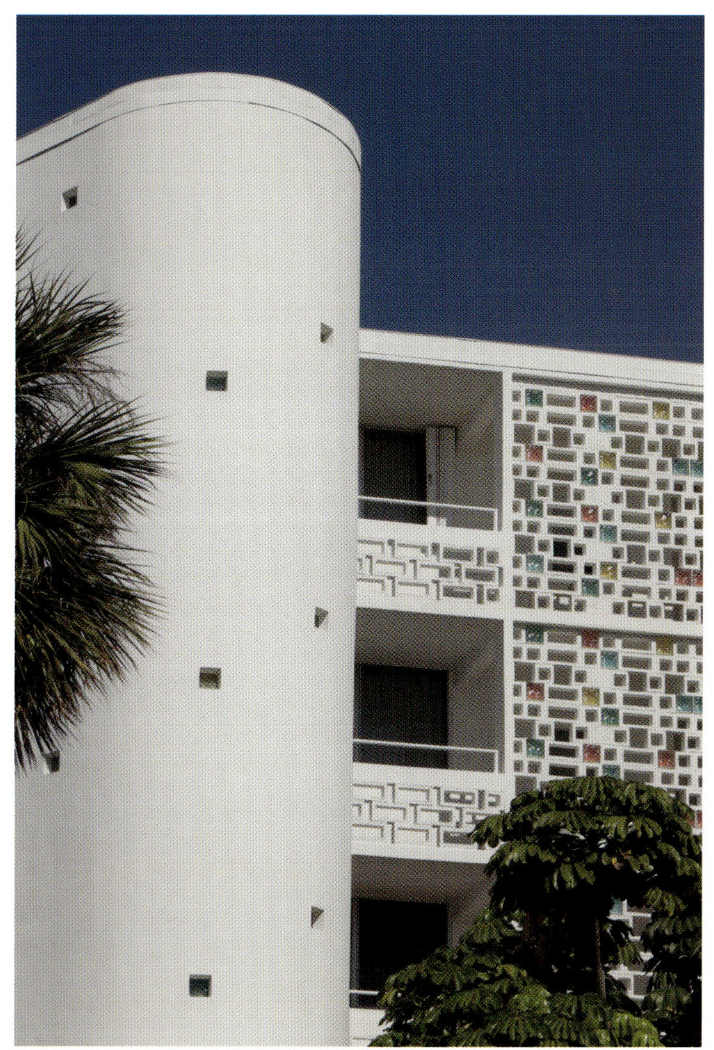

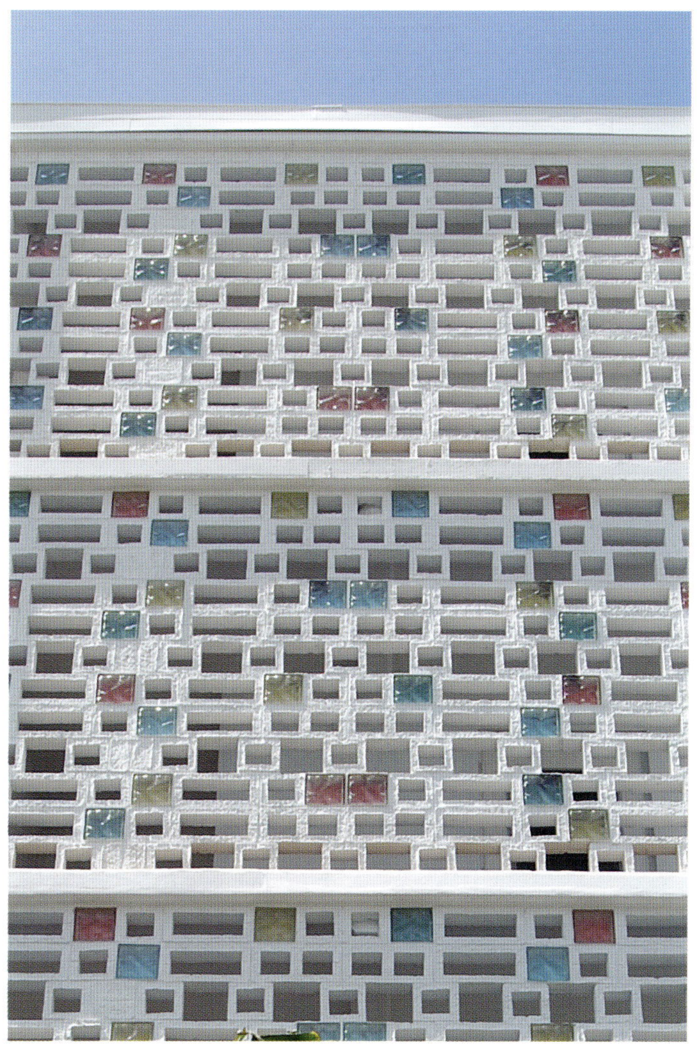

Regent Palace
9309-9317 Collins Avenue
Surfside
Architect: Leonard Glasser, 1951
Photograph: 2015

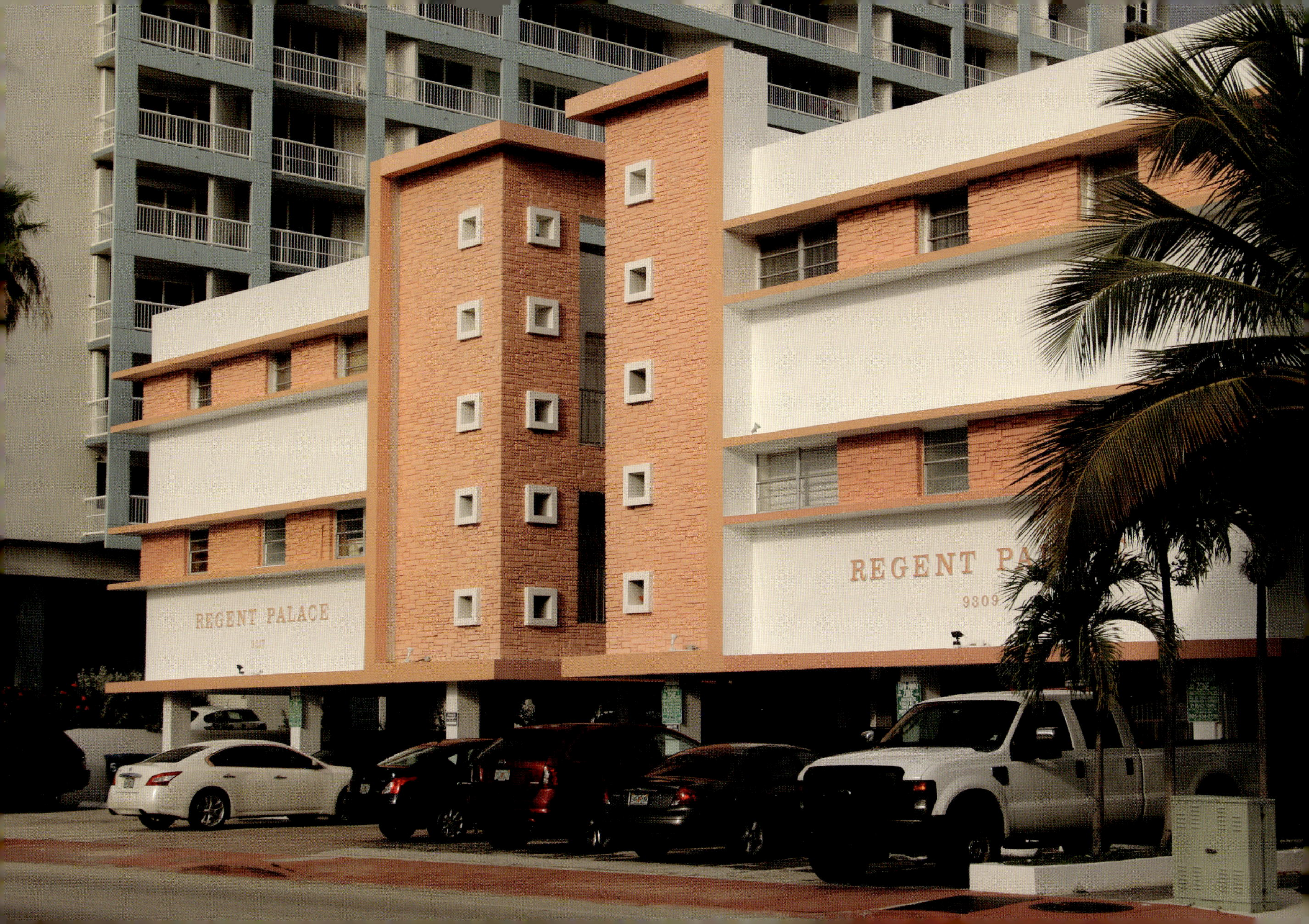
REGENT PALACE
9317
REGENT PA
9309

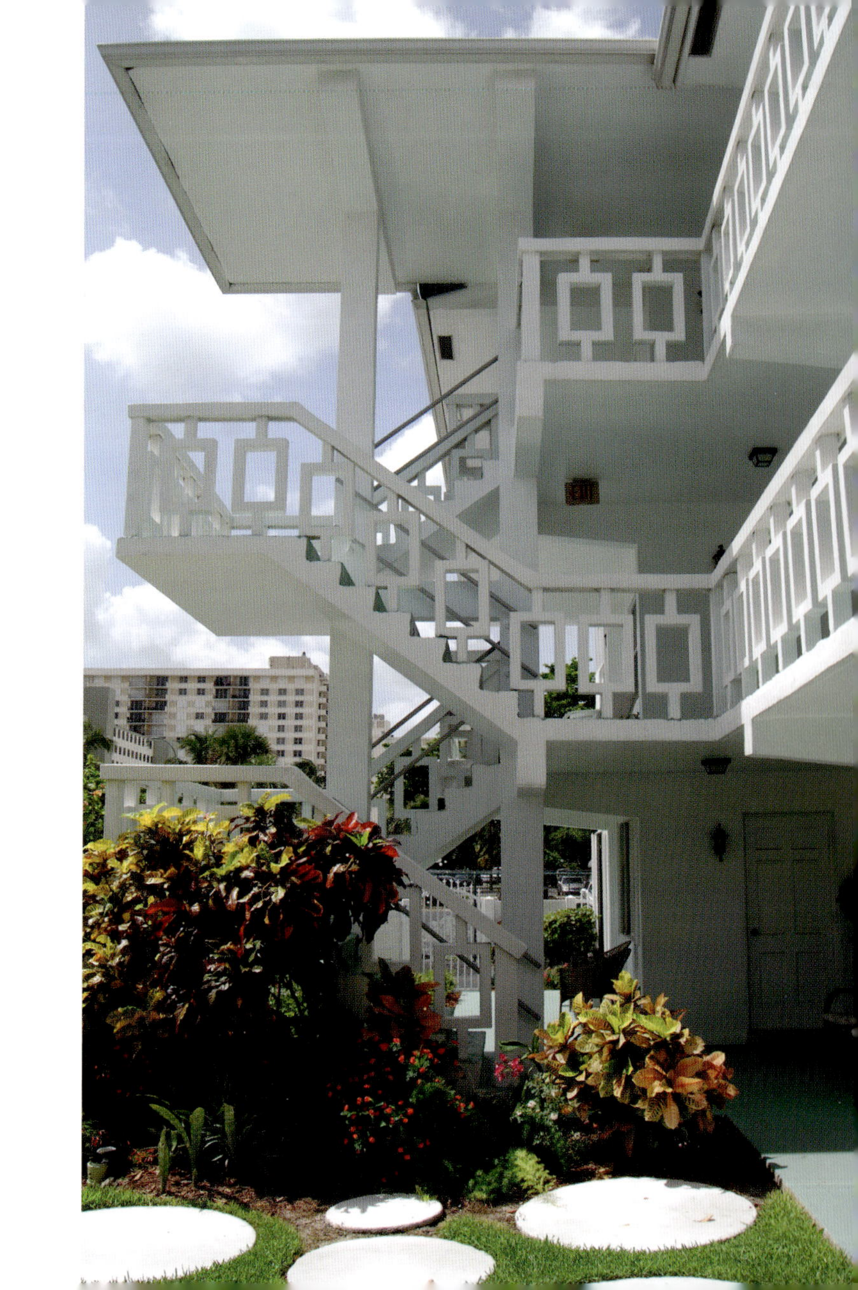

Chapter Four

LAUDERDALE-BY-THE-SEA & FORT LAUDERDALE

Jade Beach West
1900 South Ocean Drive
Lauderdale-by-the-Sea
Architect: unknown
Photograph: 2017

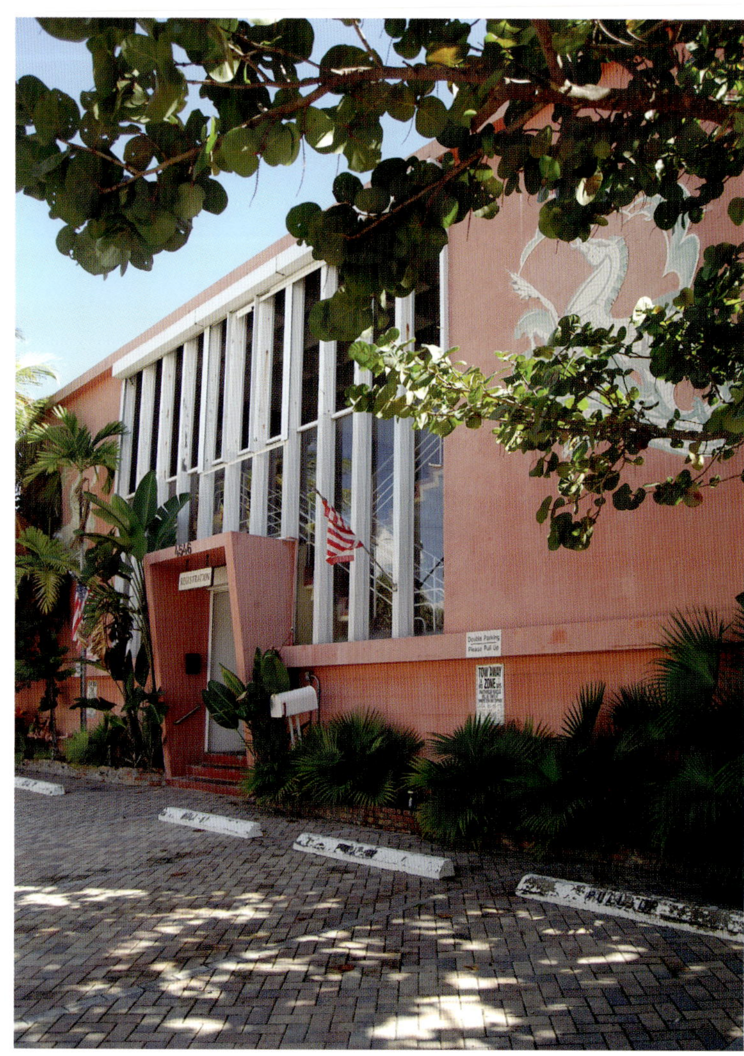

4546 El Mar Drive (demolished)
Lauderdale-by-the-Sea
Architect: Unknown, 1954
Photograph: 2014

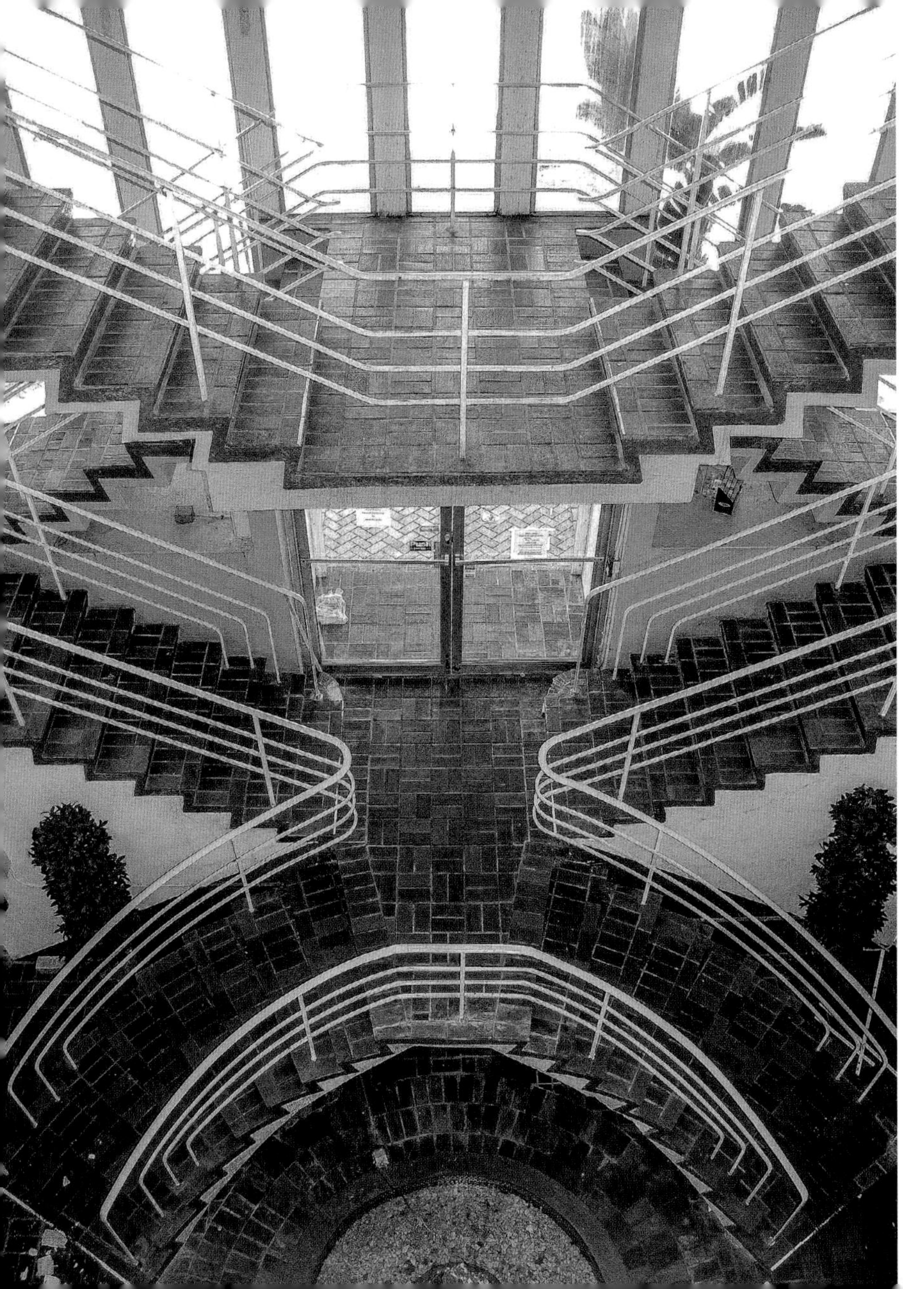

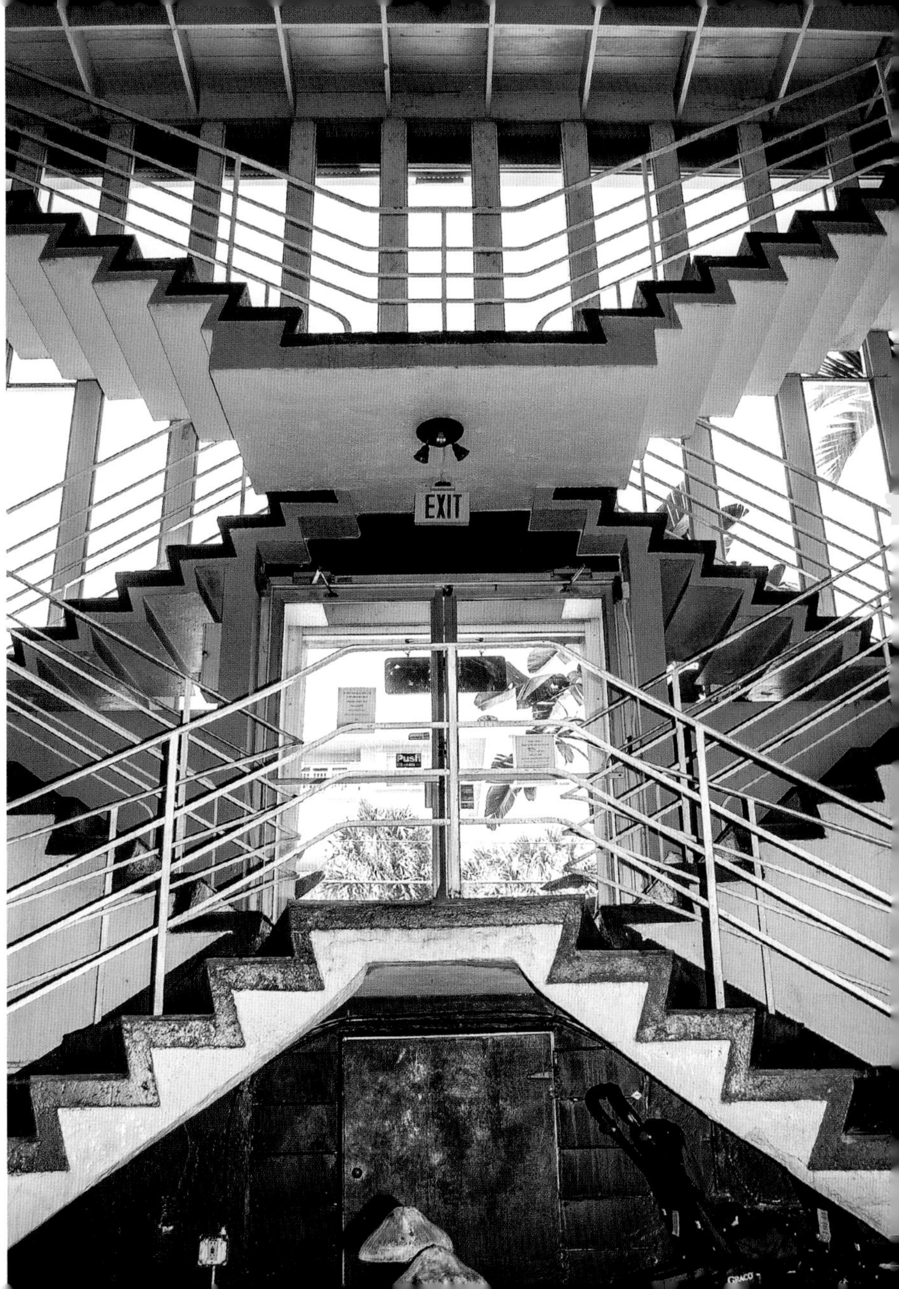

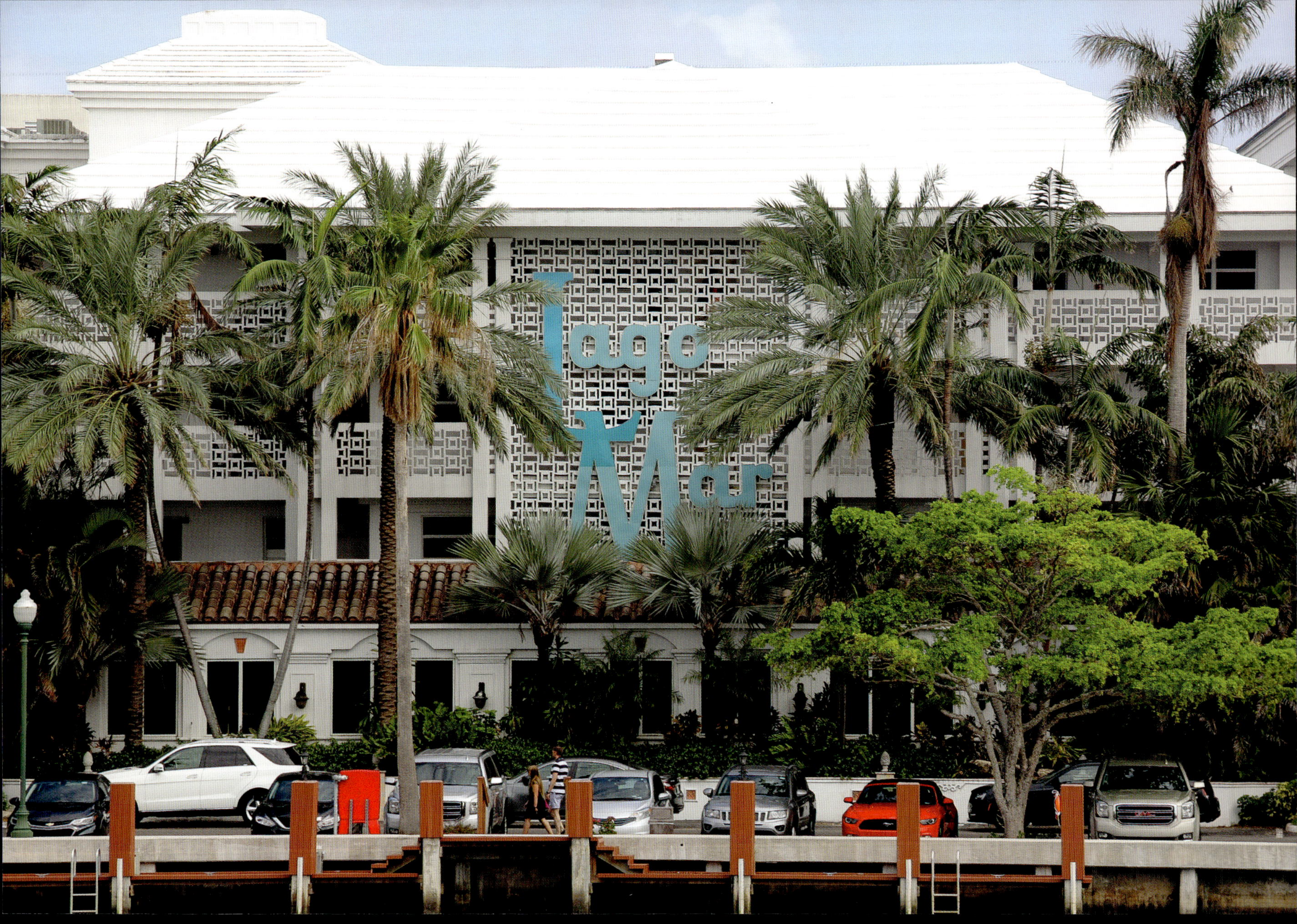
Lago
Mar

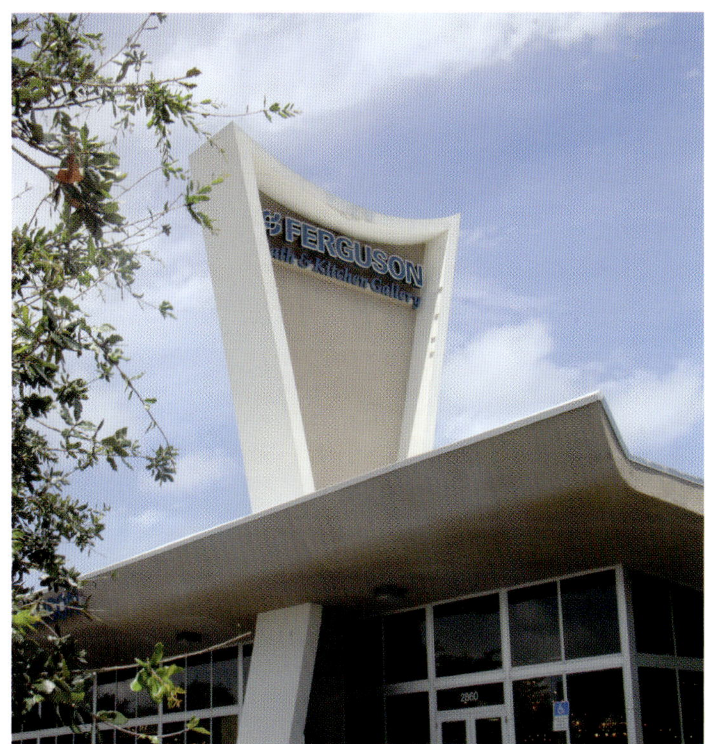

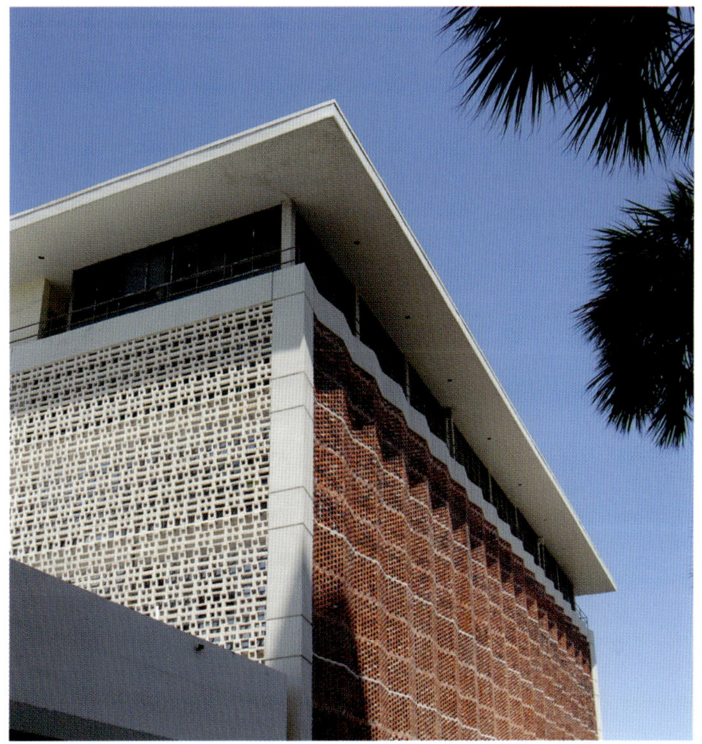

Lago Mar
1700 South Ocean Lane
Fort Lauderdale
Architect: Charles McKirahan, 1962
Photograph: 2017

Fergusons Plumbing, a.k.a. Castro Convertibles
2860 North Federal Highway
Fort Lauderdale
Architect: Charles McKirahan, 1954
Photograph: 2017

Bayview Office Building
1040 Bayview Drive
Fort Lauderdale
Architect: Charles McKirahan, 1960
Photographe: 2016

Birch House
609 Birch Road
Fort Lauderdale
Architect: Charles McKirahan, 1959
Photograph: 2017

Birch Tower
3003 Terramar Street
Fort Lauderdale
Architect: Charles McKirahan, 1960
Photograph: 2017

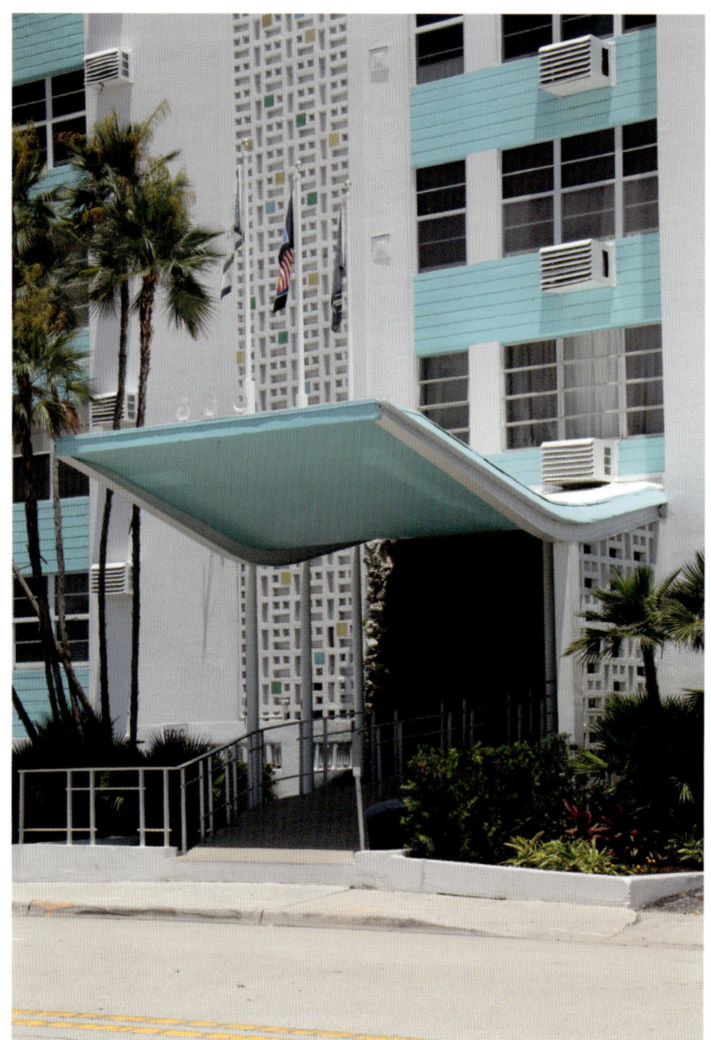

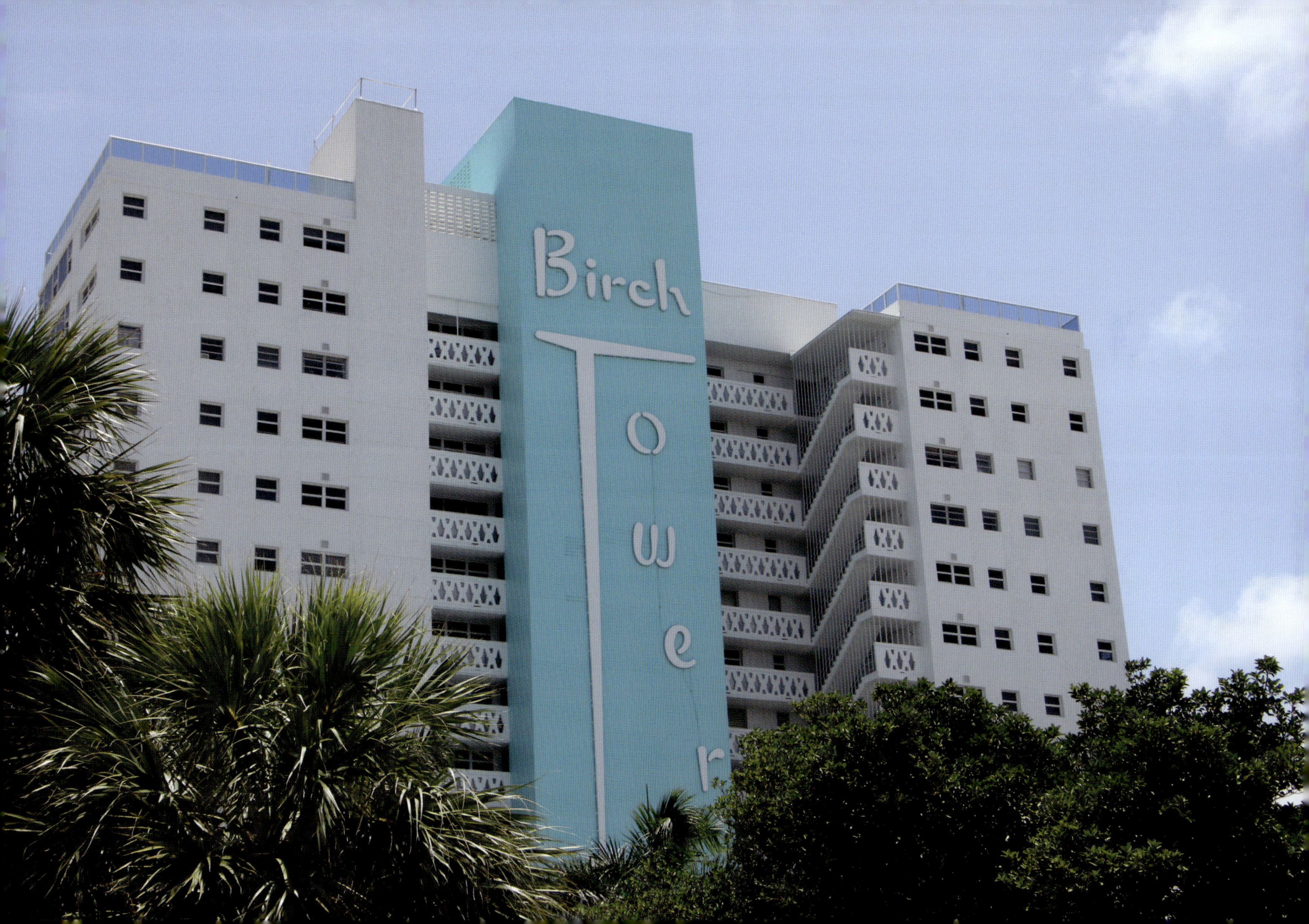
Birch
Tower

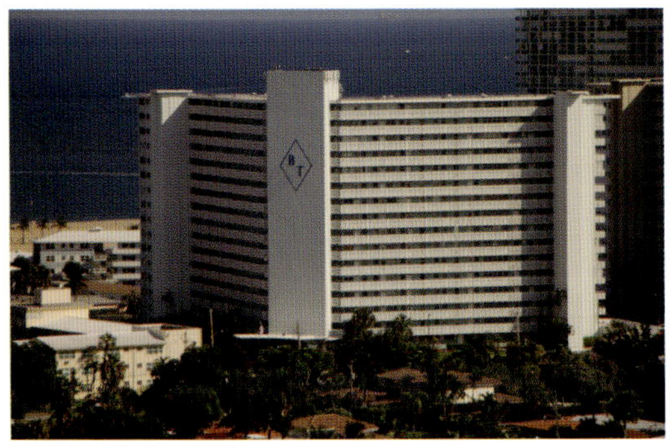

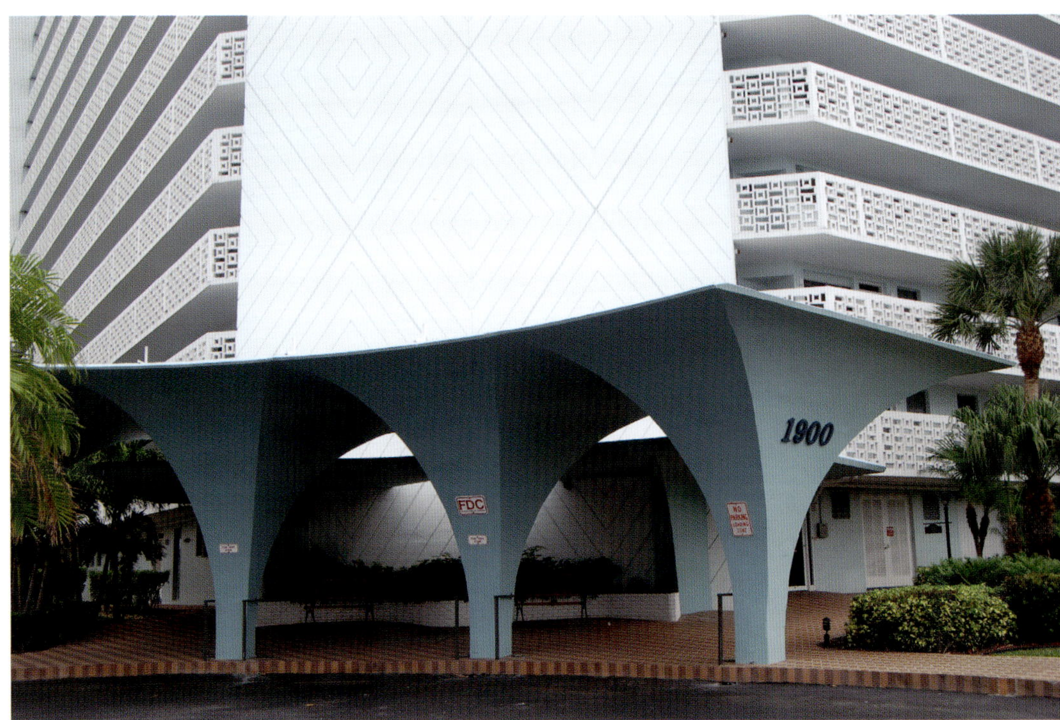

Breakwater Towers
1900 South Ocean Drive
Fort Lauderdale
Architect: Charles McKirahan, 1957
Photographs, left to right: 2018, 2013, 2015

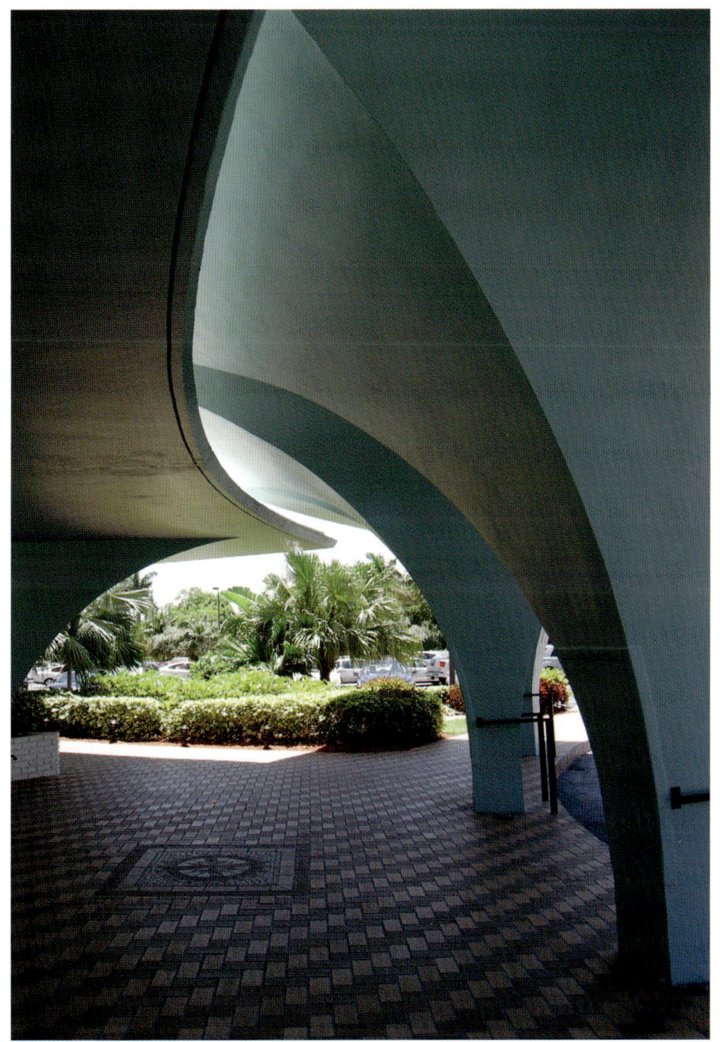

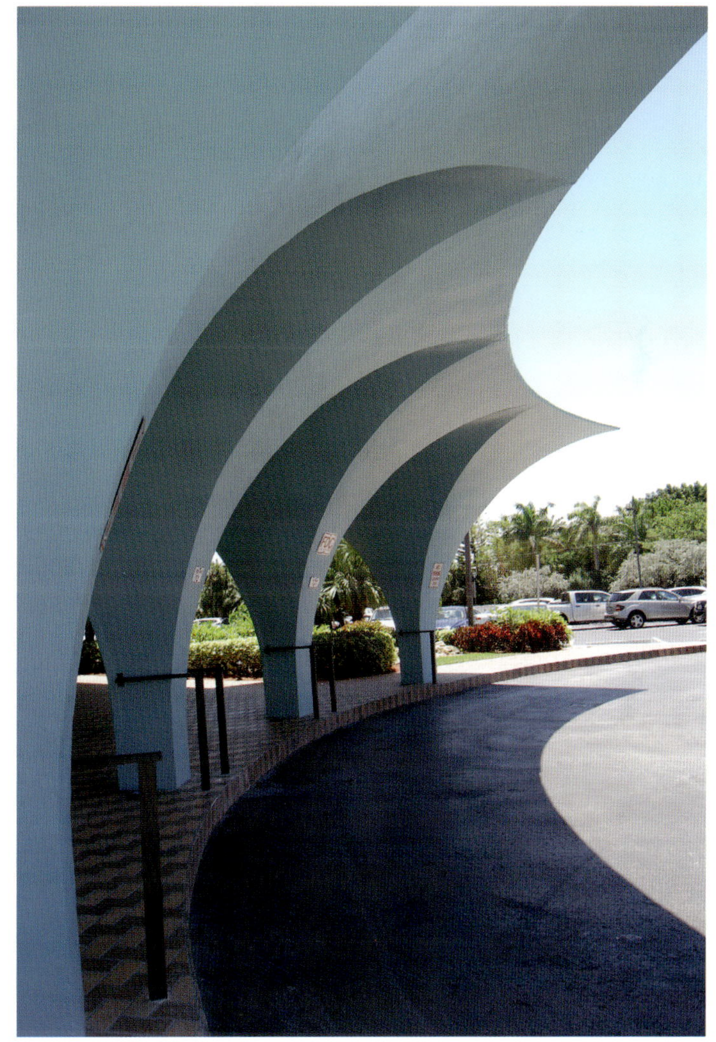

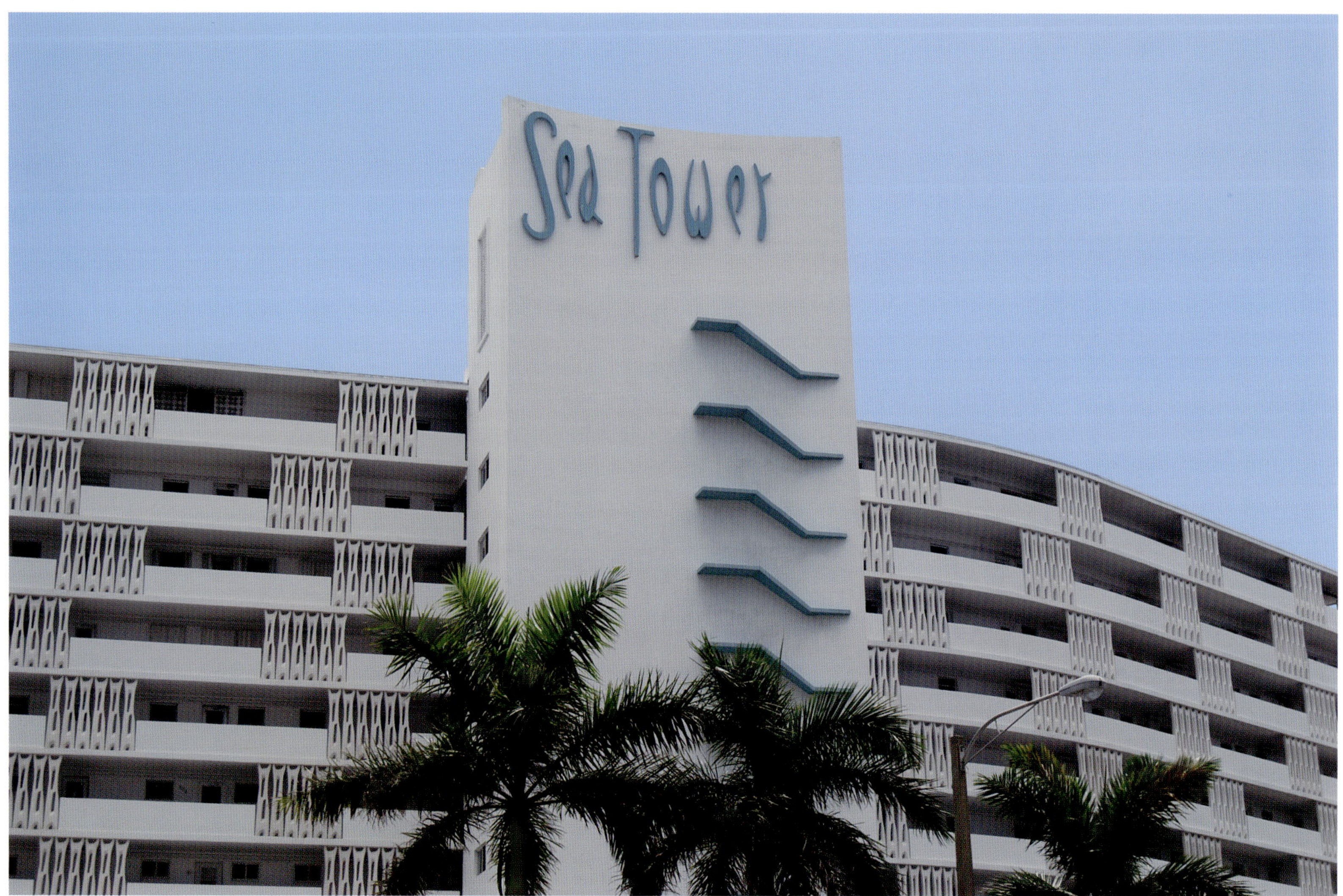
Sea Tower

Sea Tower
2840 North Ocean Boulevard
Fort Lauderdale
Architect: Igor Polevitzsky, 1957
Photograph: 2015

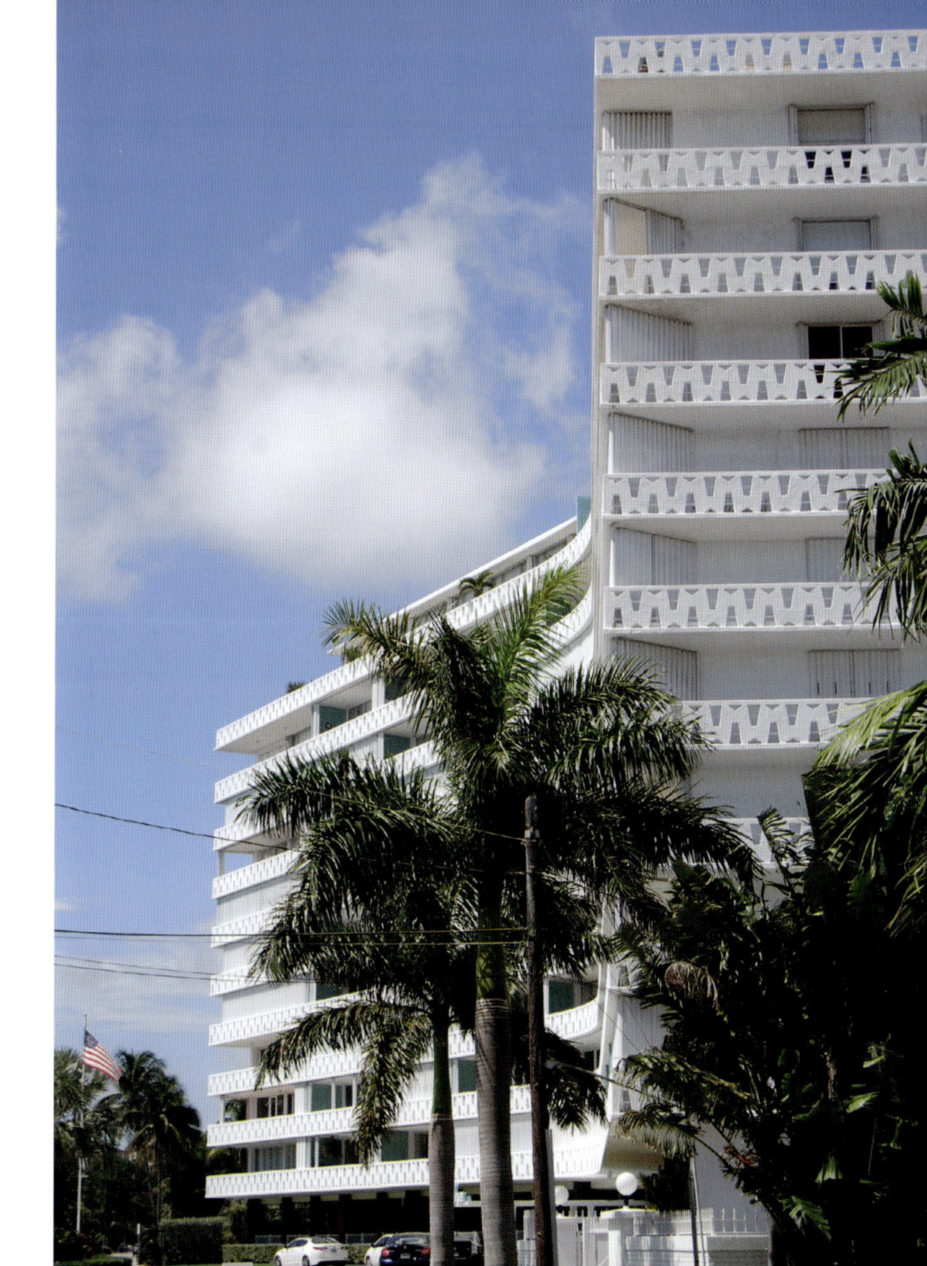

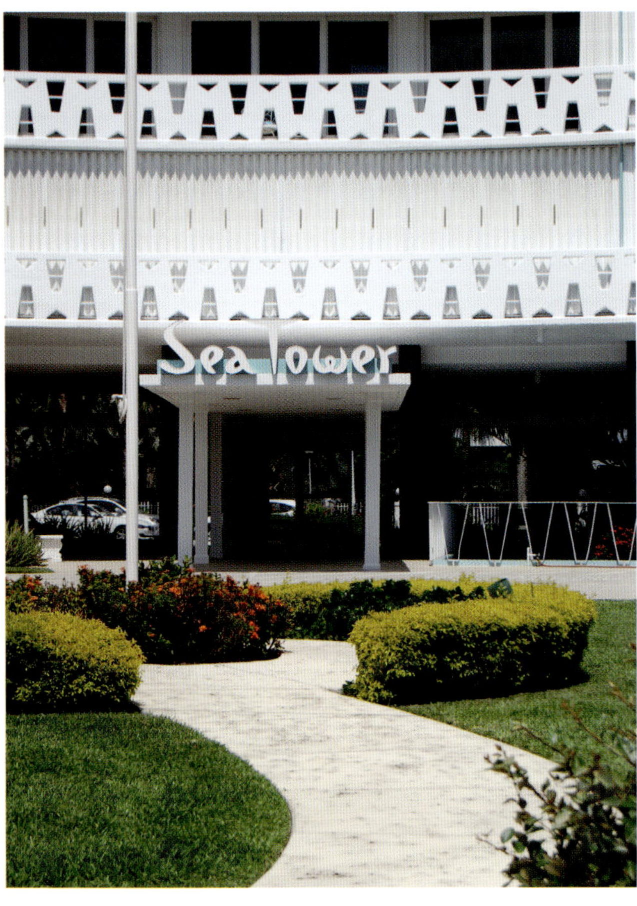
Sea Tower

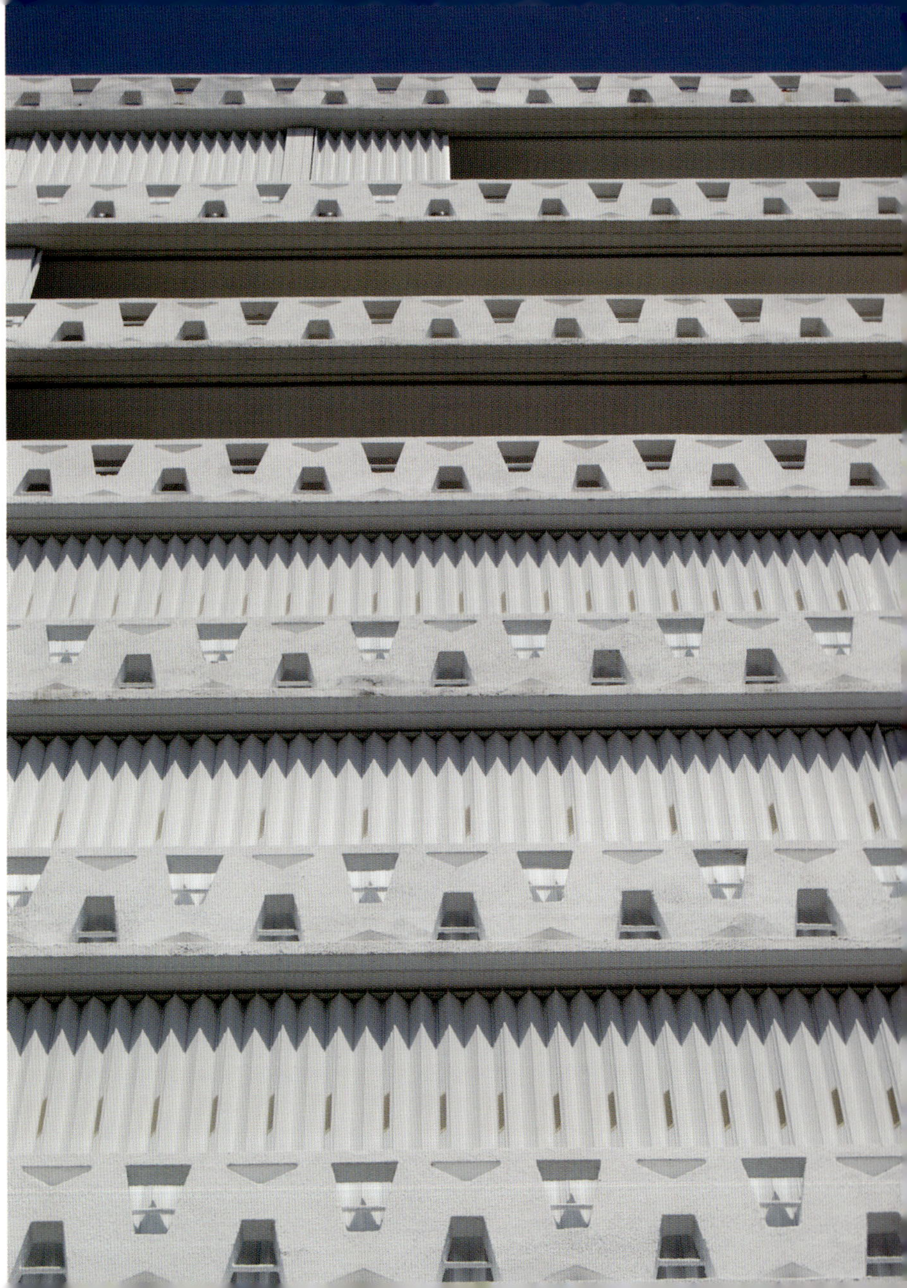

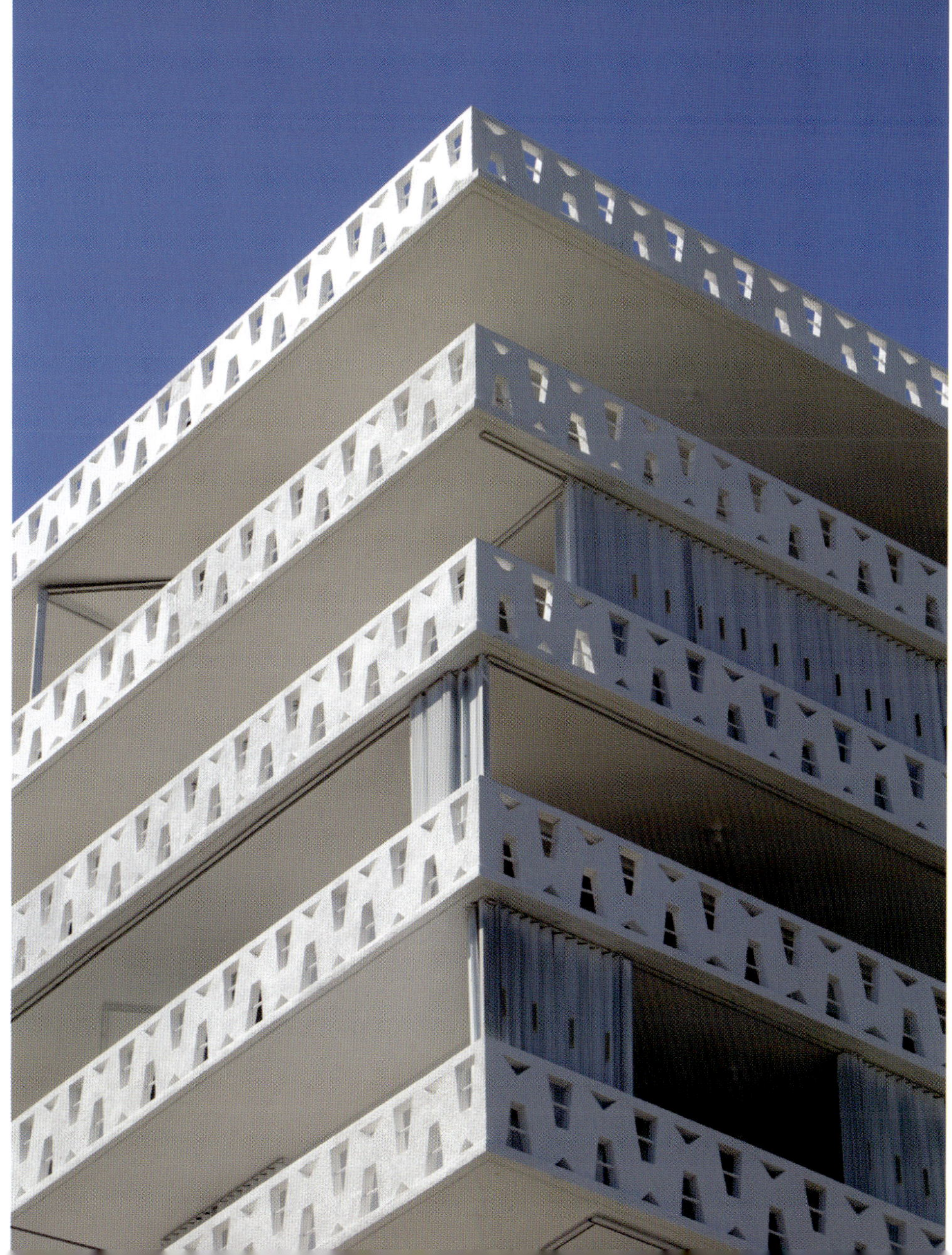

Sea Tower
2840 North Ocean Boulevard
Fort Lauderdale
Architect: Igor Polevitzsky, 1957
Photograph: 2015

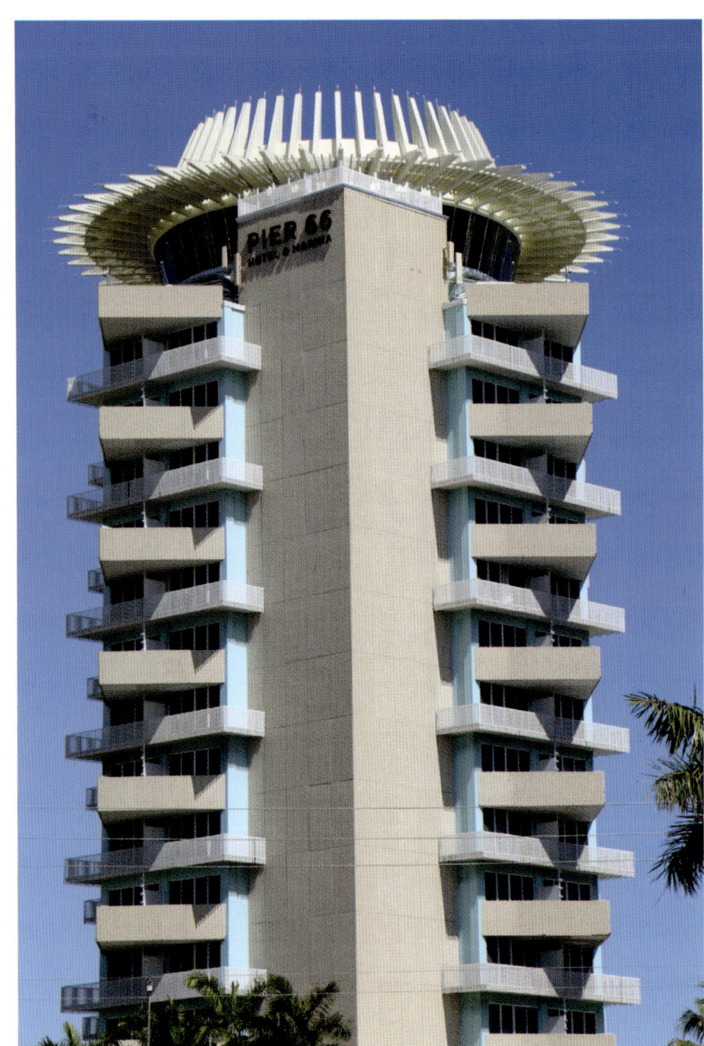

Pier 66 Hotel
2301 SE 17th Street
Fort Lauderdale
Architects: Robert F. Humble and Todd & Weisman Architects, 1964
Photographs: 2018 (left), 2015

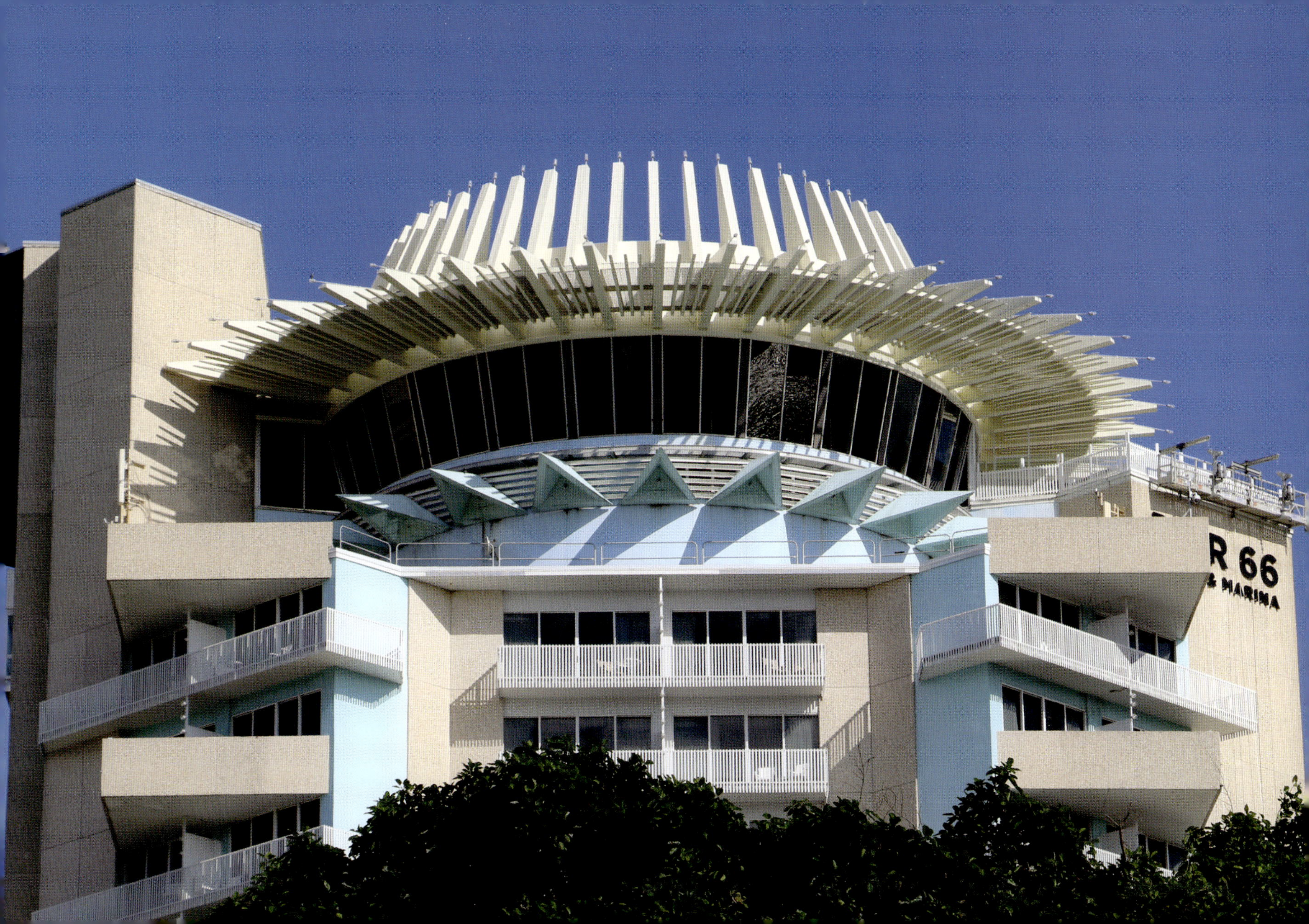
R 66
& MARINA

Pier 66 Hotel
2301 SE 17th Street
Fort Lauderdale
Architects: Robert F. Humble and Todd & Weisman Architects, 1964
Photograph: 2015

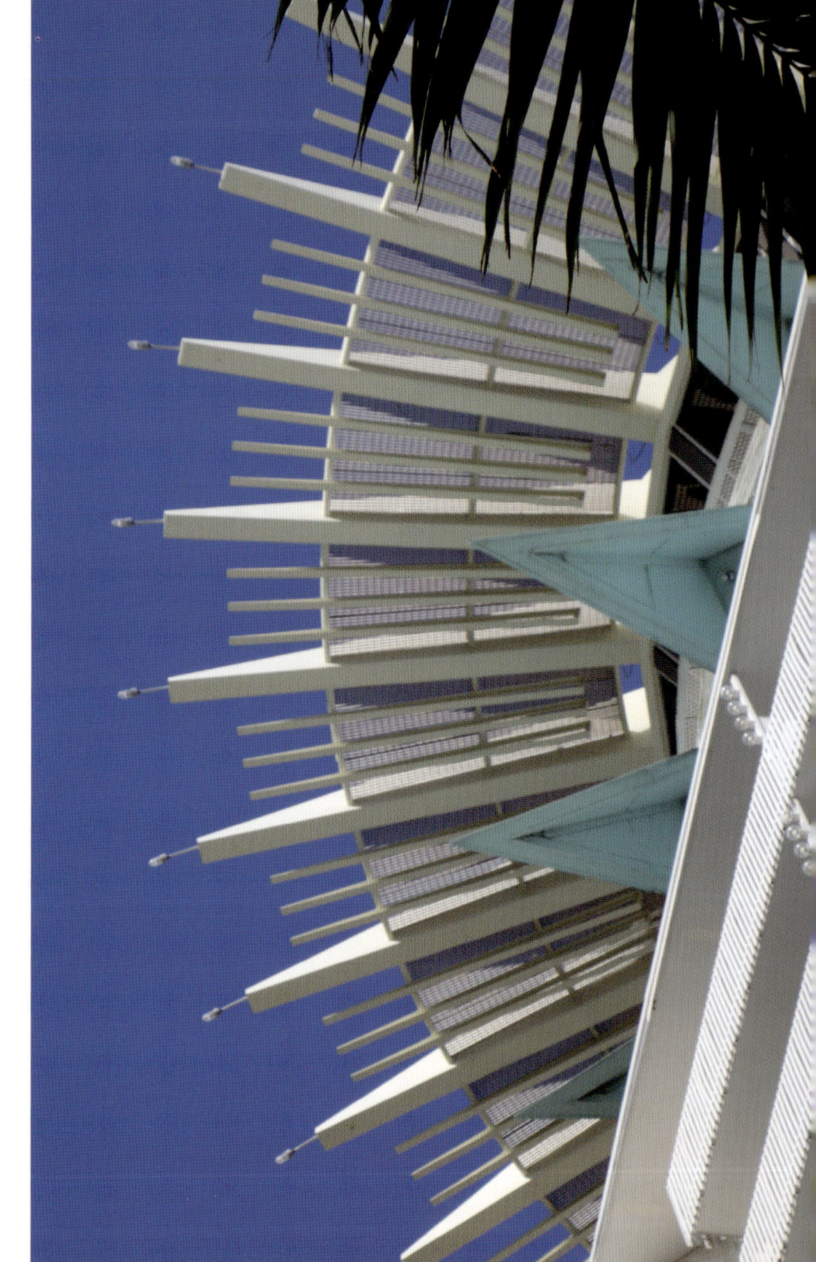

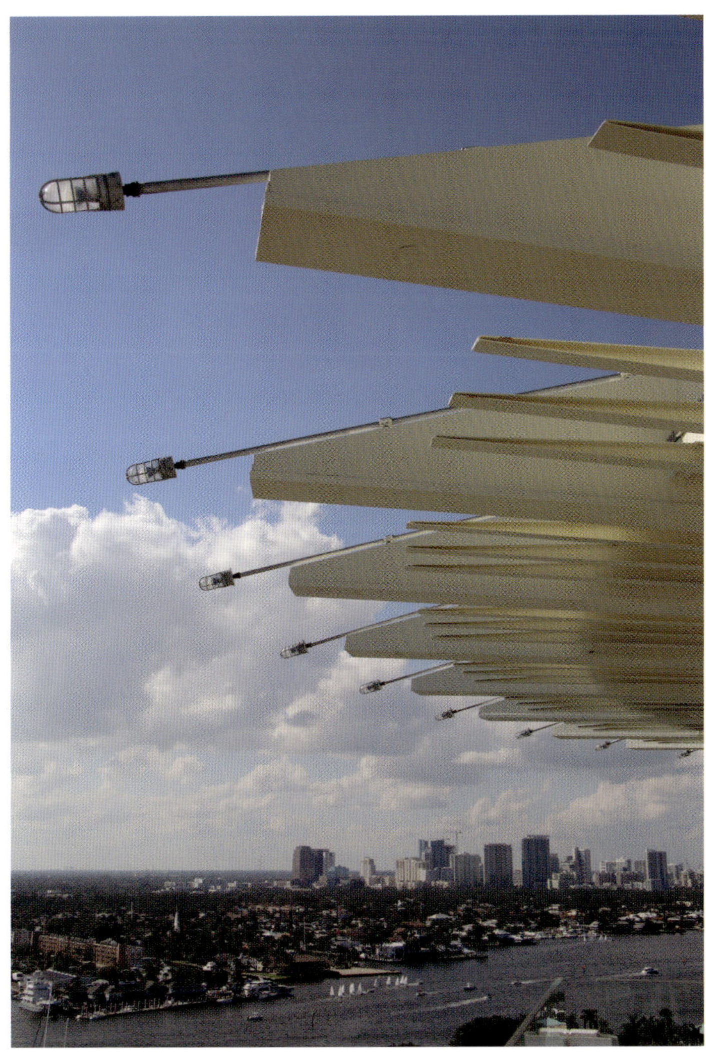

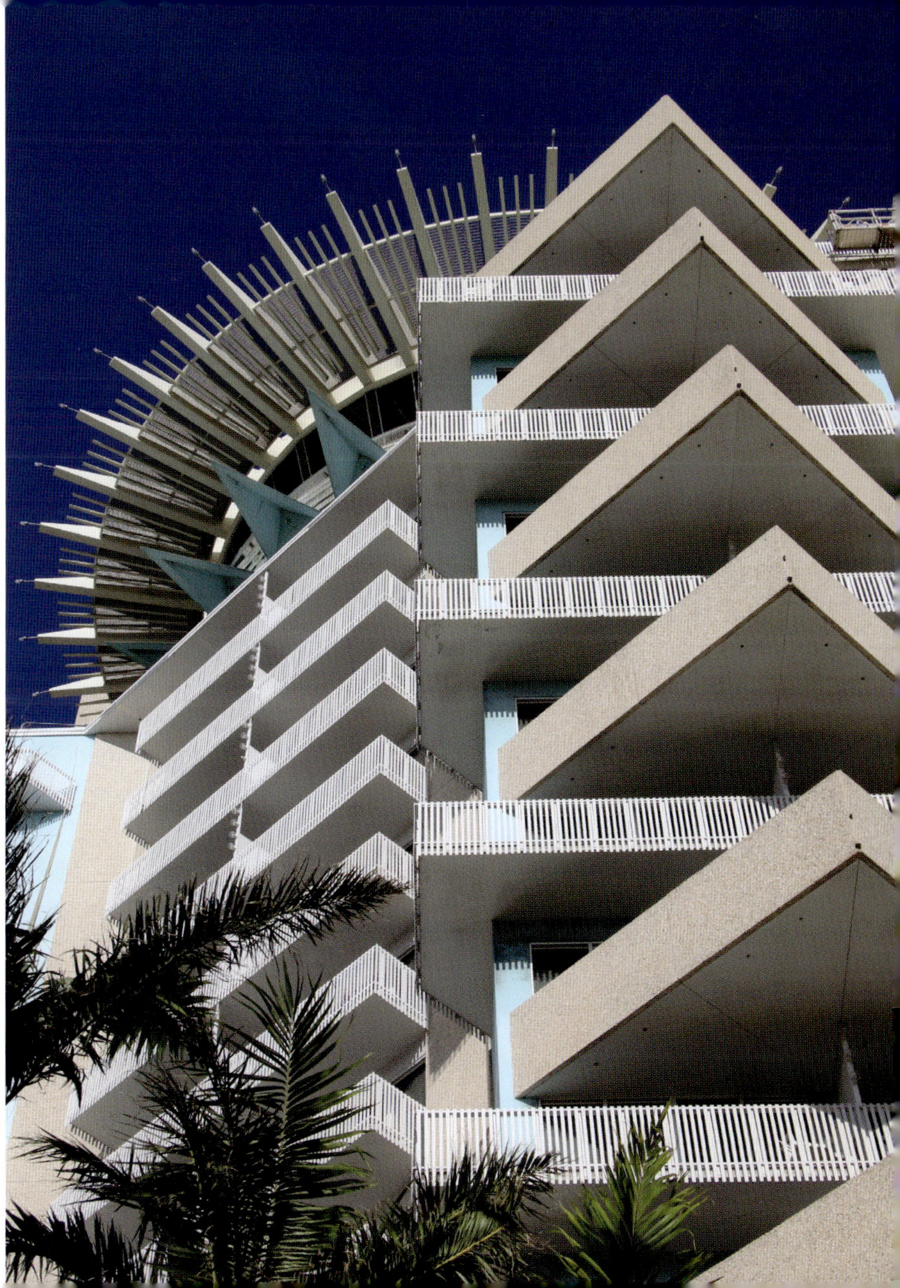

Pier 66 Hotel
2301 S.E. 17th Street
Fort Lauderdale
Architects: Robert F. Humble and Todd & Weisman Architects, 1964
Photograph: 2015

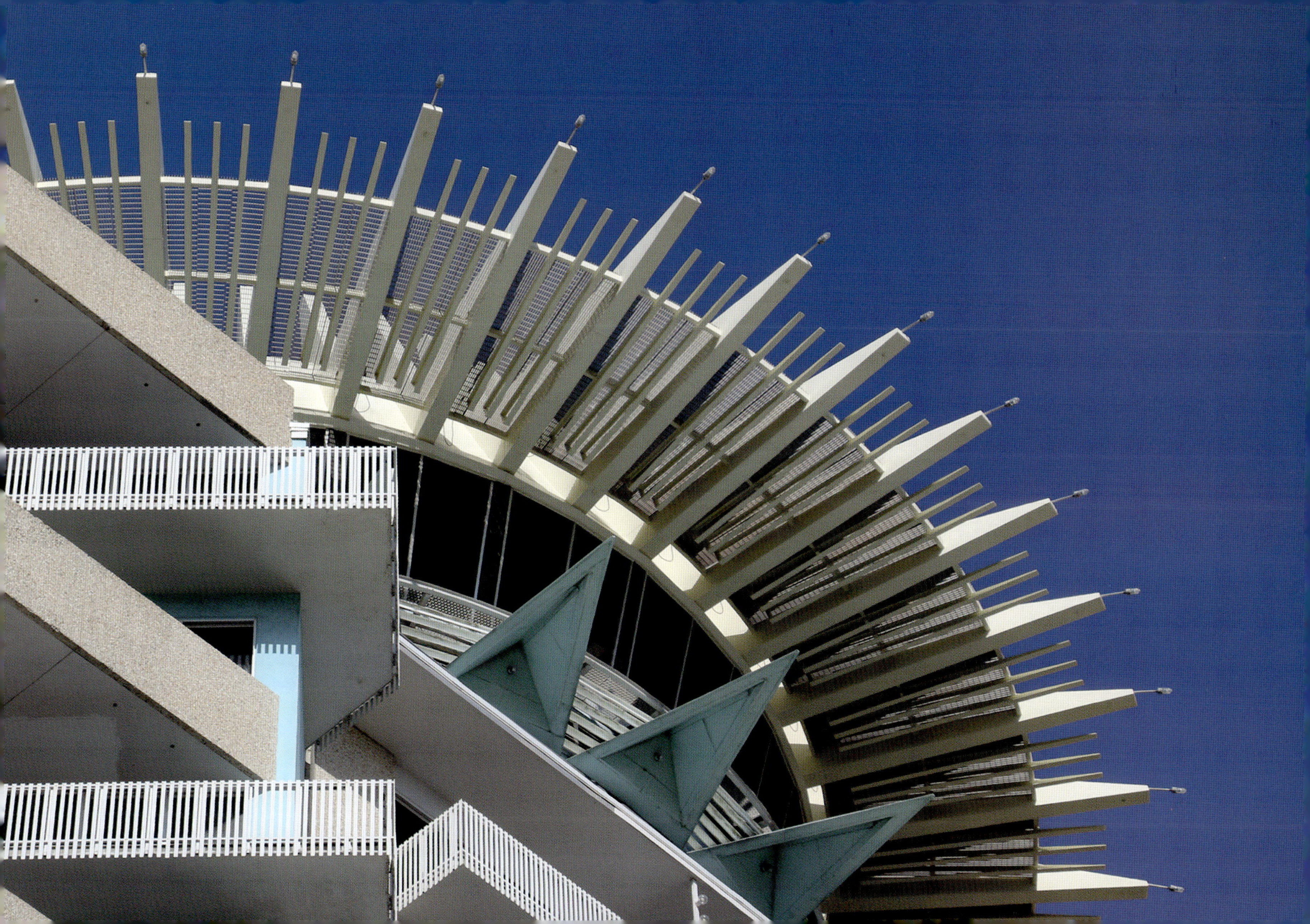

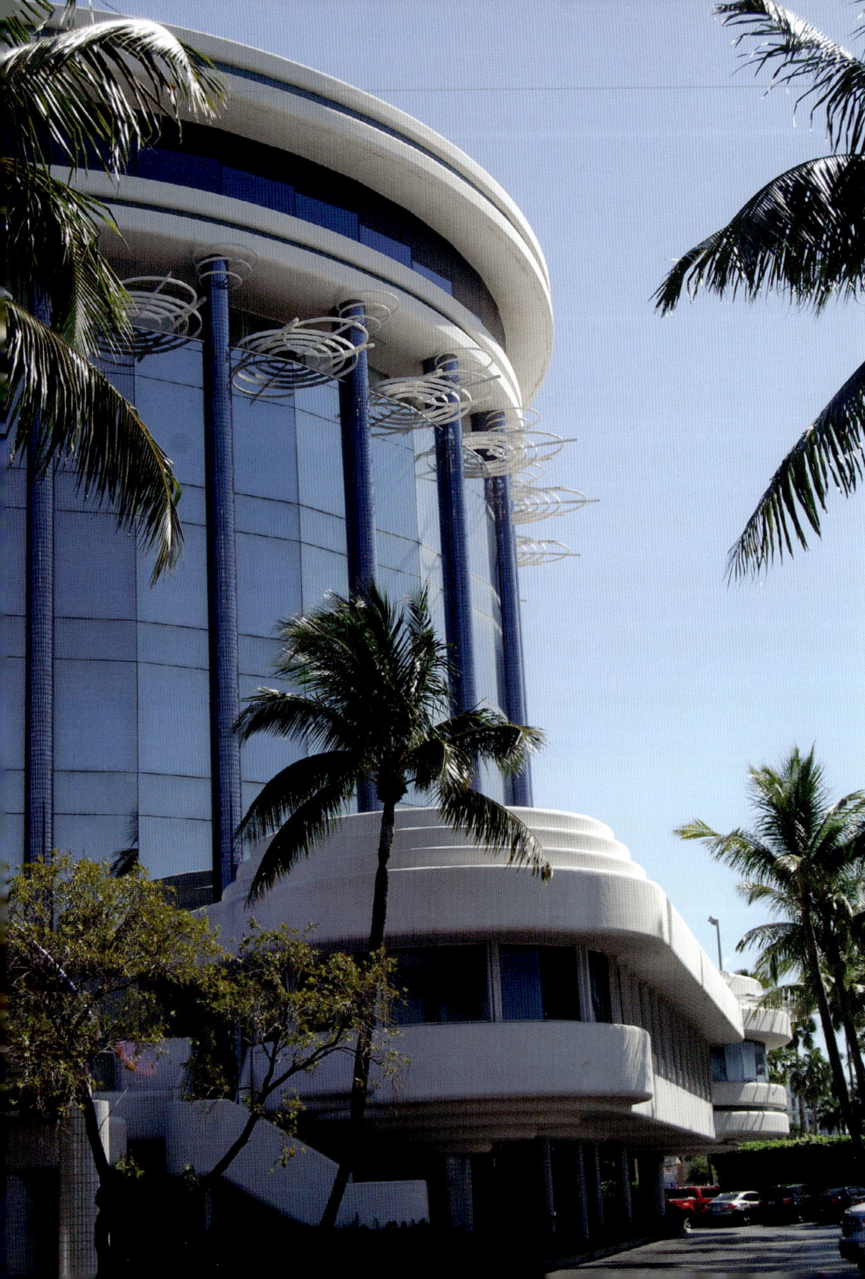

KenAnn Tower
3101 North Federal Highway at Oakland Park Boulevard
Oakland Park
Architect: Louis F. Wolff, 1968
Photograph: 2014

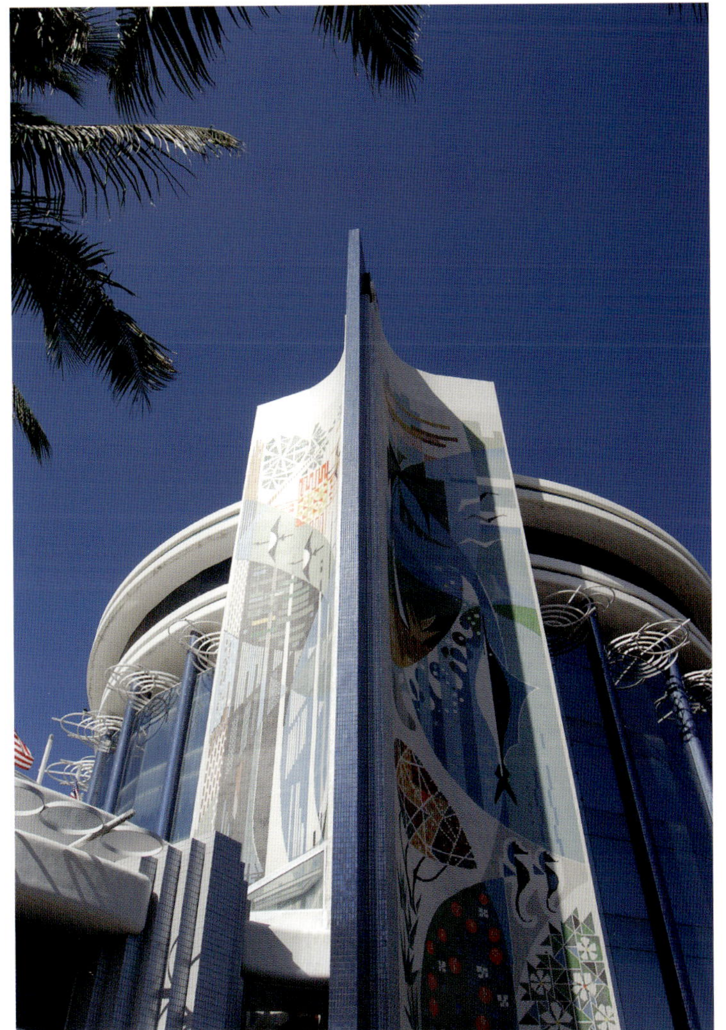

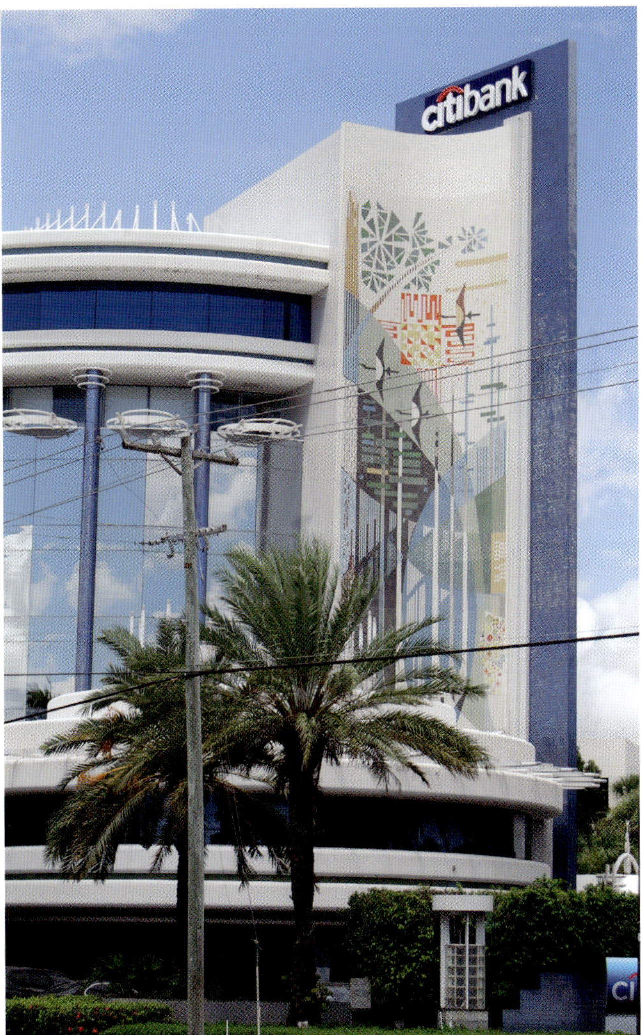
citibank

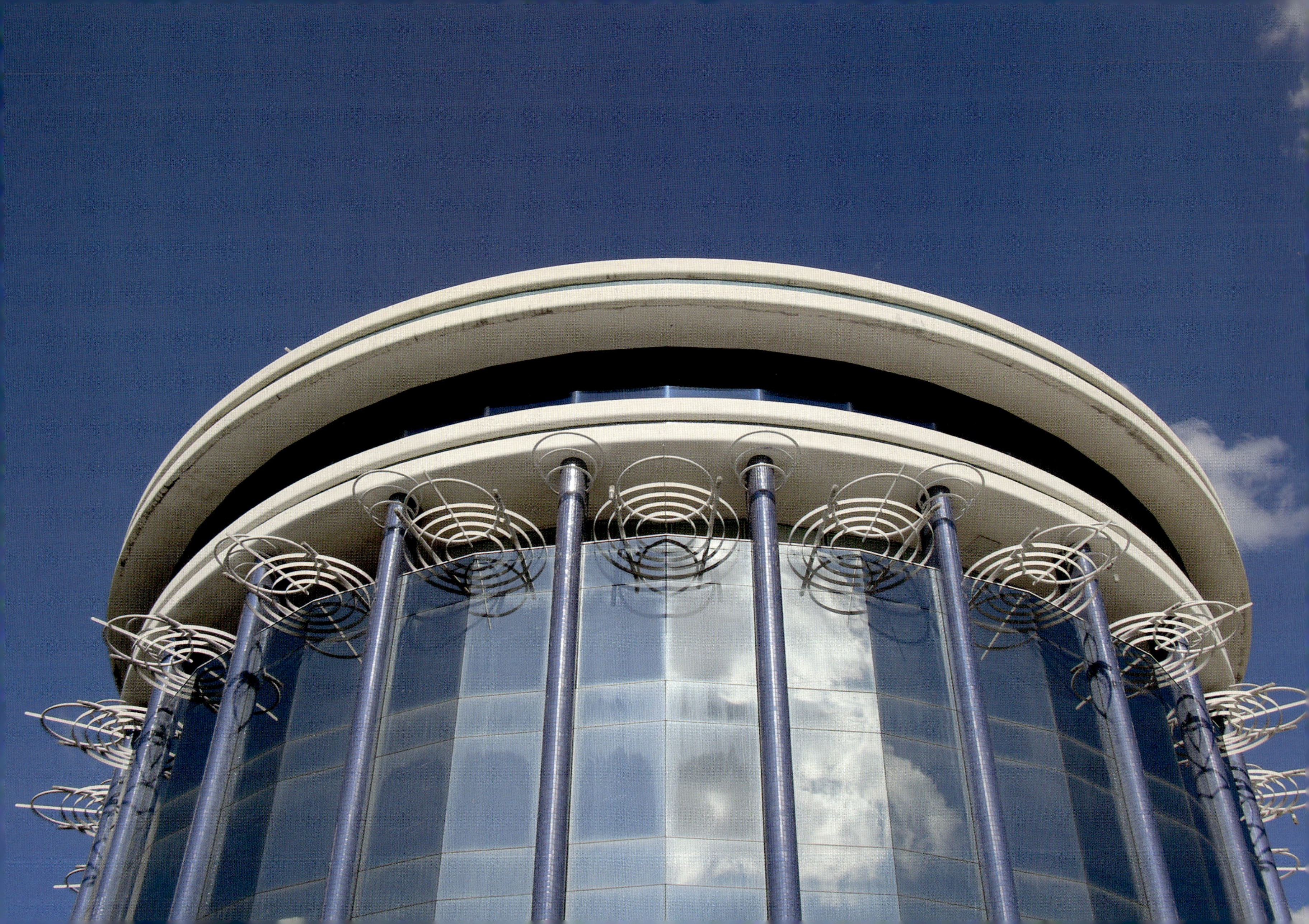

KenAnn Tower
3101 North Federal Highway at Oakland Park Boulevard
Oakland Park
Architect: Louis F. Wolff, 1968
Photograph: 2014

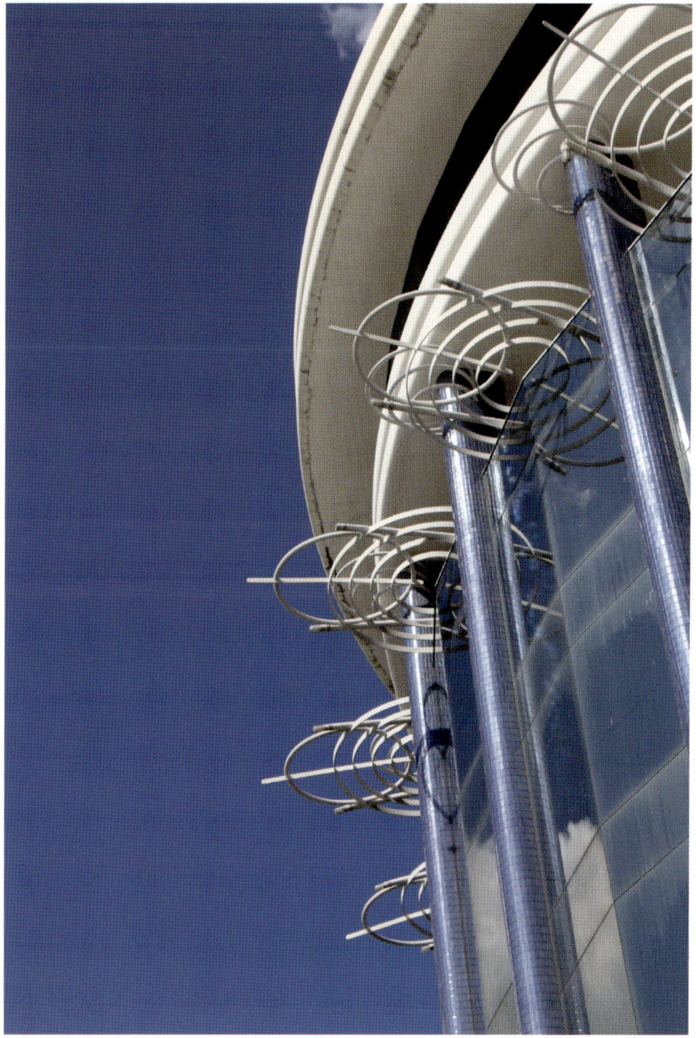

Las Olas Club
2 Hendricks Isle
Fort Lauderdale
Architect: Charles McKirahan, 1957
Photograph: 2016

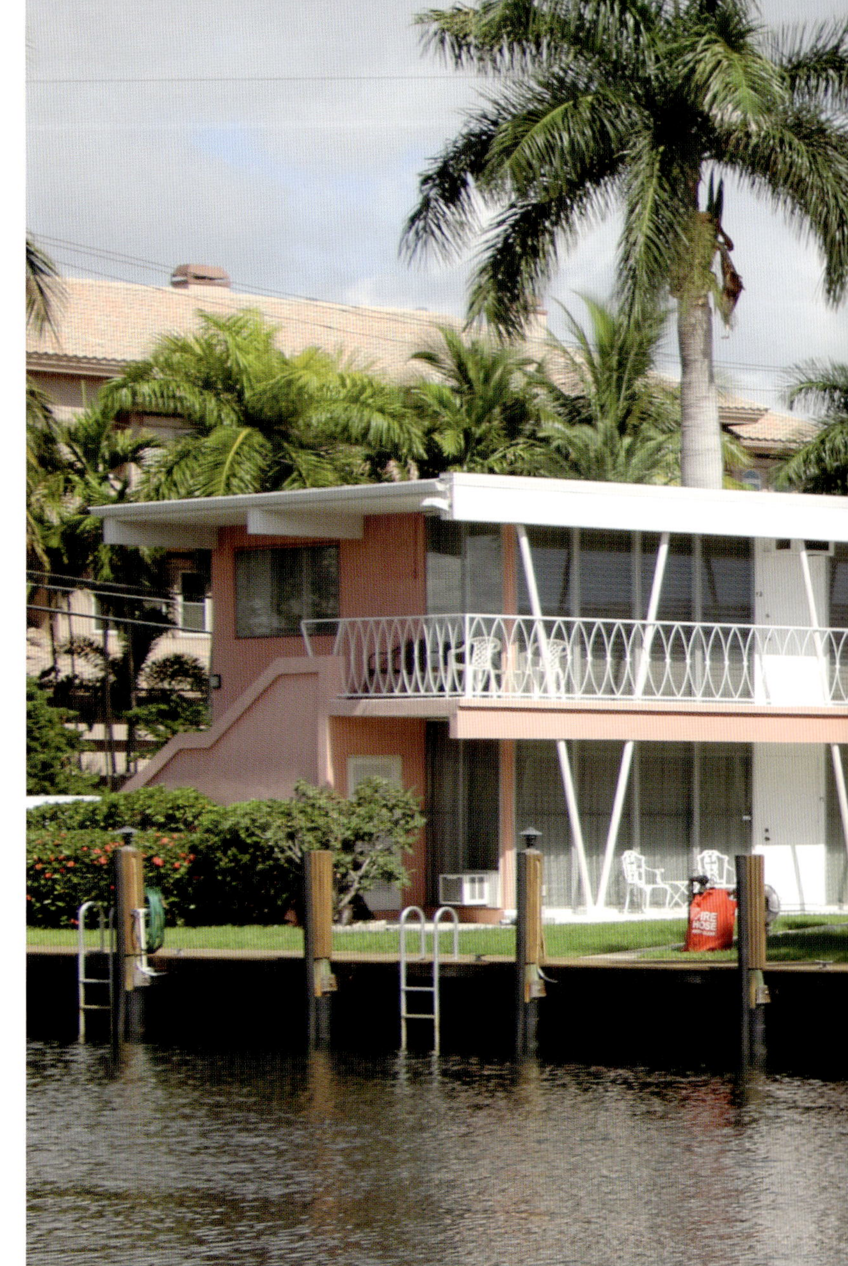

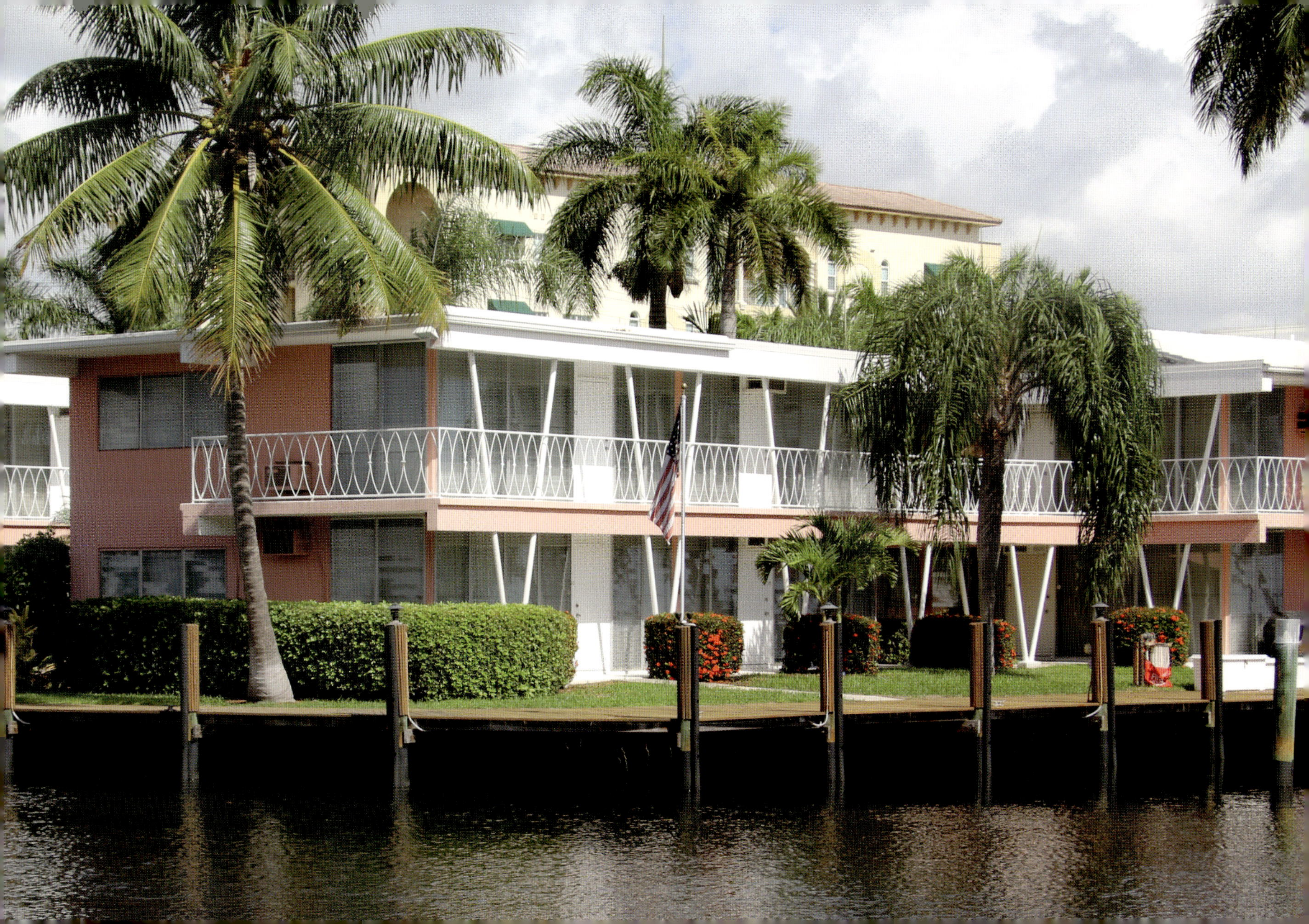

Las Olas Club
2 Hendricks Isle
Fort Lauderdale
Architect: Charles McKirahan, 1957
Photograph: 2016

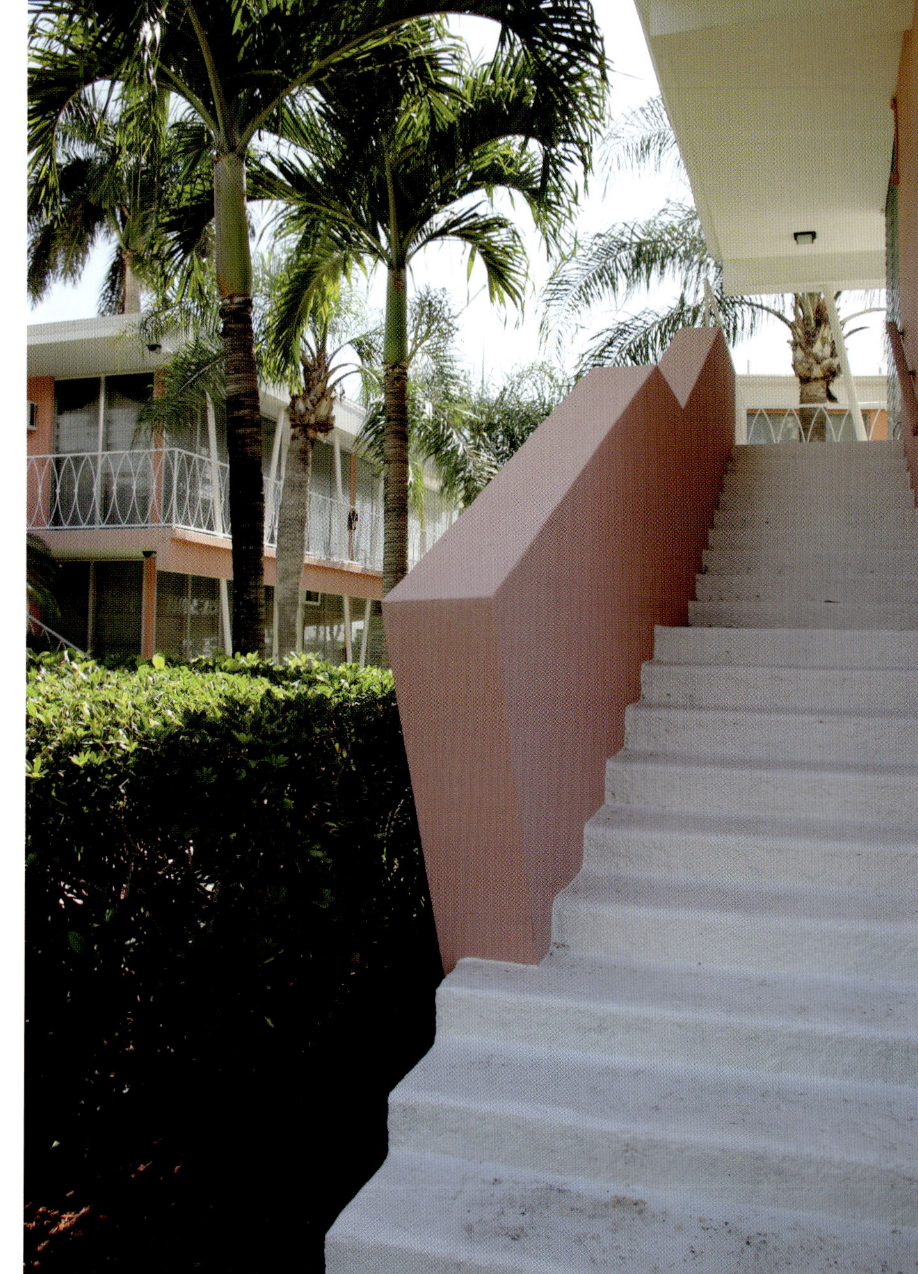

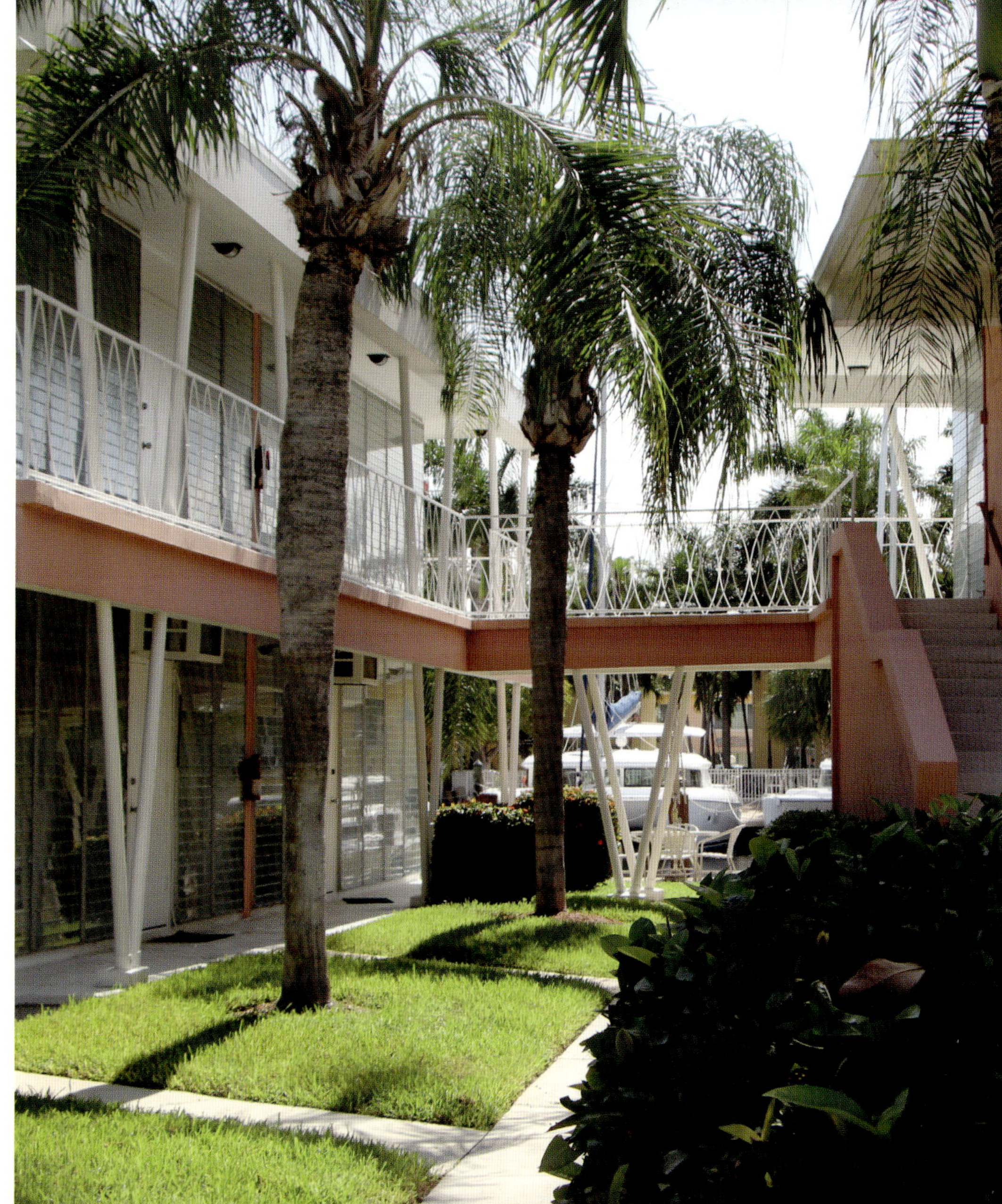

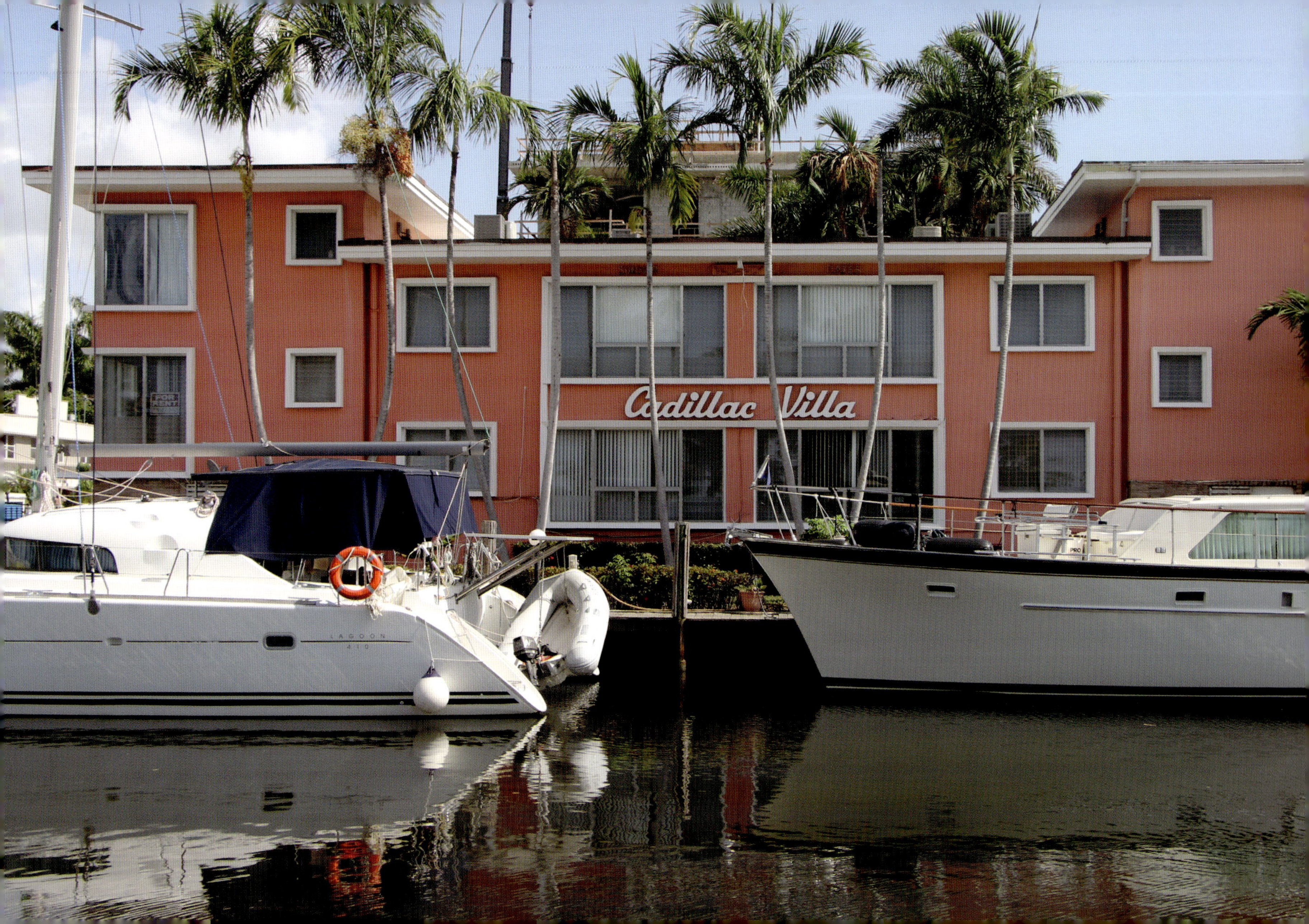
Cadillac Villa
FOR RENT

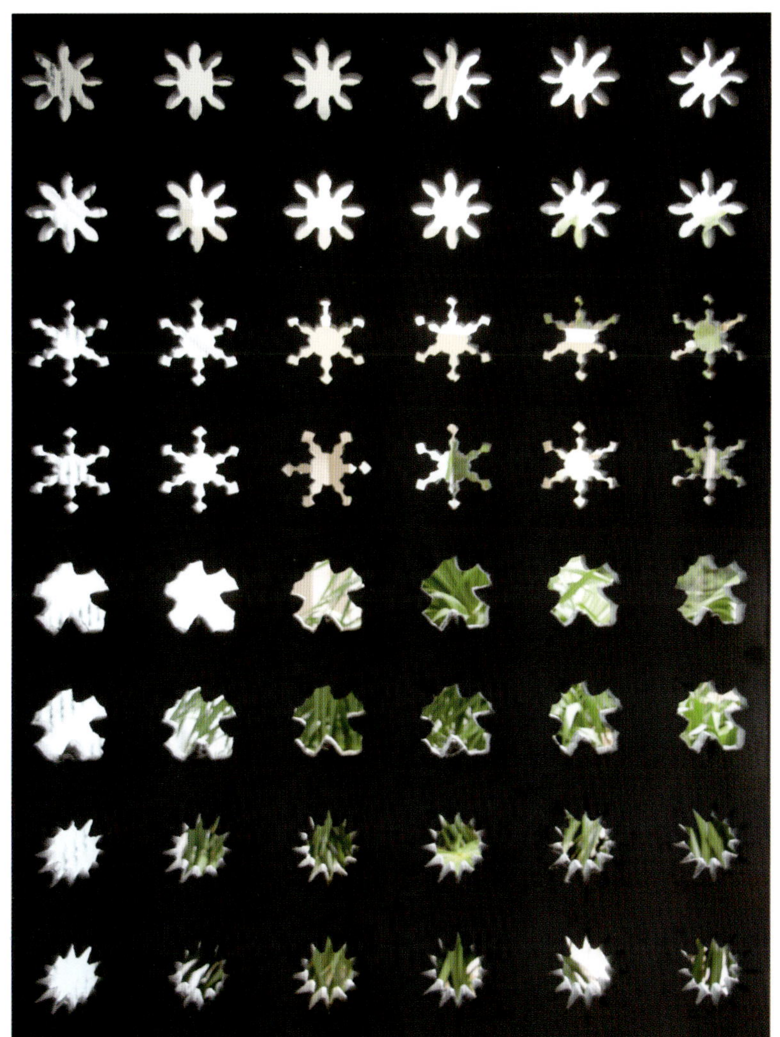

Cadillac Villa
2 Isle of Venice Drive
Fort Lauderdale
Architect: Unknown, 1958
Photograph: 2015

Four Seasons Condominium
Brise-soleil with flower, snowflake, maple leaf, and sun
333 Sunset Drive
Fort Lauderdale
Architect: William Crawford, 1958
Photograph: 2019

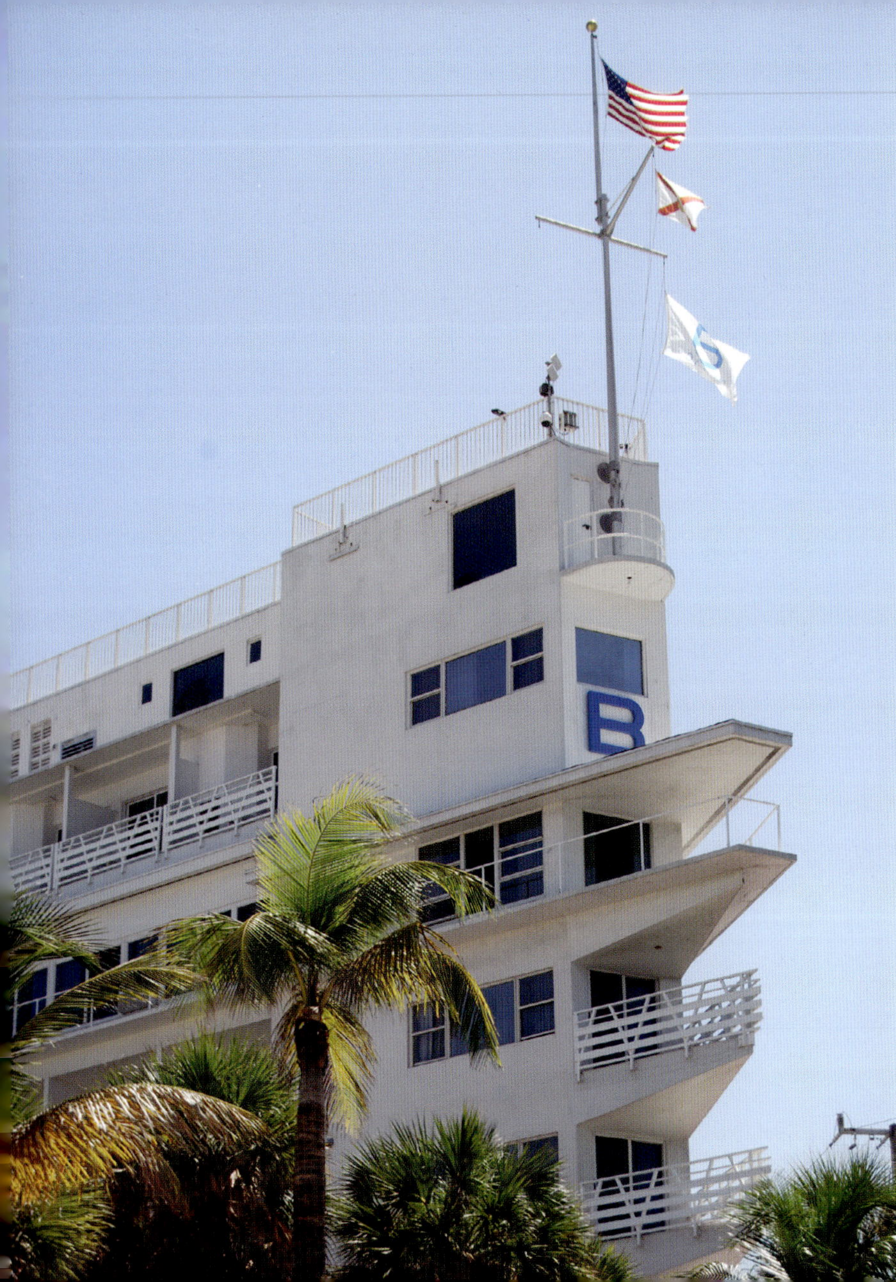

Yankee Clipper Hotel
999 North Fort Lauderdale Beach Boulevard
Fort Lauderdale
Architect: Tony Sherman, 1955
Photograph: 2015

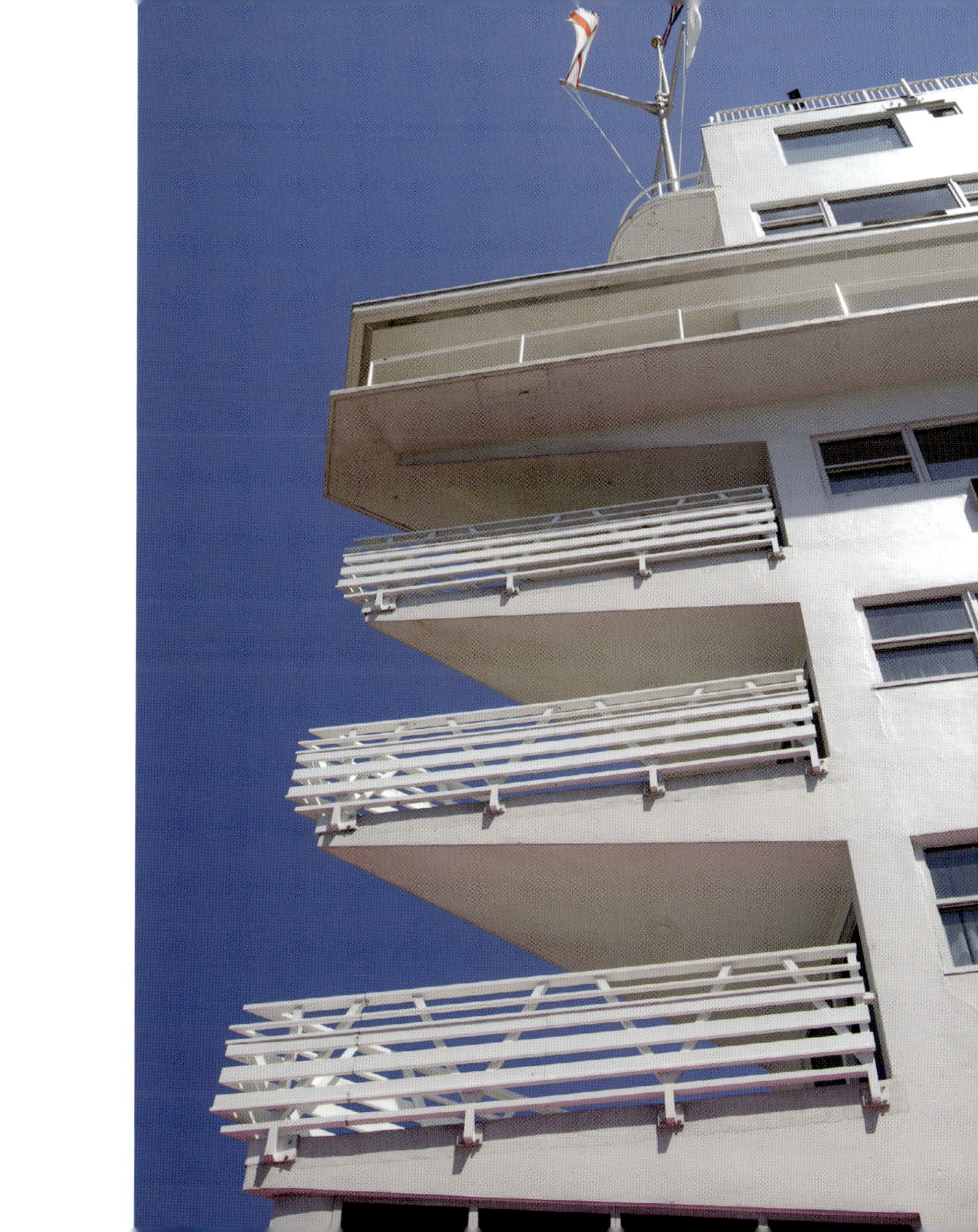

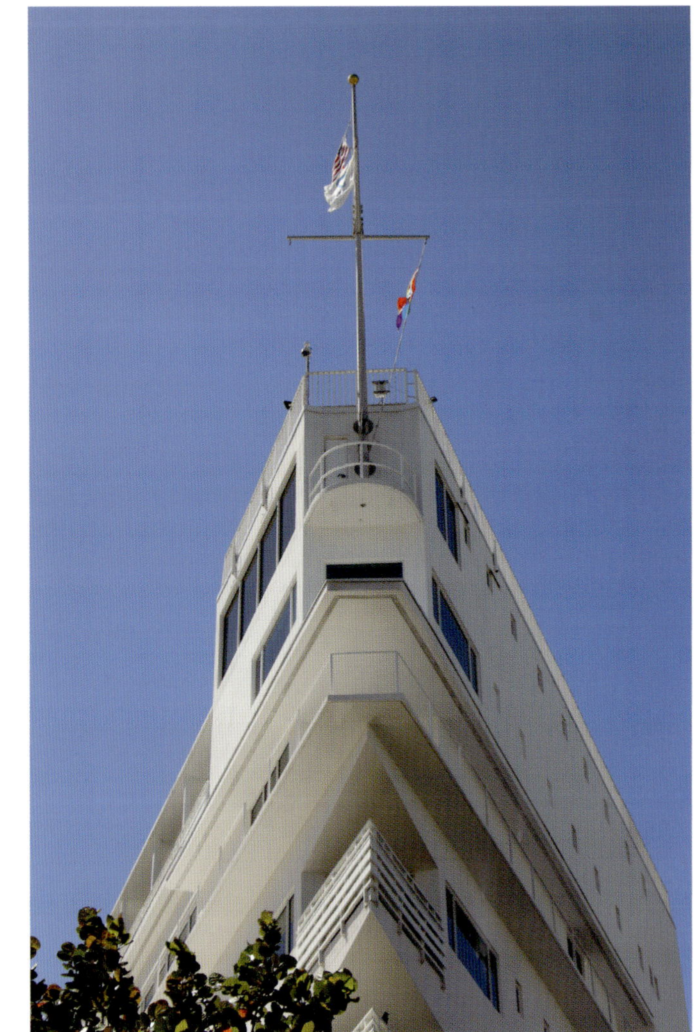

Yankee Clipper Hotel
999 North Fort Lauderdale Beach Boulevard
Fort Lauderdale
Architect: Tony Sherman, 1955
Photograph: 2015

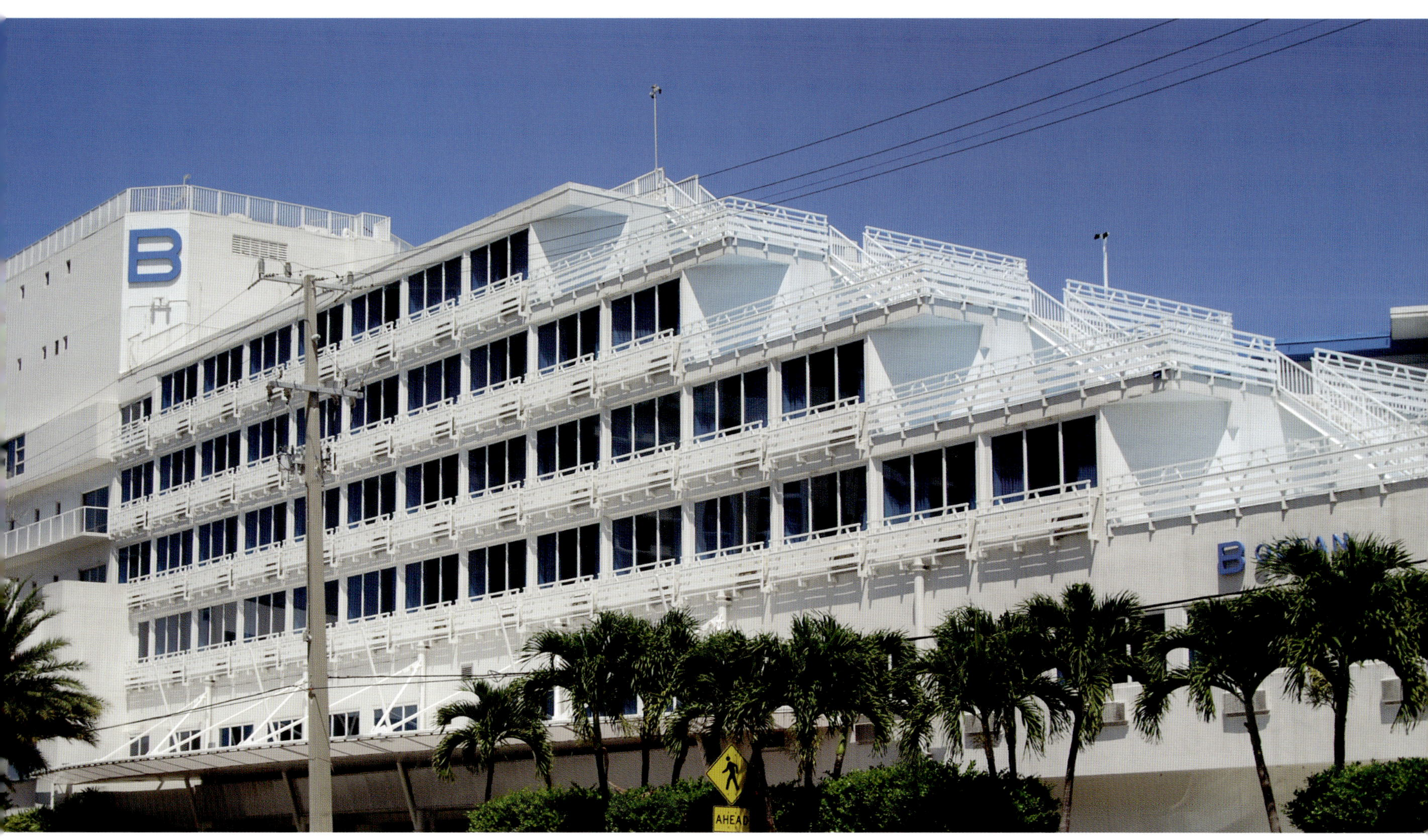
B
AHEAD

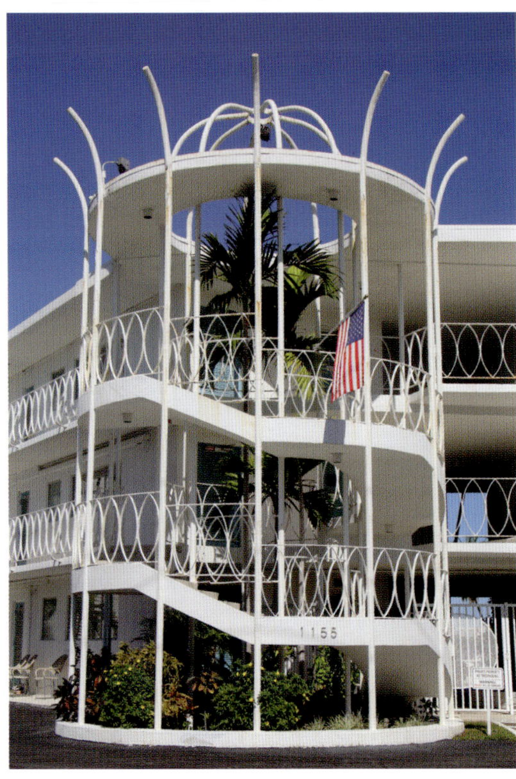

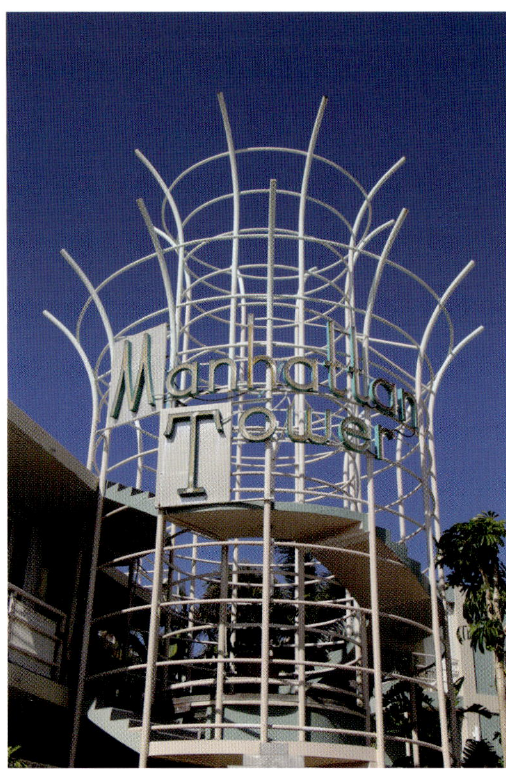

Bay Harbor Club
1155 103rd Street
Bay Harbor Islands
Architect: Charles McKirahan, 1956
Photograph: 2015

Manhattan Tower
701 Bayshore Drive
Fort Lauderdale
Architect: Charles McKirahan, 1953
Photograph: 2017

Times Square Shopping Center
Oakland Park Boulevard and Federal Highway
Fort Lauderdale
Architect: Charles McKirahan, 1954
Photograph: 2015

Circles in Circles
Sunrise Bay Club
2717 Yacht Club Boulevard
Fort Lauderdale
Architect: Charles McKirahan, 1955
Photograph: 2017

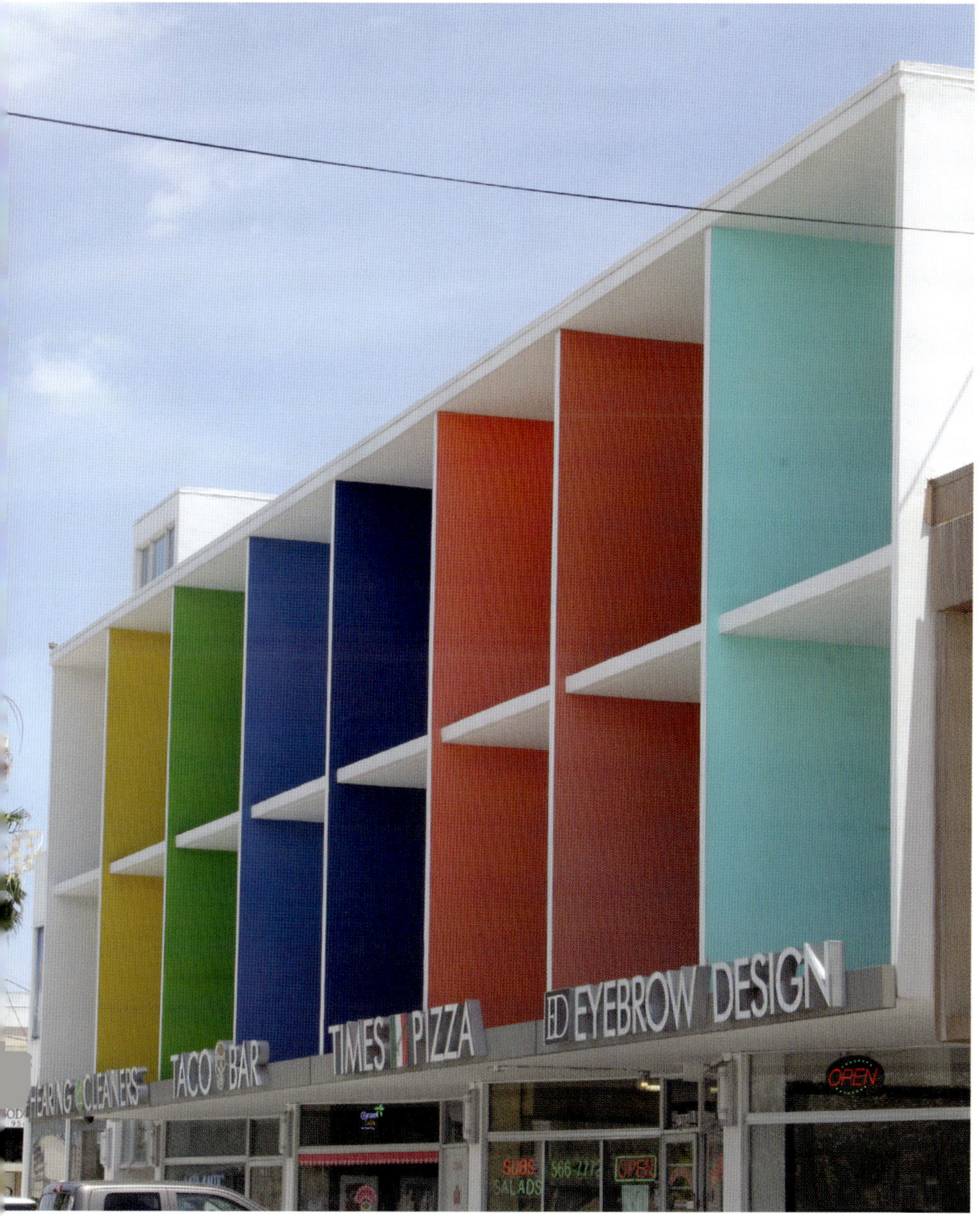
CLEANERS
TACO BAR
TIMES PIZZA
EYEBROW DESIGN
OPEN
SUBS
SALADS

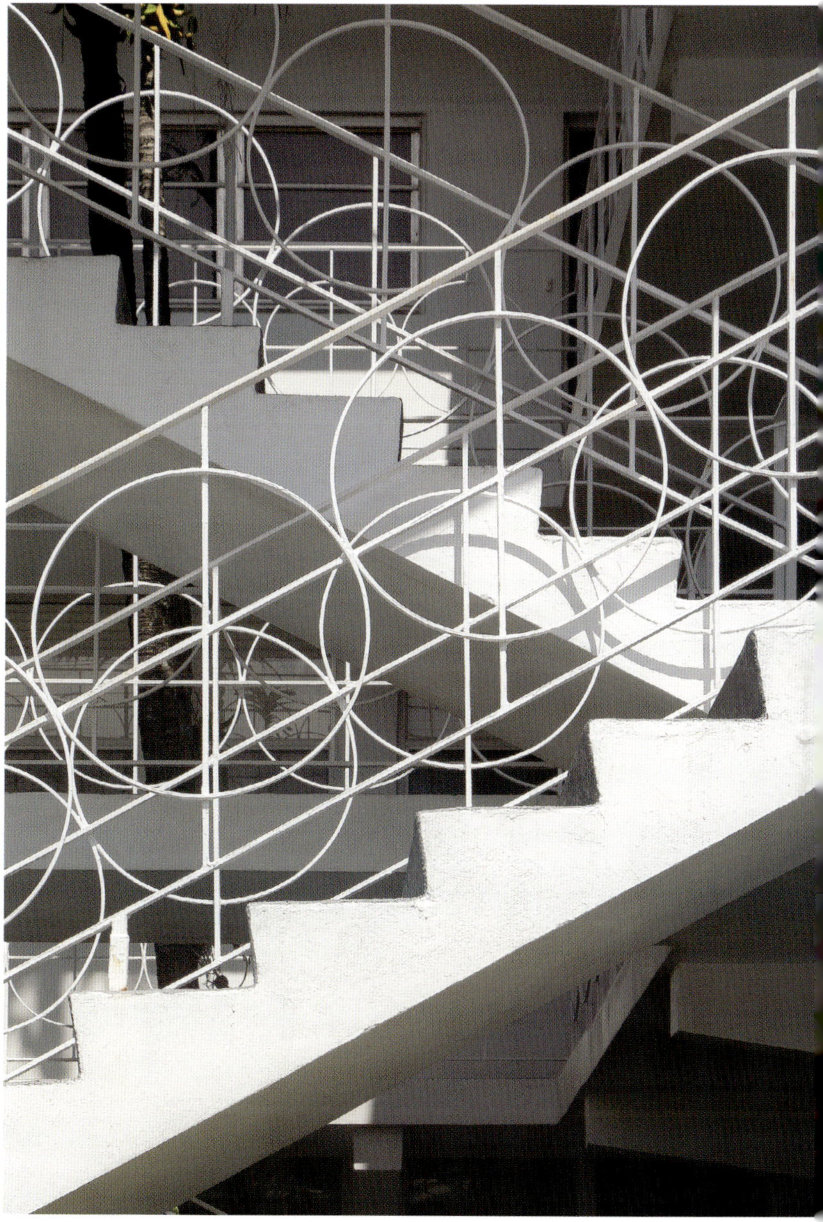

SIGNAGE AS A DESIGN ELEMENT

1
Sea Tower, Fort Lauderdale

2
Lago Mar, Fort Lauderdale

3
Alexander Hotel, Miami Beach

4
Albion Hotel, Miami Beach

5
Standard Hotel, Miami Beach

6
Delano Hotel, Miami Beach

7
Birch Tower, Fort Lauderdale

8
Premiere Hotel, Fort Lauderdale

9
Shore Club Hotel, Miami Beach

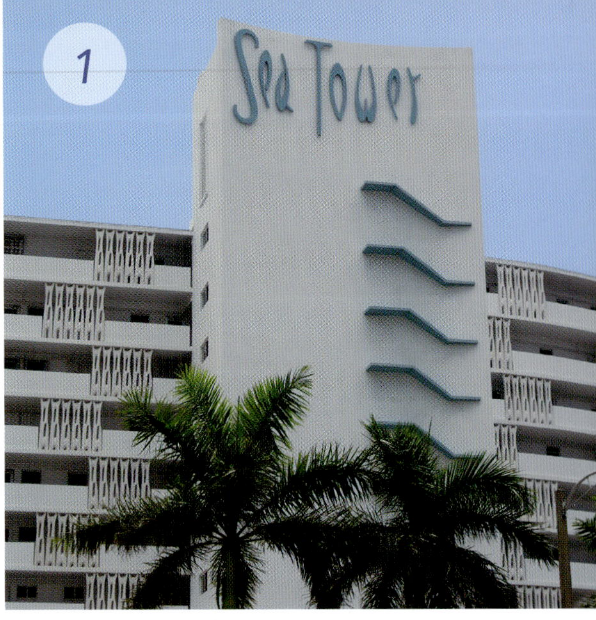

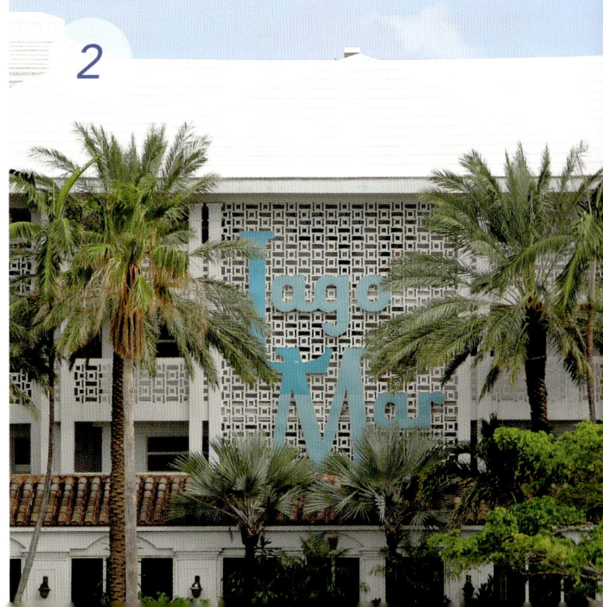

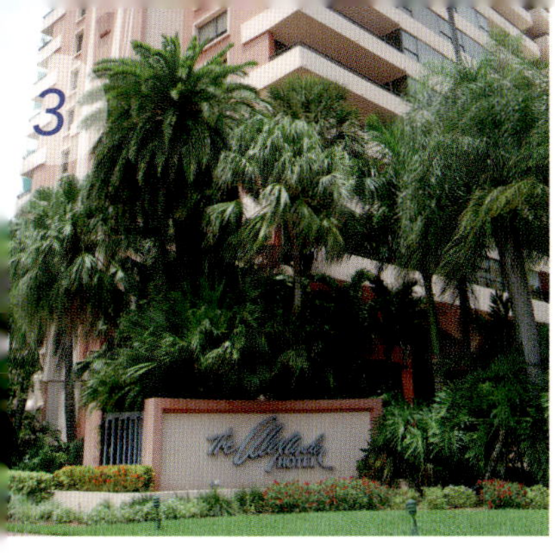
3

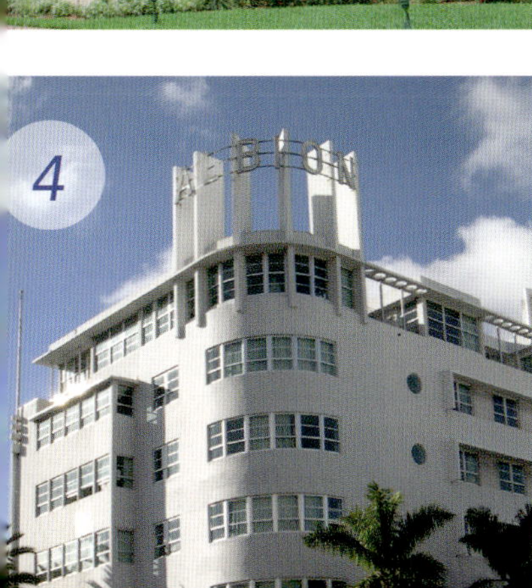
4
ALBION

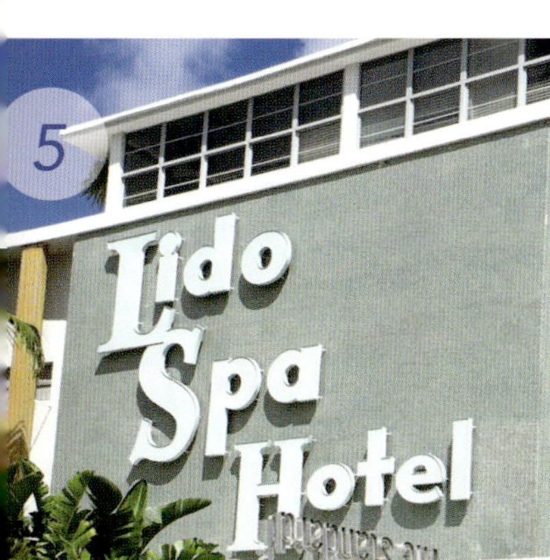
5
Lido
Spa
Hotel

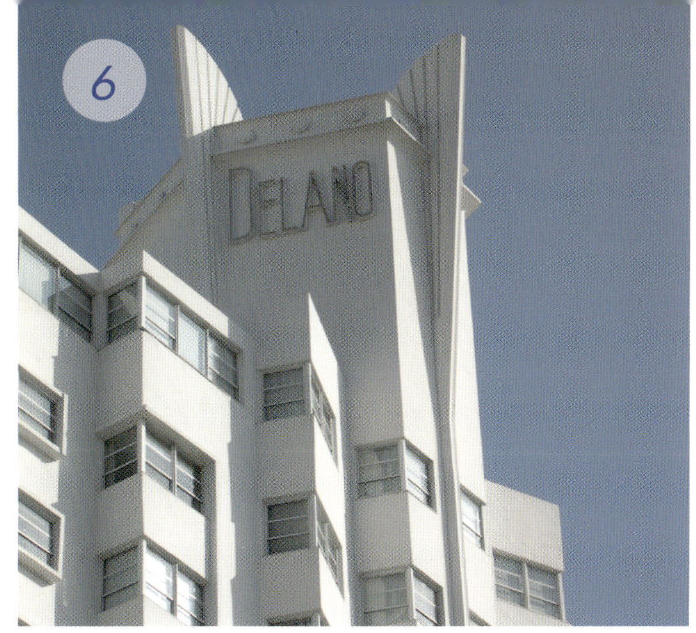
6
DELANO

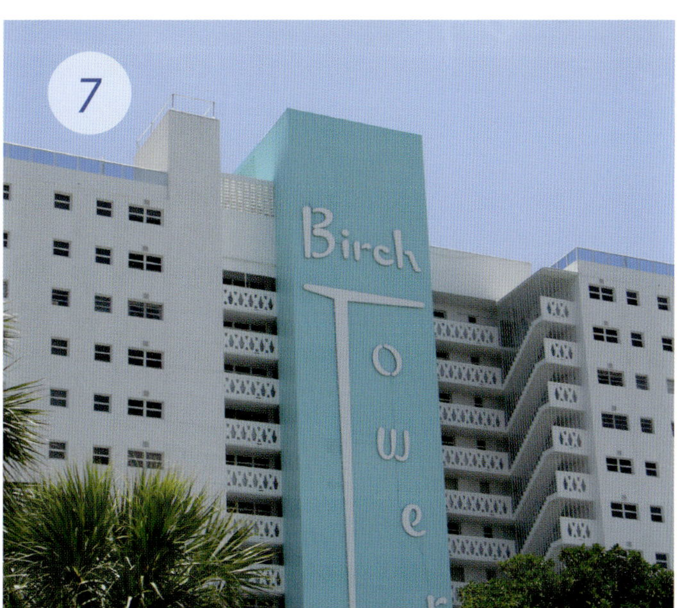
7
Birch
Tower

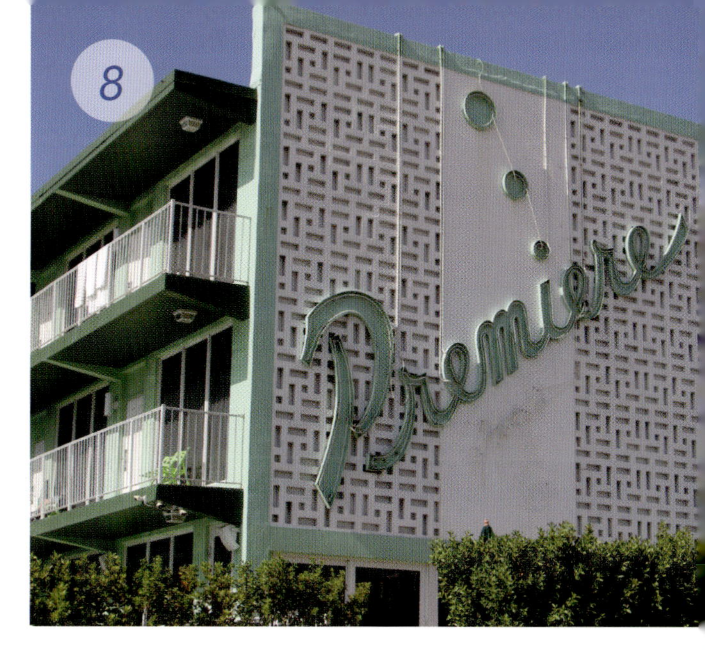
8
Premiere

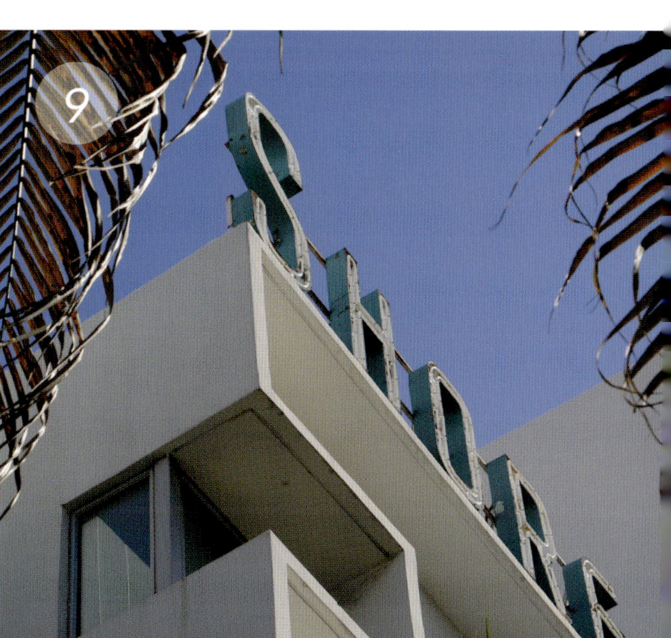
9

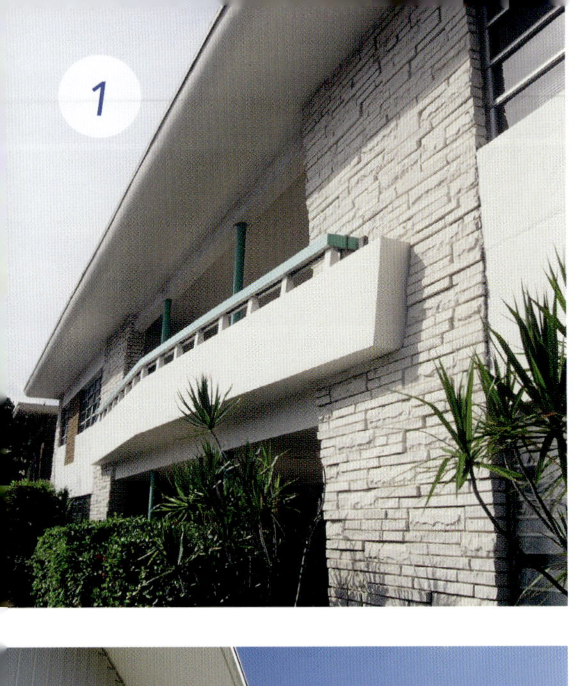
1

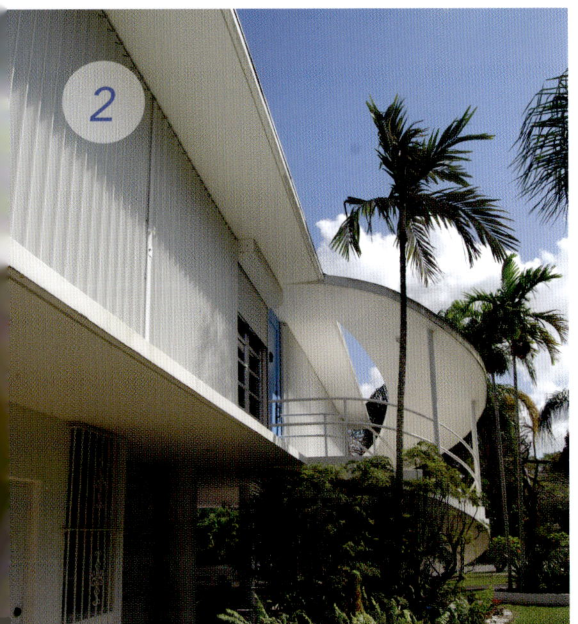
2

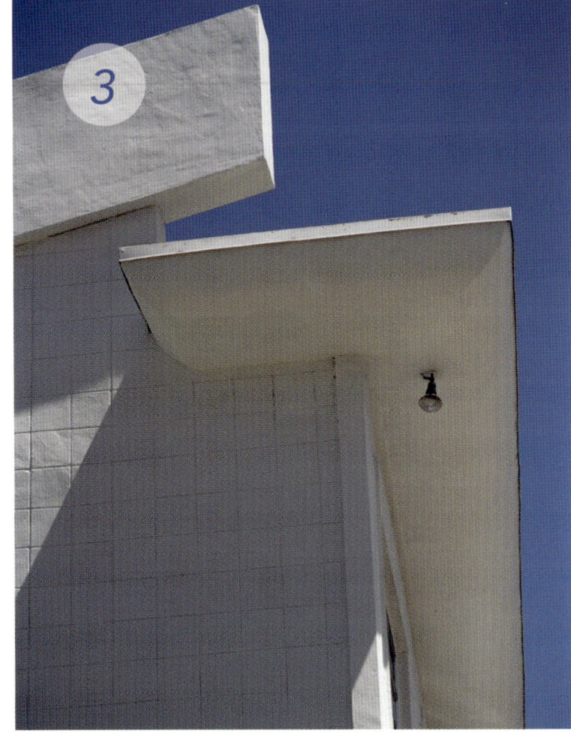
3

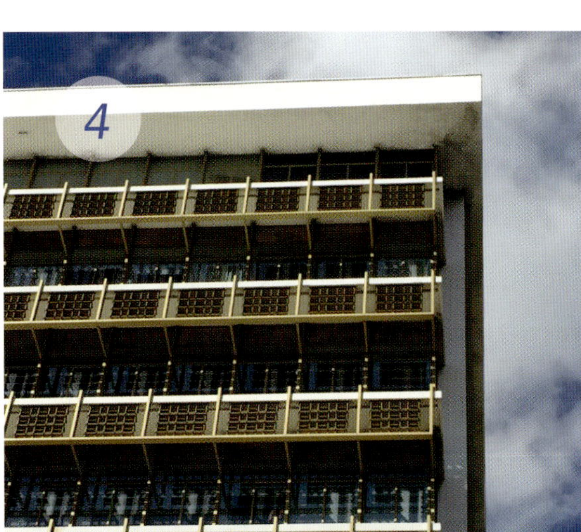
4

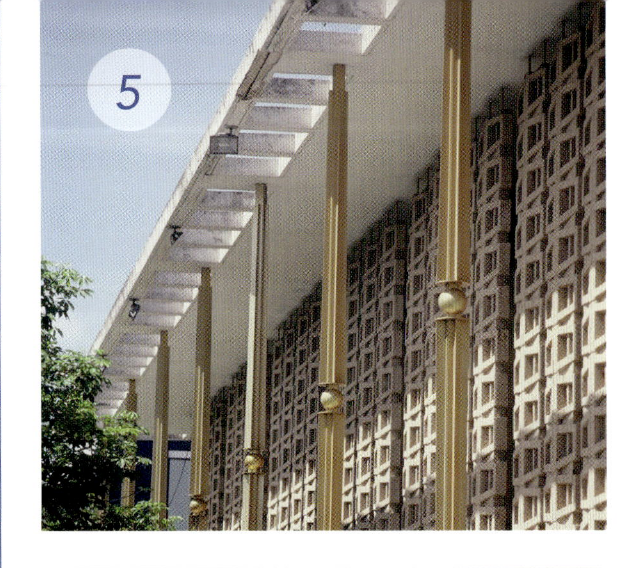
5

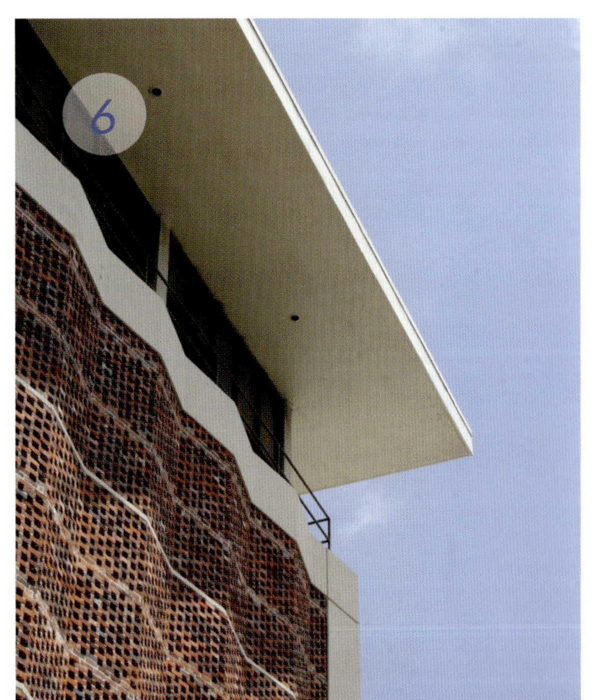
6

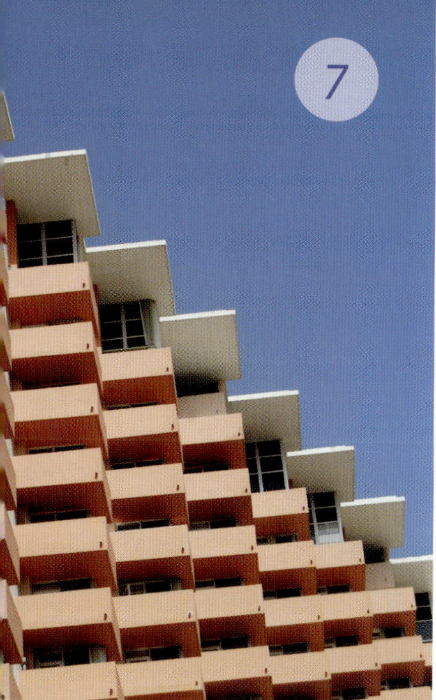

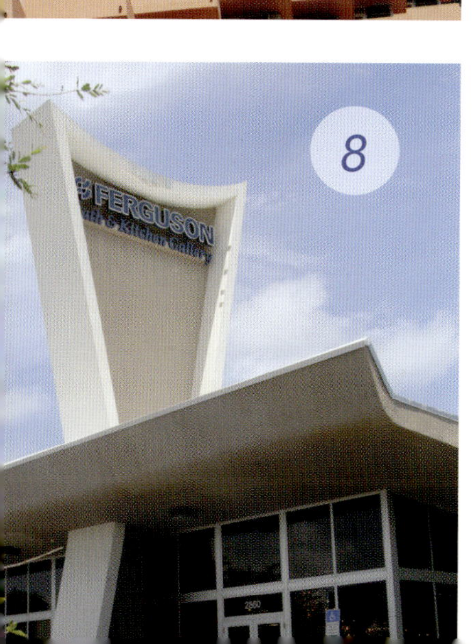

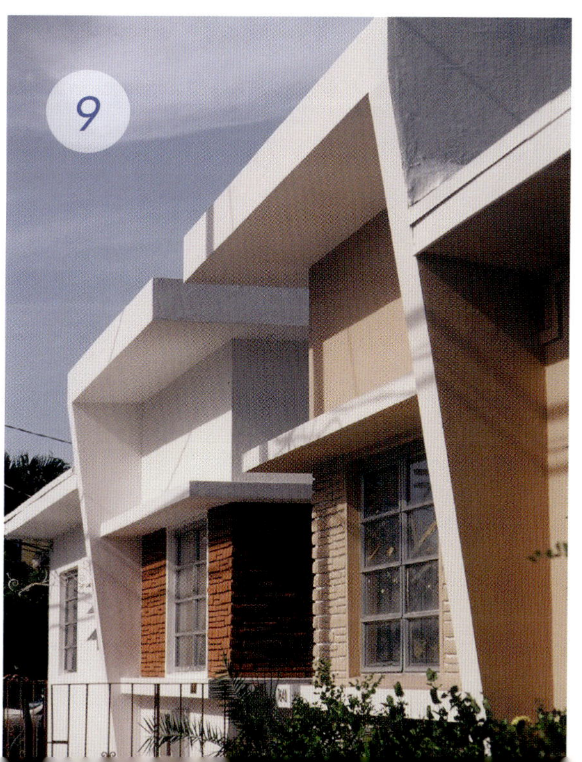

OVERHANGING ROOF PLANES

1
7291 Gary Avenue, Miami Beach

2
5261 NE 5th Avenue, Miami

3
315-321 83rd Street, Miami Beach

4
1688 Meridian Avenue, Miami Beach

5
Pan American Airlines, Miami

6
Bayview office building, Fort Lauderdale

7
Triton Towers, Miami Beach

8
Ferguson's, 2860 North Federal Highway, Fort Lauderdale

9
7630–7640 Dickens Avenue, Miami Beach

BRISE-SOLEILS & SCREEN WALLS

1
Temple Menorah Belvedere, Miami Beach

2
1751 South Ocean Boulevard, Lauderdale-by-the-Sea

3
1800 East Las Olas Boulevard, Fort Lauderdale

4
Sea Tower, Fort Lauderdale

5
9101 East Bay Harbor Drive, Bay Harbor Islands

6
Alexander Hotel, Miami Beach

7
Bay Harbor Continental, Bay Harbor Islands

8
Four Seasons, Fort Lauderdale

9
1800 Biscayne Boulevard, Miami

10
River Terrace, Oakland Park

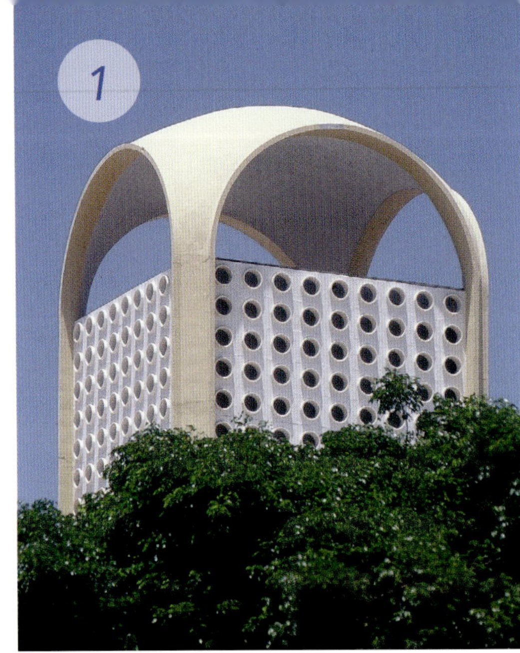

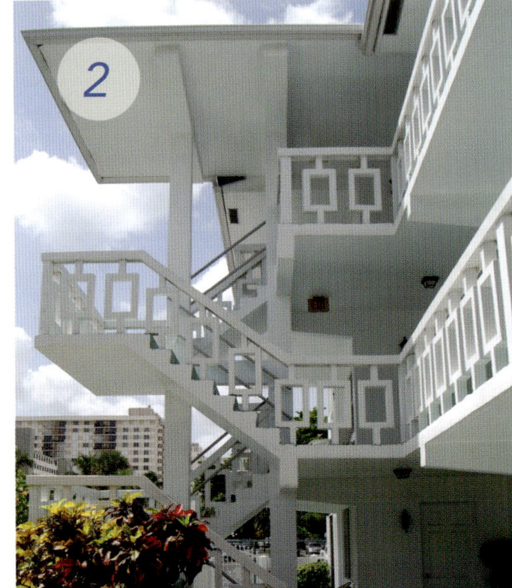

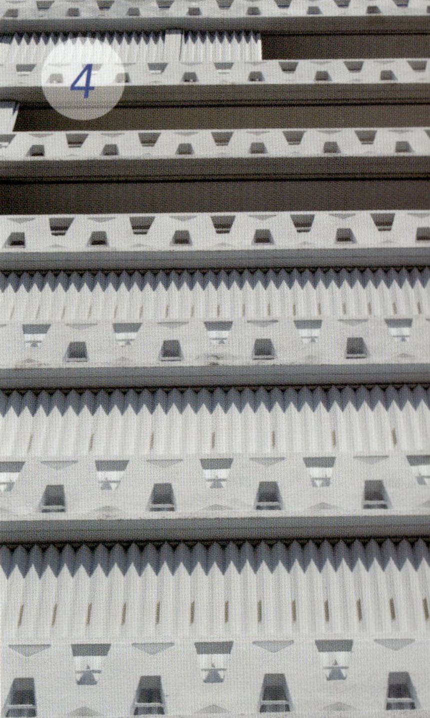

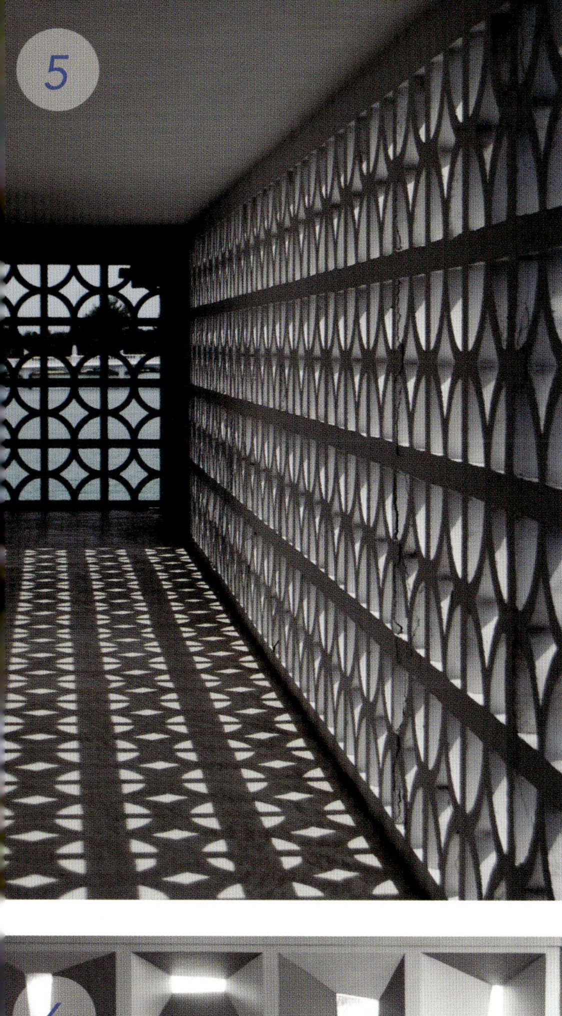
5

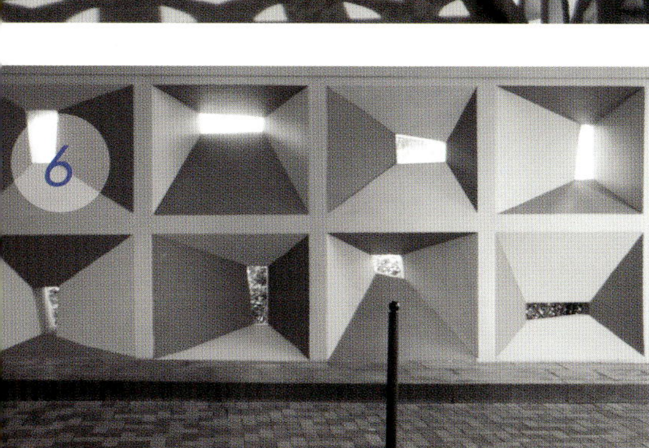
6

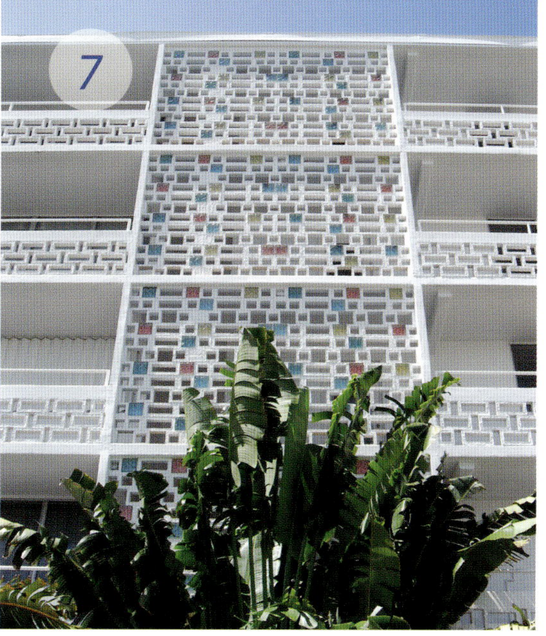
7

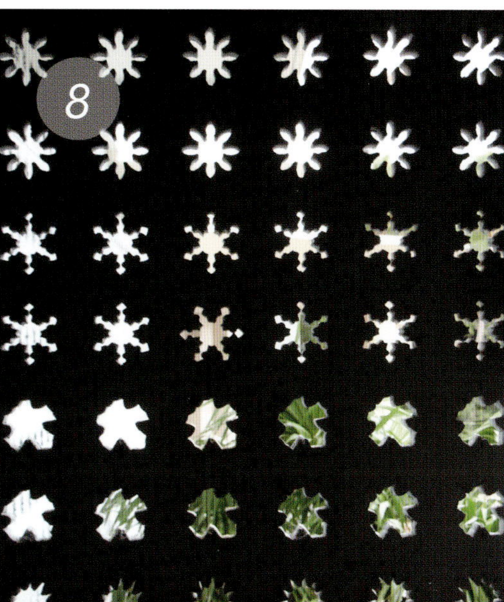
8

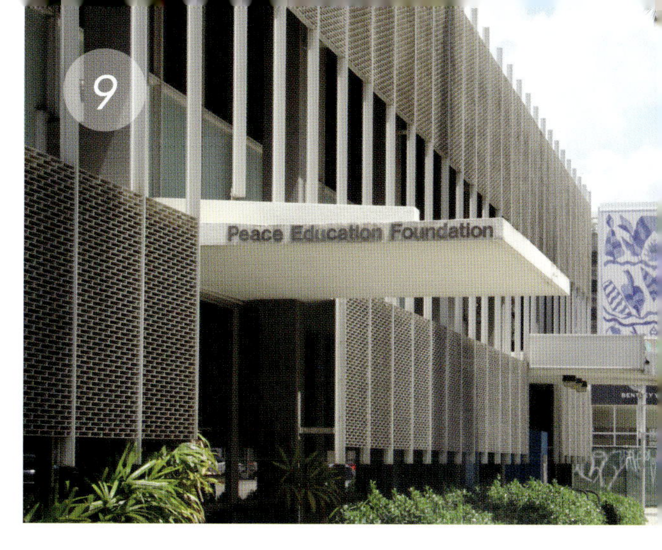
9
Peace Education Foundation

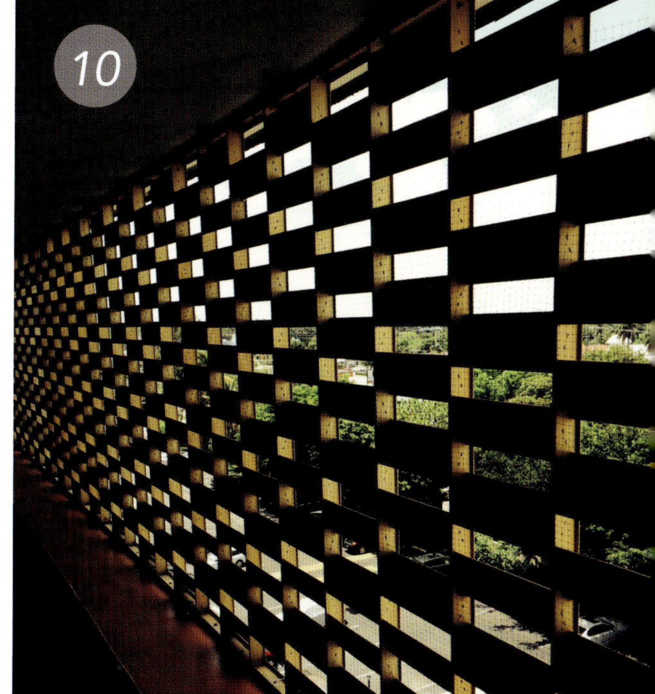
10

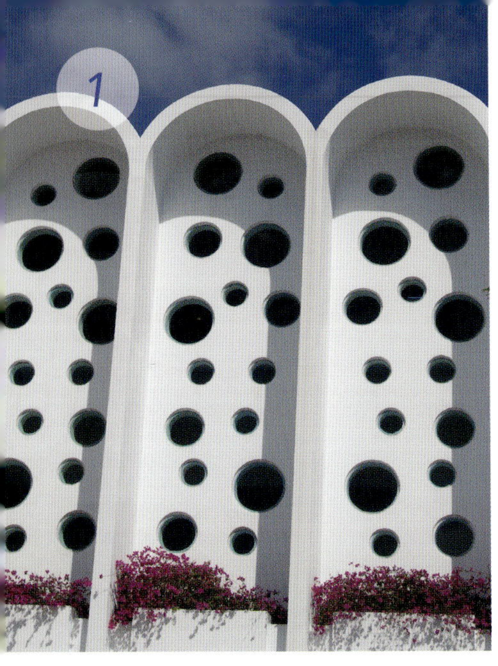
1

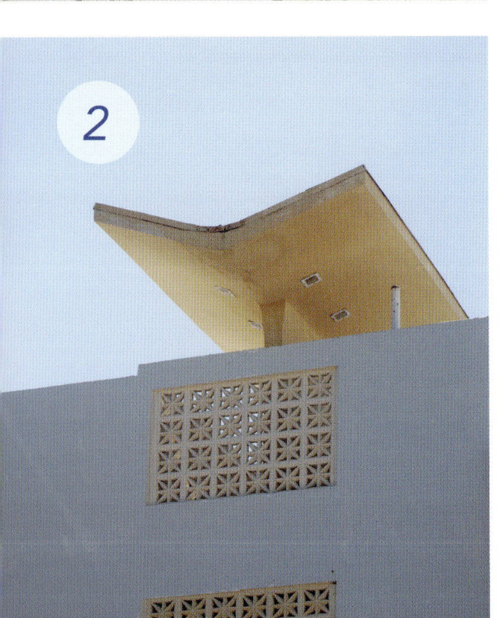
2

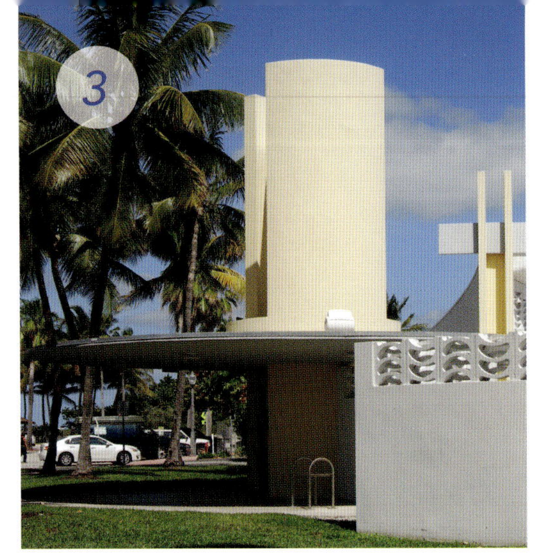
3

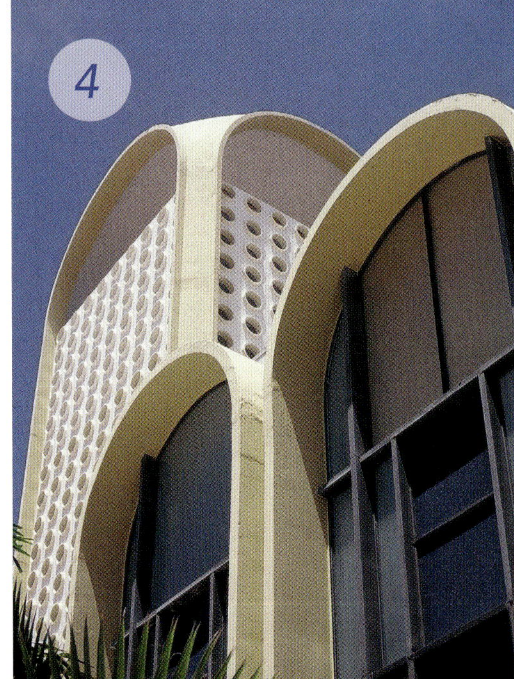
4

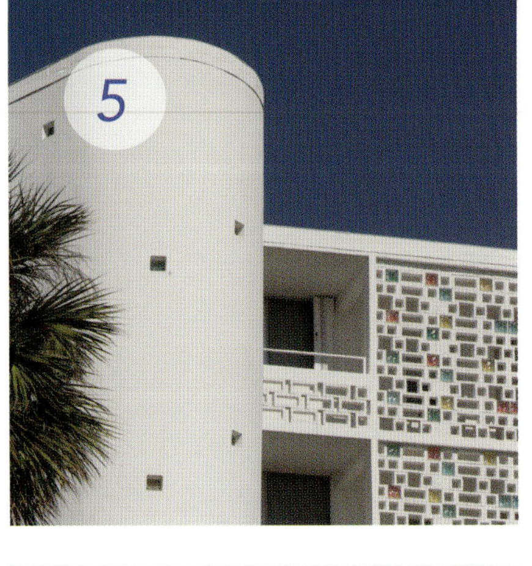
5

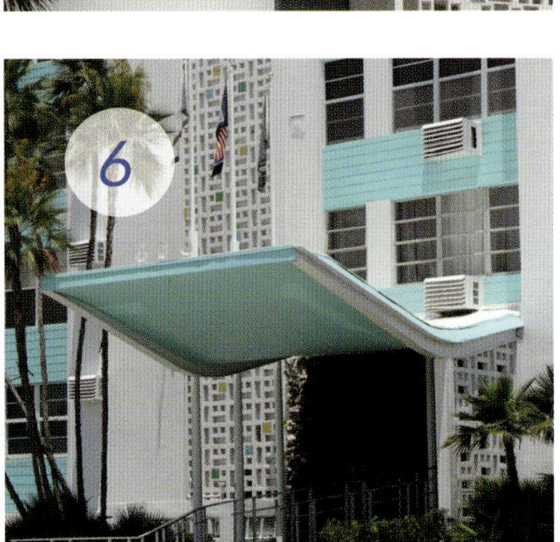
6

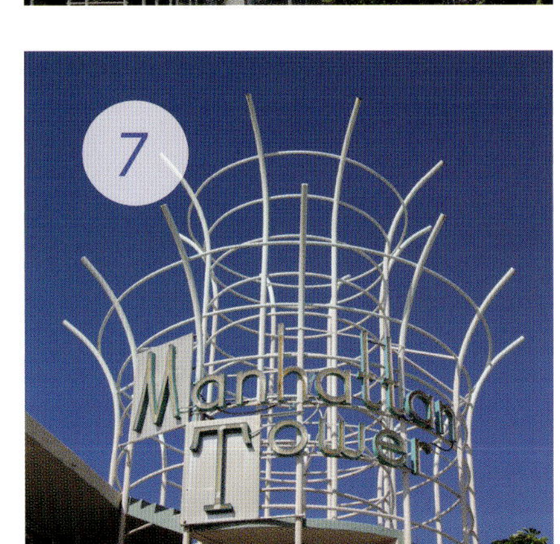
7
Manhattan
Tower

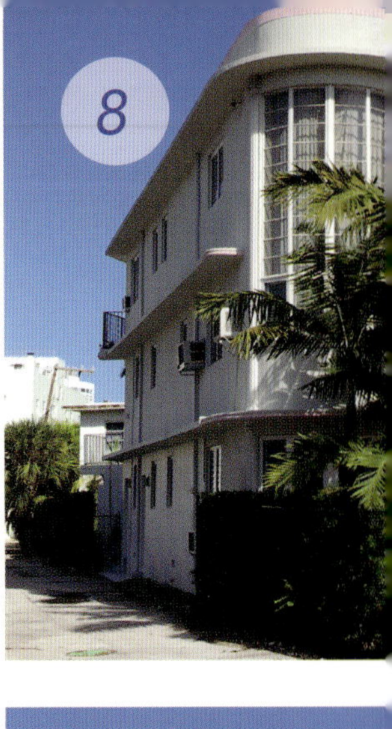
8

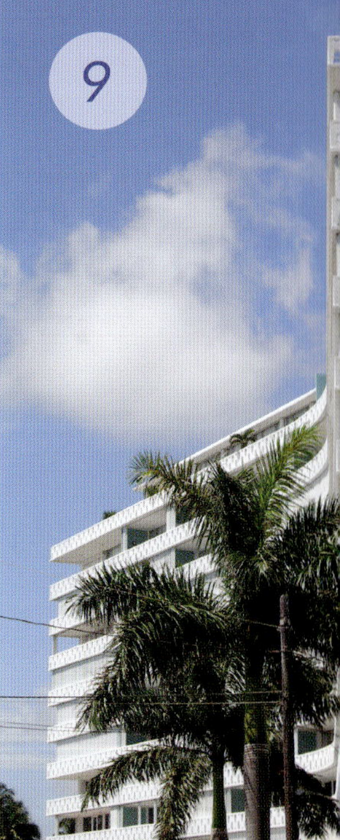
9

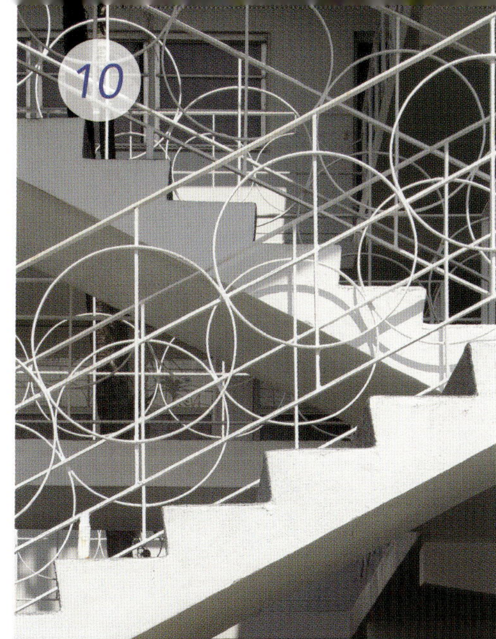

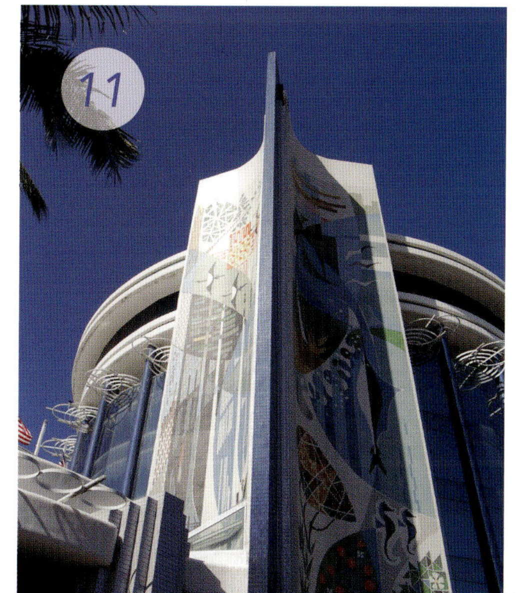

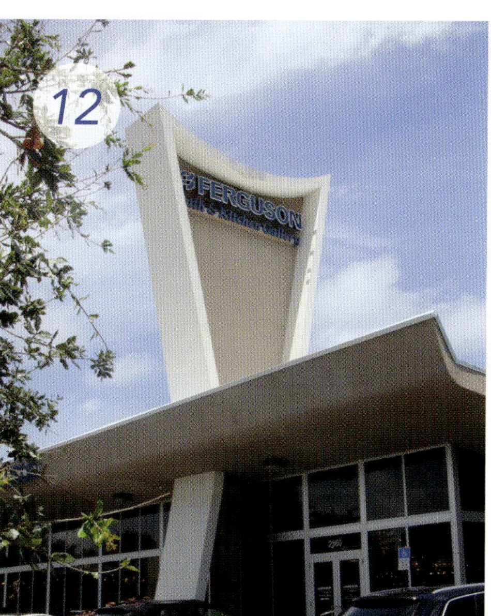

WIGGLES, WOGGLES, CURVES, ARCHES, BOOMERANGS

1
Fontainebleau Hotel, Miami Beach

2
Temple Menorah, Miami Beach

3
North Shore Band Shell, Miami Beach

4
Temple Menorah, Miami Beach

5
Bay Harbor Continental, Bay Harbor Islands

6
Birch House, Fort Lauderdale

7
Manhattan Tower, Fort Lauderdale

8
841 40th Street, Miami Beach

9
Sea Tower, Fort Lauderdale

10
Coral Cove Club, Fort Lauderdale

11
KenAnn Building, Fort Lauderdale

12
Ferguson's, a.k.a. Castro Convertibles, Fort Lauderdale

SOUTH BEACH/MIAMI BEACH, MIAMI

1 Lido Spa, South Beach / Miami Beach

2 Capri, South Beach / Miami Beach

3 Triton Towers, South Beach / Miami Beach

4 Plymouth Hotel, South Beach / Miami Beach

5 Shore Club Hotel, South Beach / Miami Beach

6 Shelborne Hotel, South Beach / Miami Beach

7 Raleigh Hotel, South Beach / Miami Beach

8 Delano Hotel, South Beach / Miami Beach

9 Albion Hotel, South Beach / Miami Beach

10 Lincoln Road Folly #1, South Beach / Miami Beach

11 Lincoln Road Folly #2, South Beach / Miami Beach

12 Sterling Building, South Beach / Miami Beach

13 Lincoln Road Folly #3, South Beach / Miami Beach

14 Clevelander Hotel, South Beach / Miami Beach

15 743 Washington Avenue, South Beach / Miami Beach

16 748 Euclid Avenue, South Beach / Miami Beach

17 5261 NE 5th Avenue, Miami

18 Bacardi Buildings, Miami

19 Gumenick Chapel @ Temple Israel, Miami

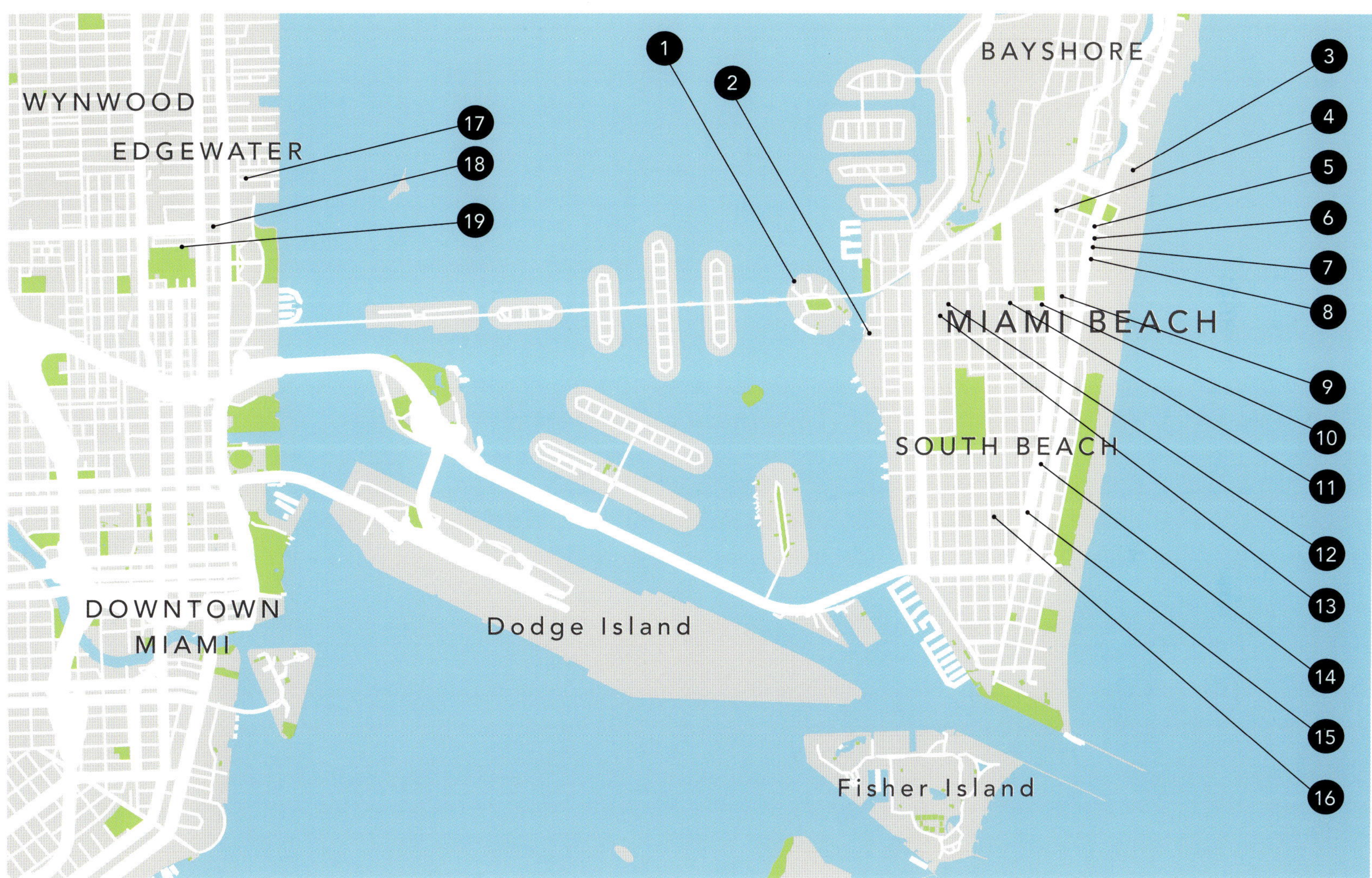

BAYSHORE
WYNWOOD
EDGEWATER
MIAMI BEACH
SOUTH BEACH
DOWNTOWN MIAMI
Dodge Island
Fisher Island
1
2
3
4
5
6
7
8
9
10
11
12
13
14
15
16
17
18
19

BAY HARBOR ISLANDS, SURFSIDE,

NORTH BEACH/MIAMI BEACH

1 The Mediterranean, Bay Harbor Islands

2 Bay Harbor Continental, Bay Harbor Islands

3 Bay Harbor Club, Bay Harbor Islands

4 Regent Palace, Surfside

5 Dezerland, North Beach / Miami Beach

6 Duane Motel, North Beach / Miami Beach

7 Temple Menorah, North Beach / Miami Beach

8 7630-7640 Dickens Avenue, North Beach / Miami Beach

9 North Shore Band Shell , North Beach / Miami Beach

10 Casablanca Hotel, North Beach / Miami Beach

11 Alexander Hotel , North Beach / Miami Beach

12 Eden Roc Hotel, Mid Beach / Miami Beach

13 Fontainebleau Hotel, Mid Beach / Miami Beach

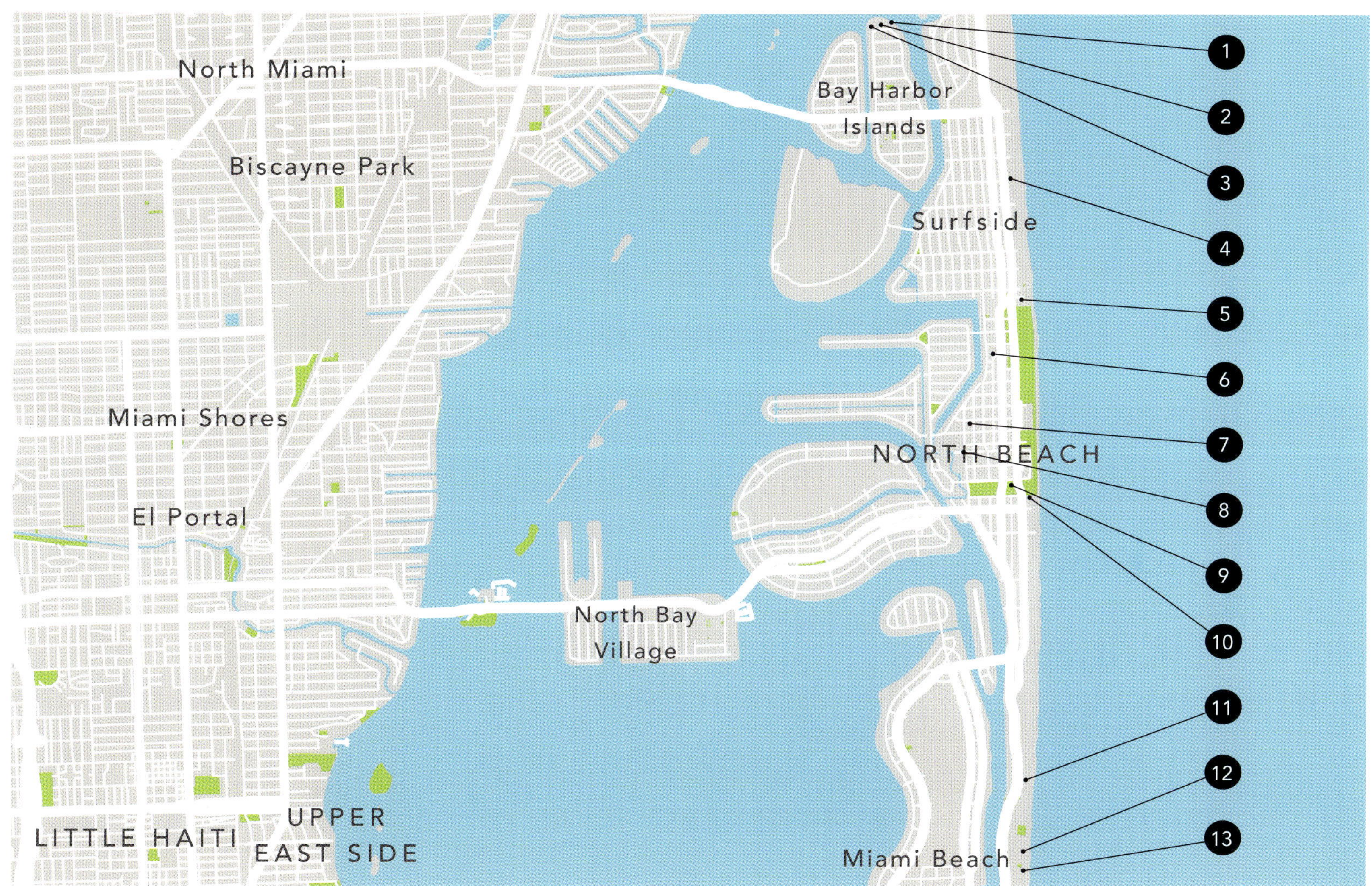
North Miami
Bay Harbor Islands
Biscayne Park
Surfside
Miami Shores
NORTH BEACH
El Portal
North Bay Village
UPPER EAST SIDE
LITTLE HAITI
Miami Beach
1
2
3
4
5
6
7
8
9
10
11
12
13

FORT LAUDERDALE

1 Jade Beach West, Lauderdale-By-The-Sea

2 4546 El Mar Drive, Lauderdale-By-The-Sea

3 Kenann Building, Oakland Park

4 Times Square Shopping Center, Fort Lauderdale

5 Ferguson, Fort Lauderdale

6 Sea Tower, Fort Lauderdale

7 Sunrise Bay Club, Fort Lauderdale

8 Bayview Office Building, Fort Lauderdale

9 Birch House, Fort Lauderdale

10 Birch Tower, Fort Lauderdale

11 Manhattan Tower, Fort Lauderdale

12 Las Olas Club, Fort Lauderdale

13 Cadillac Villa, Fort Lauderdale

14 Four Seasons Condominium, Fort Lauderdale

15 Yankee Clipper, Fort Lauderdale

16 Pier 66, Fort Lauderdale

17 Breakwater Towers, Fort Lauderdale

18 Lago Mar, Fort Lauderdale

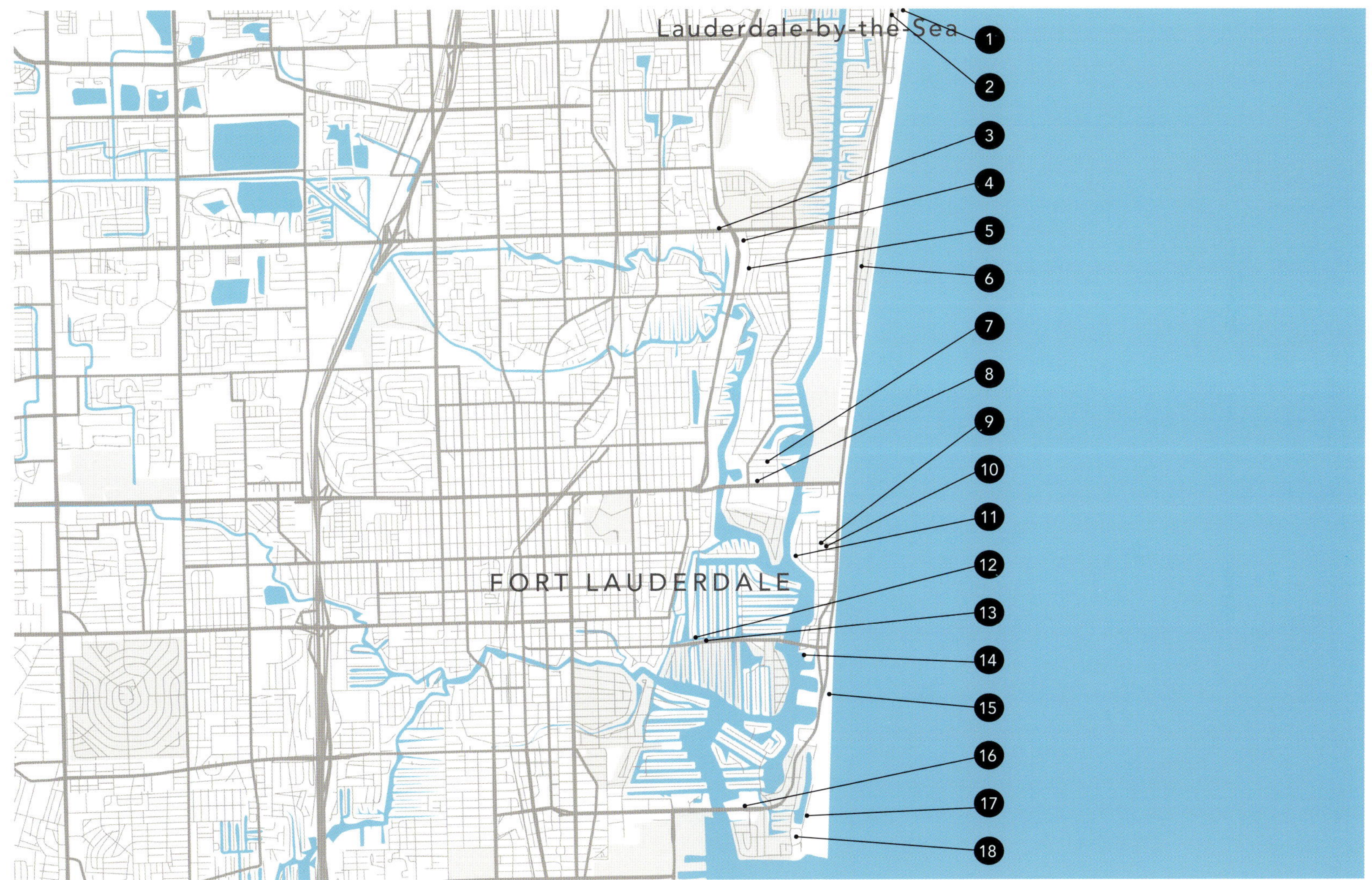

Lauderdale-by-the-Sea
FORT LAUDERDALE
1
2
3
4
5
6
7
8
9
10
11
12
13
14
15
16
17
18

THE ARCHITECTS

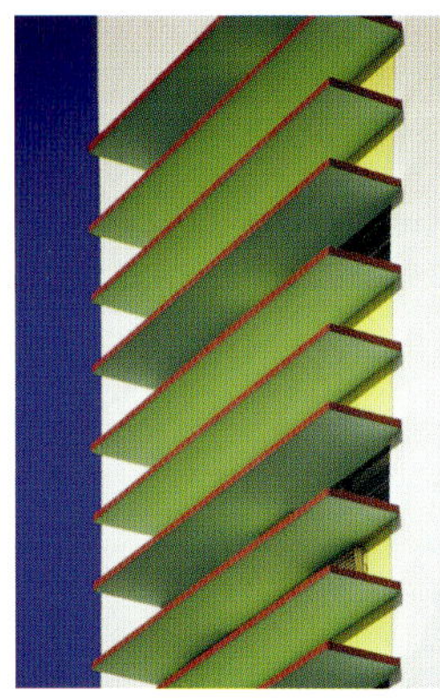

ALBERT ANIS (1889–1964) was born in Illinois and attended the Armour Institute of Technology (now the Illinois Institute of Technology) in Chicago, Illinois, from 1908 to 1910. He was certified as an architect in 1926 in Illinois and again in 1935 when he moved to Florida.

Perhaps more than any other architect, Albert Anis successfully transitioned from deco to MiMo. Although not as prolific as Dixon and Hohauser in the 1930s, Anis was a vital part of this trio of architects who helped define Miami Beach deco with influential works.

REPRESENTATIVE PROJECTS

Dezerland, a.k.a. Biltmore Terrace Hotel, Miami Beach (demolished)
Shore Club Hotel, Miami Beach
Waldorf Towers, Miami Beach
Winter Haven Hotel, Miami Beach

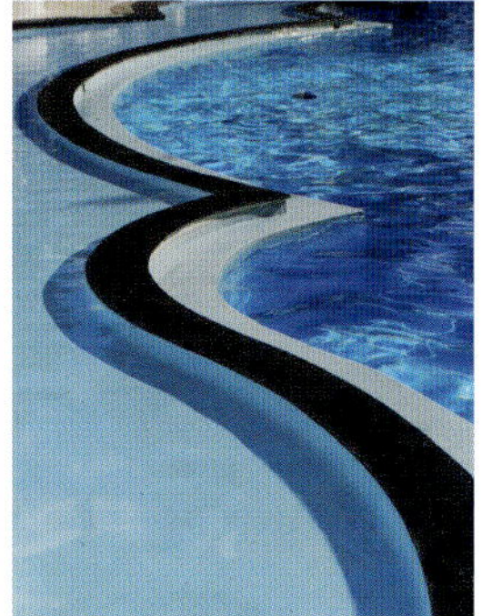

LAWRENCE MURRAY DIXON (1901–1949) was born in Live Oak, Florida, and studied at the Georgia Institute of Technology (1918–1919). Upon moving to Miami Beach and establishing his own practice, Dixon designed over a hundred buildings that still exist in Miami Beach. Although his lifetime was short, Dixon became one of Miami Beach's most notable designers of hotels, residences, and commercial buildings.

REPRESENTATIVE PROJECTS

Adams Hotel, Miami Beach
Atlantis Hotel, Miami Beach (demolished)
Beach Plaza Hotel, Miami Beach
Fairmont Hotel, Miami Beach
Grossinger Beach Hotel, a.k.a. Ritz Plaza, Miami Beach
Haddon Hall Hotel, Miami Beach
Marlin Hotel, Miami Beach
Normandy Plaza Hotel, Miami Beach
Palmer House Hotel, Miami Beach
Raleigh Hotel, Miami Beach
Seymour Building—Goldwasser's Shops, Miami Beach
Tides Hotel, Miami Beach
Tiffany Hotel, Miami Beach
Victor Hotel, Miami Beach

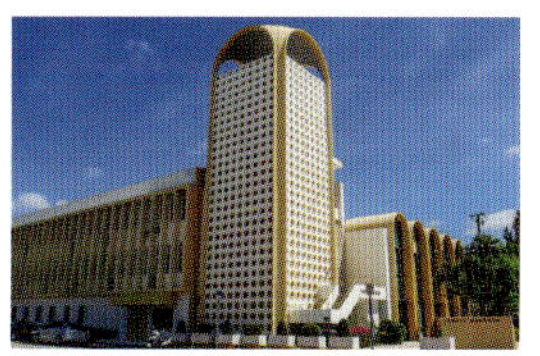

GILBERT M. FEIN (1920–2003) was born in New York City and studied architecture at New York University. During World War II he served in the Army Corps of Engineers and moved to Miami Beach after the war. He designed hundreds of residential and commercial buildings in South Florida in the new postwar modern style. Fein was known for his designs of two-story apartment buildings that mirrored each other and converged at the front elevation, enclosing a landscaped courtyard behind.

REPRESENTATIVE PROJECTS

Temple Menorah, Miami Beach
Gilbert Fein Conservation District, Miami Beach
7400 Ocean Terrace, Miami Beach
7430 Ocean Terrace, Miami Beach
8601 Harding Avenue, Miami Beach
6930 Rue Versailles, Miami Beach

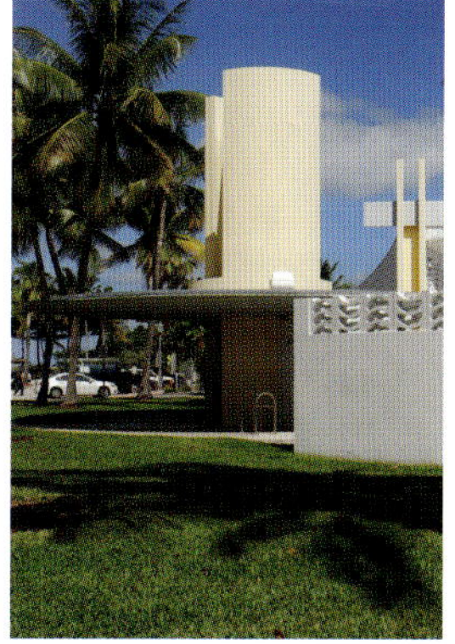

NORMAN M. GILLER (1918–2008) was born in Jacksonville, Florida, and graduated from the University of Florida in 1945 after studying with Florida's first licensed female architect, Marion Manley.

Giller was a true innovator, pioneering the use of air conditioning in South Florida. He was one of the first architects to utilize space-efficient, flat-slab concrete construction techniques in his designs, as well as the use of PVC plumbing piping. Giller also developed the two-story motel building concept, which became one of the most widely imitated building types in the US.

In 1957, *Architectural Forum* magazine ranked his firm as the tenth largest architectural firm in the country, with six offices in Central and South America. He also worked in Canada, in Europe, and throughout Florida, designing more than 11,000 buildings during his career. Giller was also instrumental in establishing a design review board in Miami Beach and served as its first chair.

REPRESENTATIVE PROJECTS

Bombay Hotel, a.k.a. Golden Sands, Miami Beach
Carillon Hotel, Miami Beach (altered)
Davis Motel, Miami Beach
Diplomat Hotel, Hollywood (demolished)
Driftwood Motel, Sunny Isles (demolished)
Giller Building, Miami Beach
Jewish Museum of Florida, Miami Beach
Miami Beach Chamber of Commerce
Monterrey Motel, a.k.a. The Standard, Miami Beach
North Beach Elementary School, Miami Beach
North Shore Band Shell, Miami Beach
Ocean Palm Hotel, Sunny Isles (demolished)
Thunderbird Motel, Sunny Isles (demolished)

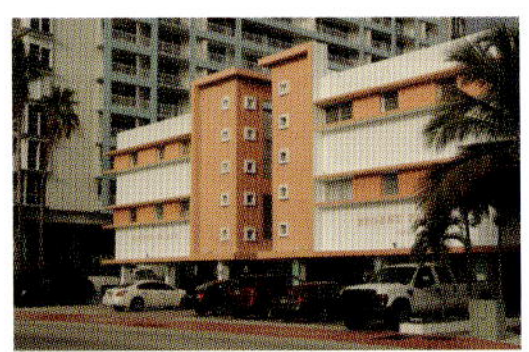

LEONARD H. GLASSER (1922–1982) and his brother Robert L. Glasser served in World War II after graduation from Miami Beach High School. They shared an office on Lincoln Road in Miami Beach and designed a wide variety of buildings. They moved their offices to Puerto Rico in 1961 to work on projects there and in Central America. While in Puerto Rico the Glassers formed a partnership with Enrique Gutierrez and his firm, SACMAG International, on the design of the Bacardi buildings in Miami.

REPRESENTATIVE PROJECTS

Regent Palace, Surfside
Oceanfront Auditorium, Miami Beach
Coral Gables Post Office, Coral Gables
990 Insurance Building, Miami
Fun Fair Drive-In Theater, Miami Beach

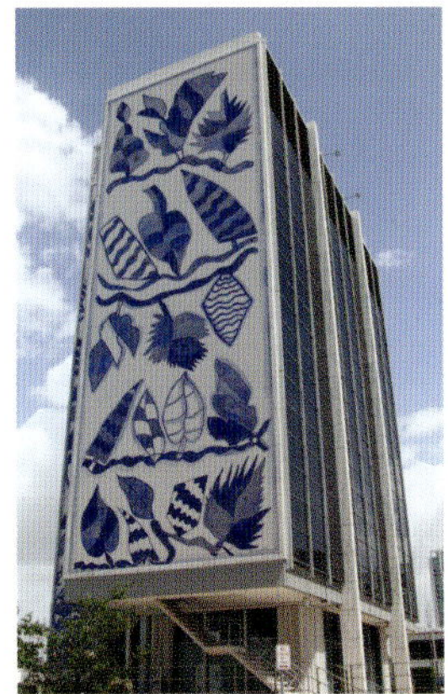

ENRIQUE GUTIERREZ (1931–2017) was born in Cuba and graduated from the University of Havana School of Architecture in 1956. After moving his architectural practice to Puerto Rico, his firm, SACMAG International, became one of the island's most prolific architects and opened an office in Miami after completing the Bacardi buildings.

REPRESENTATIVE PROJECTS

Bacardi Buildings, a.k.a. Young Arts Foundation, Miami
El Caribe Building, Puerto Rico
One Biscayne Building, Miami

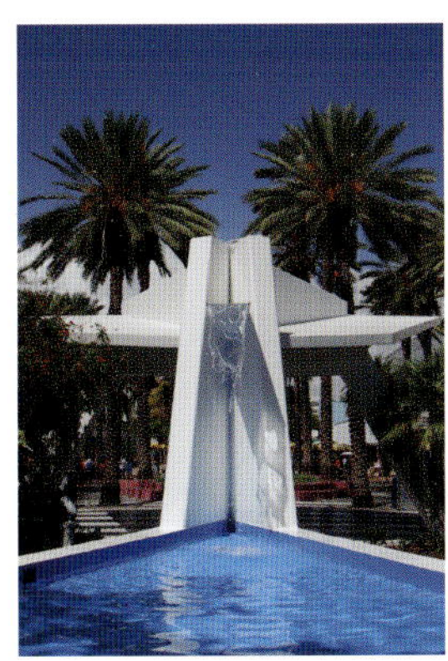

MORRIS LAPIDUS (1902–2001) was born in Russia and immigrated to New York as a child. He graduated from Columbia University and began working in New York City as a retail designer. His storefronts were noted for their innovative forms, curves, and receding show windows, designed to draw in shoppers.

He first visited Miami Beach in 1929 on his honeymoon and returned after World War II to design hotels. His first major project was the interior of the Sans Souci Hotel, with additional interior work on the Algiers, Nautilus, DiLido, and Biltmore Terrace hotels.

In 1954, Lapidus was retained to design an entirely new hotel on the oceanfront site of the former Firestone estate. The Fontainebleau Hotel was destined to become one of Miami Beach's most famous hotels. His designs were initially panned by architecture critics as being overly decorative, yet the public loved the fantasy environments he created.

In 1955, he received a commission for the Eden Roc Hotel next door to the Fontainebleau, which began a famous battle between the owners of these two properties. In 1958 the Fontainebleau constructed a high-rise North Tower designed by A. Herbert Mathes, with a blank wall facing the Eden Roc property, blocking the sun from the Eden Roc pool. This new North Tower was nicknamed the Spite Wall.

Lapidus became one of Miami Beach's most well-known and respected architects. The titles of two of his books summarize his approach to design: *The Architecture of Joy* and *Too Much Is Never Enough*.

REPRESENTATIVE PROJECTS

Algiers Hotel, Miami Beach
Americana Hotel, Bal Harbour (demolished)
Aruba Caribbean Hotel, Aruba
Biltmore Terrace, a.k.a. Dezerland Hotel, Miami Beach
Crystal House, Miami Beach
Daniel Tower Hotel, Israel
Fontainebleau Hotel, Miami Beach
Eden Roc Hotel, Miami Beach
International Inn, Washington, DC
Lincoln Road Pedestrian Mall, Miami Beach
Sans Souci Hotel, Miami Beach
Saxony Hotel, Miami Beach
Seacoast Towers, Miami Beach
Summit Hotel, New York, New York
Temple Menorah, Miami Beach
Trelawny Hotel, Jamaica

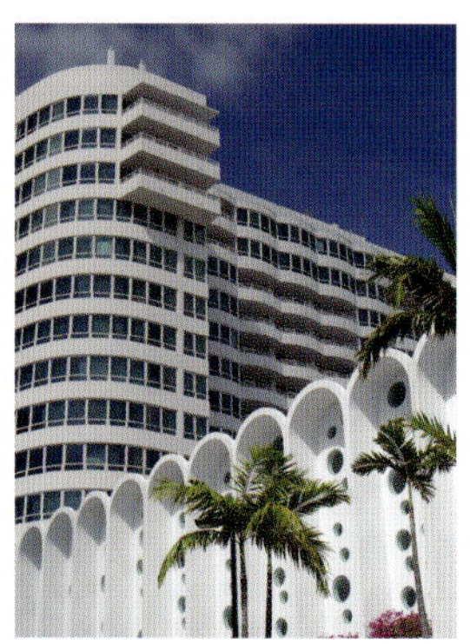

A. HERBERT MATHES (1912–1977) graduated from New York University in 1937 and settled in Miami Beach in 1944. Mathes had a varied background, having designed stores for the National Show Company, shoe exhibits at the 1939 New York World's Fair, packing plants in Kansas, film labs for 20th Century Fox, and ships for the US Navy during World War II.

REPRESENTATIVE PROJECTS

Parisian Hotel, Miami Beach
Continental Hotel, Miami Beach
Allison Hotel, Miami Beach
Fontainebleau North Tower, Miami Beach

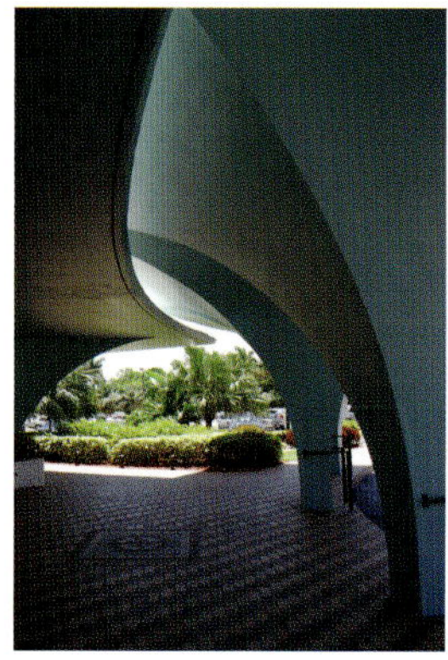

CHARLES FOSTER MCKIRAHAN (1919–1964) was born in Tulsa, Oklahoma, and attended Oklahoma State University. He served as a captain with the US Army Corps of Engineers during World War II in Australia, Hawaii, Guam, Japan, and the South Pacific. These travels and the cultures he encountered strongly influenced his later work.

In 1947, he received an architecture degree from the University of Illinois, where he met his future wife, Lucille. She became a partner, producing artistic renderings for client presentations. He formed Wilmer & McKirahan in 1951 but opened his own practice in 1953 in Fort Lauderdale.

McKirahan worked throughout the Caribbean and Central and South America. He designed homes for the actor Raymond Burr and for the artist Alexander Calder. His life was tragically cut short in an automobile accident in 1964, when he was forty-four years old and at the height of his career.

REPRESENTATIVE PROJECTS

Alexander Hotel, Miami Beach
Bay Harbor Continental, Bay Harbor Islands
Bayview Office Building, Fort Lauderdale
Birch House, Fort Lauderdale
Birch Tower, Fort Lauderdale
Castaways Island Hotel, Sunny Isles (demolished)
Castro Convertibles, a.k.a. Ferguson, Fort Lauderdale
Coral Ridge Communities, Fort Lauderdale
Coral Ridge Country Club, Fort Lauderdale
Coral Ridge Towers (north and east), Fort Lauderdale
Everglades House, Fort Lauderdale
Lago Mar Apartments, Fort Lauderdale
Las Olas Club, Fort Lauderdale
Mai Kai Restaurant, Fort Lauderdale
Manhattan Tower, Fort Lauderdale
Ocean Manors Hotel, Fort Lauderdale
Point of America Condominium, Fort Lauderdale
Times Square Shopping Center, Fort Lauderdale

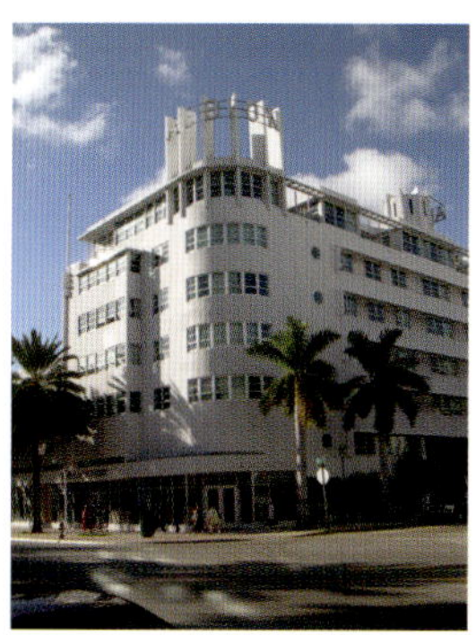

IGOR B. POLEVITZSKY (1911–1978) was born in St. Petersburg, Russia, and immigrated to America with his family in 1922. Polevitzsky's mother, Katherine, worked as a researcher at the University of Pennsylvania in Philadelphia, and he enrolled in 1929.

After beginning studies in civil engineering, he was directed to the school of architecture, studying under the well-known architect Paul Phillippe Cret, who was credited with having a major influence on young Igor. Polevitzsky graduated cum laude from Penn in 1934.

After graduation, Polevitzsky moved to Miami and soon began a partnership with fellow Penn graduate Thomas Triplett Russell. Polevitzsky and Russell maintained their partnership from 1936 to 1945. Polevitzsky later formed Polevitzsky, Johnson & Associates.

His architecture was known for its avant-garde futuristic modeling. The work focused on the merging of interior and exterior spaces to take advantage of the tropical climate. Polevitzsky designed more than 500 buildings during his career.

REPRESENTATIVE PROJECTS

Albion Hotel, Miami Beach
Arthur Murray Dance Studio, Miami Beach
Castaways Motel, Sunny Isles (demolished)
First Unitarian Church, Miami
Fontainebleau Motor Inn, New Orleans
Frank and Bun Fast Food restaurant, Miami
Gulf Service Station & Hotel, Miami Beach (demolished)
Habana Riviera Hotel, Havana, Cuba
Jamaica Inn, Key Biscayne
Jolly Roger, Fort Lauderdale
One Lincoln Road Office Building, Miami Beach
Plaza Building, Miami
Saks Fifth Avenue, Miami Beach
Sans Souci Estates, Miami
Sea Tower, Fort Lauderdale
Seaview Realty Building, Miami
1069–1085 Kane Concourse, Bay Harbor Islands

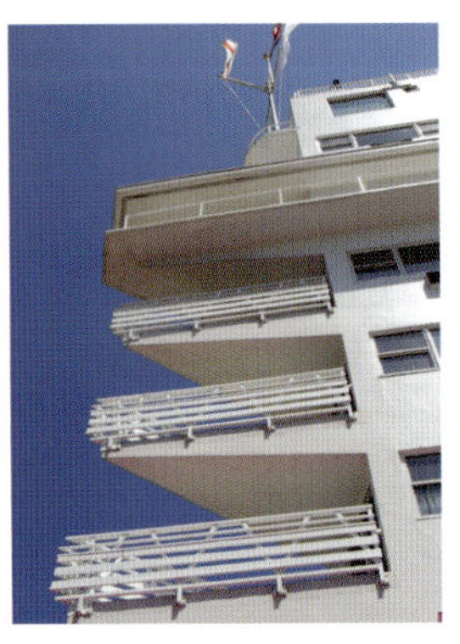

M. TONY SHERMAN (1910–1989) worked in New York City for thirteen years before moving to Miami in 1947 and eventually opening his own firm.

The Yankee Clipper Hotel, a.k.a. B Ocean Resort in Fort Lauderdale, is Sherman's homage to the nautical, roughly taking the form of a beached ocean liner. Its Wreck Bar still features underwater windows facing into the pool.

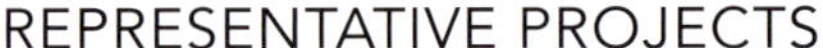

REPRESENTATIVE PROJECTS

Yankee Clipper Hotel, Fort Lauderdale
7455 Byron Avenue, Miami Beach
7818 Harding Avenue, Miami Beach
Catalina Motel, Miami Beach
Adrian Apartments, Miami Beach
425 20th Street, Miami Beach

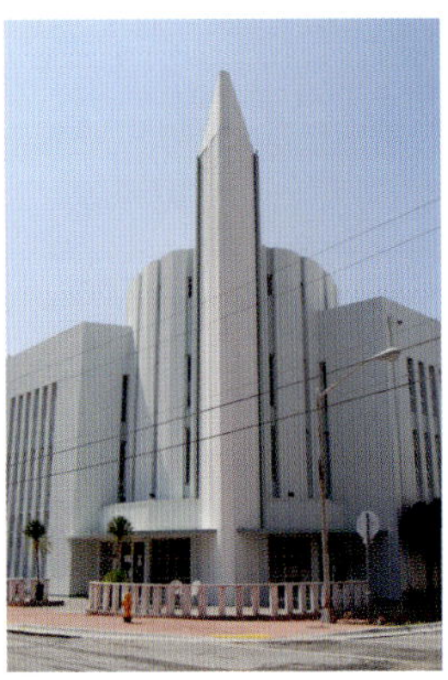

ANTON SKISLEWICZ (1895–1980) was born in Dubrovnick, Yugoslavia, and was a World War I aviator. He immigrated to New York after the war and graduated from Columbia University in 1929.

Drawn by the building boom in Miami Beach during the 1930s, he opened a practice in Miami Beach in 1934, bringing a European sensitivity to local architecture. His earlier work in naval architecture and aviation clearly shows in his streamlined buildings. He also designed a limited-edition limousine for Lincoln Motors in 1938. During the war he closed his practice and returned to shipbuilding in Tampa, Florida.

REPRESENTATIVE PROJECTS

Breakwater Hotel, Miami Beach
Di Lido, a.k.a. Ritz Carlton Hotel, Miami Beach
Kenmore Hotel, Miami Beach
Lord Balfour Hotel, Miami Beach
Lincoln Center buildings, Miami Beach
Ocean Surf Hotel, Miami beach
Plymouth Hotel, Miami Beach

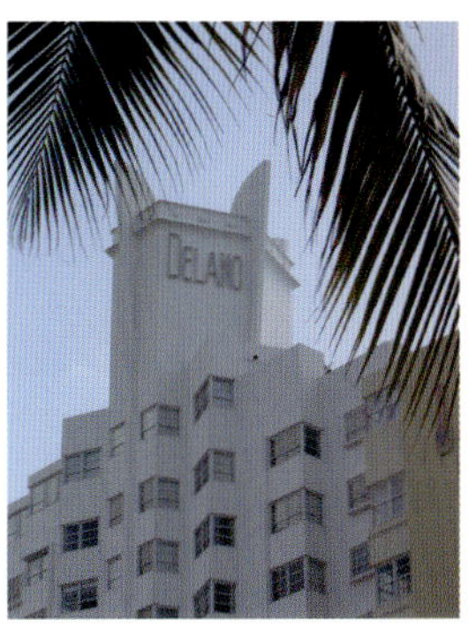

B. ROBERT SWARTBURG (1895–1975) was born in New York City and studied at Columbia University, the American Academy in Rome, and the Ecole des Beaux Arts in Paris. After practicing architecture in New York City for several years, he moved to Miami in 1944. He designed more than 1,000 buildings and was a well-known artist.

REPRESENTATIVE PROJECTS

Belle Towers, Miami Beach
Cleveland Hotel, Miami Beach
Delano Hotel, Miami Beach
Executive House, Miami Beach
Garden Bay Manor, New York City
Ojus Elementary School, Miami
Riviera Junior High School, Miami
Sorrento Hotel, Miami Beach
Vagabond Motel, Miami

BIBLIOGRAPHY

City of Miami Beach. "MiMo on the Beach: Futuristic, Flamboyant and Fun; Post–World War II–Era Architecture of Miami Beach." www.mimoonthebeach.com, 2011.

D'Amico, Teri, and David Framberger. *Beyond the Box: Mid-century Architecture in Miami and New York*. Miami Beach, FL: Urban Arts Committee of Miami Beach, 2002.

Giller, Norman M., and Sarah Giller Nelson. *Designing the Good Life: Norman M. Giller and the Development of Miami Modernism*. Gainesville, FL: University Press of Florida, 2007.

Kleinberg, Howard, and Carolyn Klepser. *Miami Beach: A Centennial History*. Miami, FL: City of Miami Beach, 2016.

Lapidus, Morris. *Too Much Is Never Enough: An Autobiography*. New York: Rizzoli International, 1996.

Lejeune, Jean Francois, and Allan T. Shulman. *The Making of Miami Beach, 1933–1942: The Architecture of Lawrence Murray Dixon*. New York: Rizzoli International, 2000.

Miami Dade Historic Neighborhood Preservation Coalition. *Bay Harbor Islands MiMo: Architecture of a Mid-century Town*. Miami, FL: Miami Dade Historic Neighborhood Preservation Coalition, 2009.

Nash, Eric P., and Randall C. Robinson Jr. *MiMo: Miami Modern Revealed*. San Francisco: Chronicle Books, 2004.

O'Connor, John, and Diane Smart. *Going, Going, Gone? Mid-century Modern Architecture in South Florida*. Fort Lauderdale, FL: North Beach Development Corporation and Broward Trust for Historic Preservation, 2005.

Shulman, Allan T., ed. *Miami Modern Metropolis: Paradise and Paradox in Midcentury Architecture and Planning*. Princeton, NJ: Princeton Architectural Press, 2009.

Shulman, Allan T., Randall C. Robinson, and James F. Donnelly. *Miami Architecture: An AIA Guide Featuring Downtown, the Beaches and Coconut Grove*. Gainesville, FL: University Press of Florida, 2010.

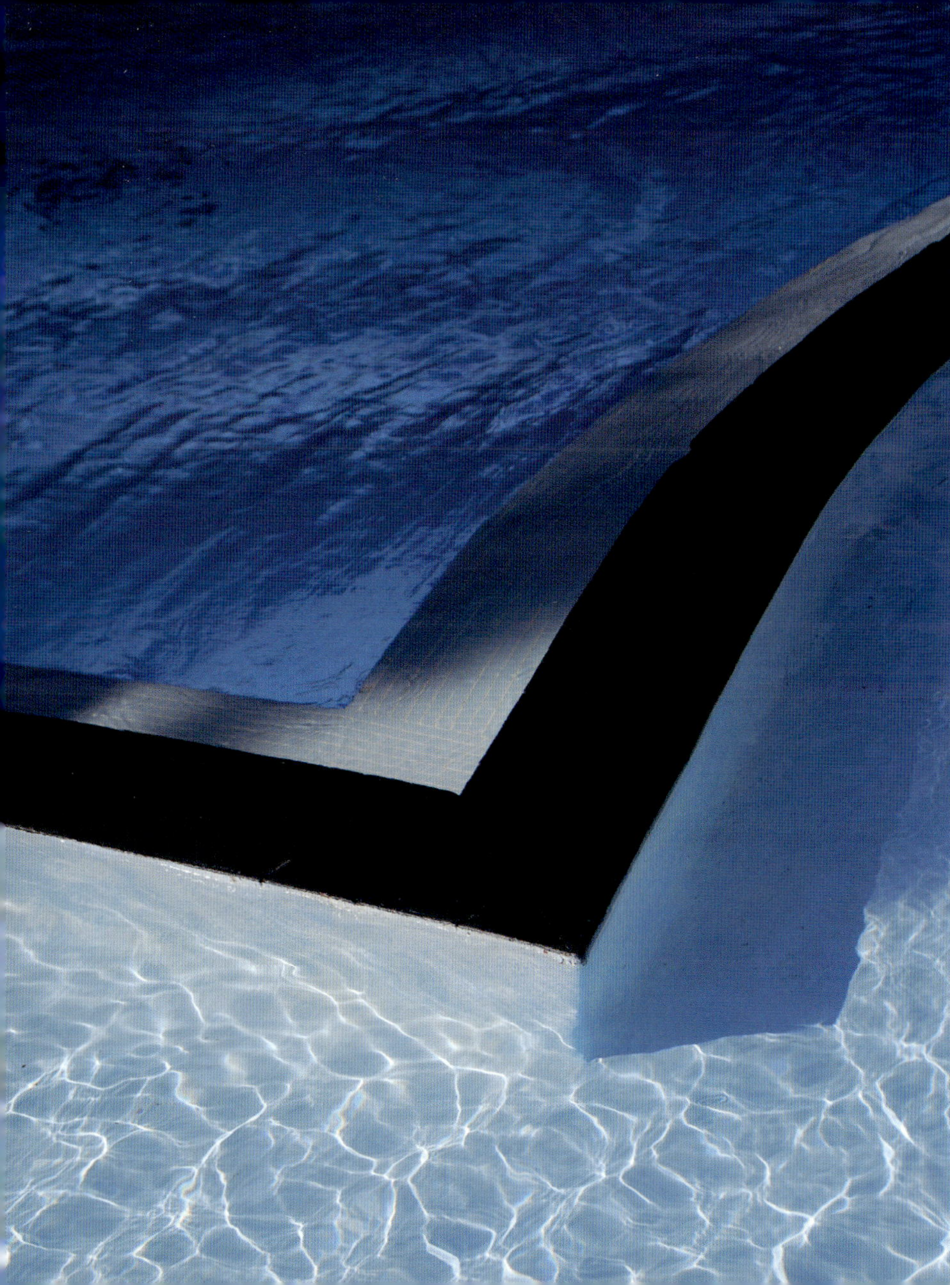

Raleigh Hotel Pool
1775 Collins Avenue
Miami Beach
Architect: Lawrence Murray Dixon 1940
Photograph: 2013

the Author

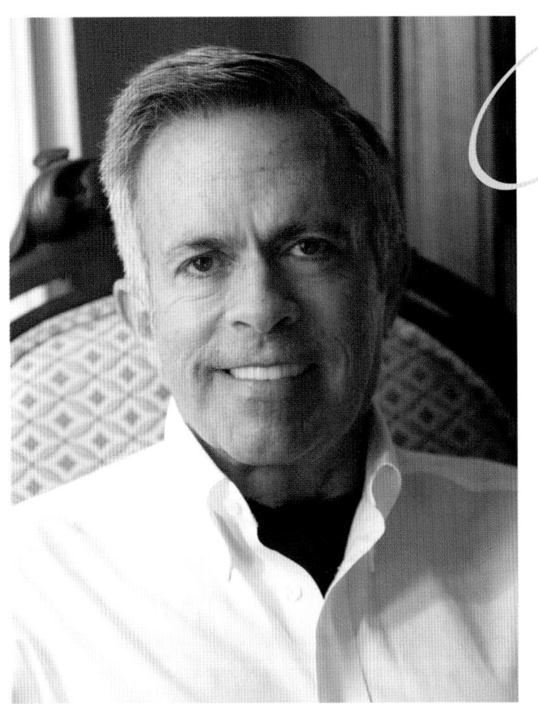

Arthur Jay Marcus is an architect, photographer, and historical preservationist living in South Florida since 1992. A native of Philadelphia, he received a BA from Temple University and a master's degree in architecture from Carnegie Mellon University. Arthur is also a self-taught photographer specializing in abstracted views of the built environment. His lifelong passions, architecture and photography, have informed each other over the course of his career. www.arthurmarcus.com

Peggy Abrams Photography

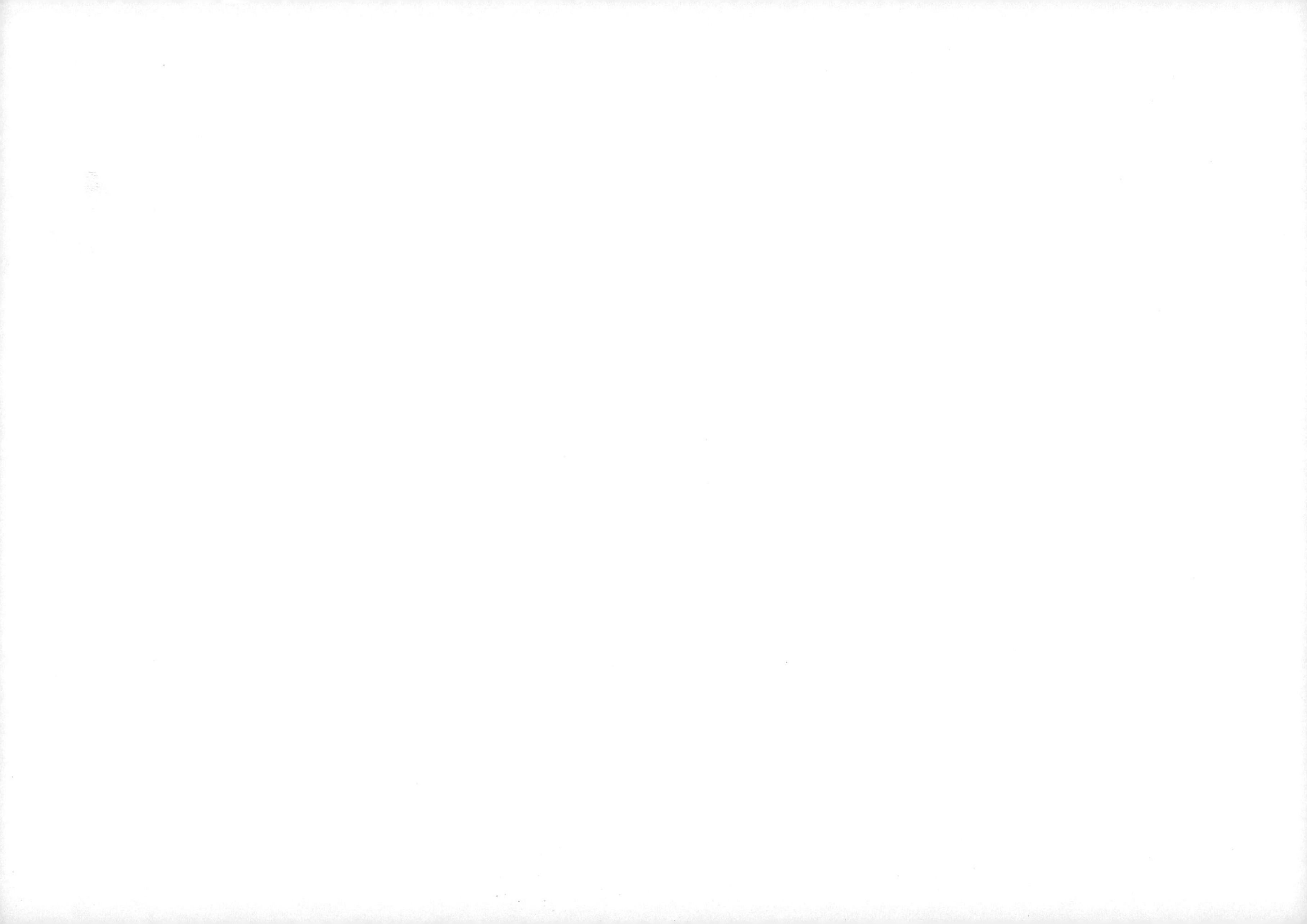